Return from the World

Return from the World

Economic Growth and Reverse Migration in Brazil

GREGORY DUFF MORTON

The University of Chicago Press
Chicago and London

The University of Chicago Press, Chicago 60637
The University of Chicago Press, Ltd., London
© 2024 by The University of Chicago
All rights reserved. No part of this book may be used or reproduced in any manner whatsoever without written permission, except in the case of brief quotations in critical articles and reviews. For more information, contact the University of Chicago Press, 1427 E. 60th St., Chicago, IL 60637.
Published 2024
Printed in the United States of America

33 32 31 30 29 28 27 26 25 24   1 2 3 4 5

ISBN-13: 978-0-226-83290-6 (cloth)
ISBN-13: 978-0-226-83292-0 (paper)
ISBN-13: 978-0-226-83291-3 (e-book)
DOI: https://doi.org/10.7208/chicago/9780226832913.001.0001

Library of Congress Cataloging-in-Publication Data

Names: Morton, Gregory Duff, author.
Title: Return from the world : economic growth and reverse migration in Brazil / Gregory Duff Morton.
Description: Chicago ; London : The University of Chicago Press, 2024. | Includes bibliographical references and index.
Identifiers: LCCN 2023050517 | ISBN 9780226832906 (cloth) | ISBN 9780226832920 (paperback) | ISBN 9780226832913 (ebook)
Subjects: LCSH: Movimento dos Trabalhadores Rurais sem Terra (Brazil) | Urban-rural migration—Brazil. | Migration, Internal—Economic aspects—Brazil. | Economic development—Social aspects—Brazil. | Agricultural laborers—Brazil—Social conditions. | Farmers—Brazil—Social conditions. | Brazil—Social conditions—21st century. | Brazil—Economic conditions—21st century. | Brazil—Rural conditions. | BISAC: SOCIAL SCIENCE / Anthropology / Cultural & Social | SOCIAL SCIENCE / General
Classification: LCC HT381 .M67 2024 | DDC 307.2/60981—dc23/eng/20231214
LC record available at https://lccn.loc.gov/2023050517

♾ This paper meets the requirements of ANSI/NISO Z39.48-1992 (Permanence of Paper).

*To Siloe, Raissa, and Jamile de Thamires
and to Ranieri and Jamile de Renan:
for you, we have to build a better world*

From an interview with Jaqueline and Oziel, peasant farmers and landless activists at Maracujá

OZIEL: You wrote down everything there. But look. When you get to your country, you say, "The solution for ending hunger in Brazil—"
JAQUELINE: Ending deprivation.
OZIEL: "—for ending deprivation, ending hunger, ending poverty—is land reform." [. . .]
JAQUELINE: It's the solution.
OZIEL: It's what takes the poor person out of the slum. Takes the child out of social exclusion. Out of drugs. Come to the fields, to the land. And for this, we have to occupy land so the government will buy it and give it to us to work. We have to occupy land. [. . .] You can say that in your country to the big people—the authorities, that the solution, in Brazil, to end hunger and deprivation, to take the poor person out of the slums of the city, is land reform. Give land for the poor person to work. And tell them that if they do this over there, it lessens the needs of the poor person.

You can say that we get into the struggle for real. We strive. We strive to reach our objectives. You know? And we struggle for real. We don't sit around with our arms crossed. We get aggressive with the government—and we achieve our goals. [. . .]

And another thing, Duff, that you have to say. If—if you give land and no credit, it doesn't work. [. . .]

You can say that it was a landless person who sent this message to—to a big person who's going to hear your presentation.

Contents

Introduction 1
1 The Phone Call Home: Forms of Speech in the Growth Process 35
2 The Roads: Histories of Growth as Histories of Cooperation 67
3 The Bus Ride: Making and Unmaking Abstract Labor 93
4 The Cargo: Marketplaces, Labor at a Distance, and Distance from Labor 117
5 The Money: Asset Chains, Class Consciousness, and the Transfer of Value Out of the City 139
6 The Things You Hold: Against Saving 173
Conclusion: Wait for the Coffee 203
Afterword 211

Acknowledgments 215
Notes 221
References 237
Index 253

Introduction

> The road from home leads out to the world and back.
> CAROL STACK, *Call to Home* (1996: 16)

The call came at the worst time. Alexandra had just days to go before she graduated from her business class. As she held the phone in her hand, she was one person among the 2.5 million living in Belo Horizonte, the city where she learned how to chat with drug dealers, the city where she ran into soap opera stars at the supermarket. On the other end of the line was her mother, talking to her from a village in the dust of the high plains.[1]

"Oh, Alexa," her mother implored, "you come back, because—I'm sick. I'm not, I'm not managing to do anything anymore."[2] Then she mentioned Alexandra's children. "Come and take care of the kids. And Anastacia, she's starting to cause me trouble. So you've got to come back."

Anastacia was not the only problem, as it turned out. Alexandra's sister Selma had recently traveled to the village with an infant son, and along the way, somehow, a suitcase had gone missing. Selma lost all her belongings.

It was, as Alexandra described it to me later, "one tribulation after another."

Alexandra hung up the phone. She contacted the bus station and bought a ticket, then went down to the business school. At the school, unhelpful staff explained to her that she still needed to finish a little maze of tasks: complete her work in various subject areas, submit her school identity card, pick up the actual diploma.

Alexandra calculated that it would take her all afternoon. The bus left before then. The ride to the village lasted nineteen hours in total, including transfers, with the last stretch on a coughing behemoth driven by a local who did not work every day. If Alexandra did not use the ticket she had, if she stayed to graduate, she would have to wait maybe a week or more to travel—it was unclear how long.[3]

"And there," Alexandra remembered afterward, "I had to choose."

Alexandra could remain in the city and have her mother continue to raise the children in the countryside. Many young people from the village did exactly that. Or she could go back.

The first time I heard this story from Alexandra, we were both in transit, camped out for the night in the back of an echoing warehouse. People could sleep there for free on their way to or from the city. The cement floor had been weighed down with doughy bags of manioc meal, the excess flour rising to the rafters like white incense. Evening sun spilled in from a courtyard where migrants washed their clothing in a deep sink. Bedrolls were unfurled a few feet from truck tires. It was 2012, and I had come to that place to study the zigzag migrations that people were making, town to city to village, all across the geography of boom-time Brazil. Alexandra was just looking for someone to listen. That day, she agonized to me while I lay on a hard wooden bed, nodding my sympathy. It was not the last time I would hear the story. Over the next several years, Alexandra told me bits and scraps. Finally, one night, I had the presence of mind to tape it on a tiny silver voice recorder. What is written above is what I taped.

Moving Back, in Boomtime and in Recession

When Alexandra received the phone call from her mother, Brazil was in the middle of an extraordinary episode of economic growth. This growth was accompanied by a notable *decrease* in income inequality. The lowest paid workers were growing the most. From 2001 to 2011, the people in the wealthiest tenth of the nation's population saw their real incomes rise by 16.6 percent. Over that same decade, the people in the poorest tenth of the population raised their real incomes by 91.2 percent.[4] The poor were increasing their incomes at five times the rate of the rich. Brazil was growing and becoming more equal at the same time.

But during those same years, every week, ramshackle buses carried waves of people like Alexandra out of the city and into the villages of Maracujá and Rio Branco, in the *sertão*, or drylands, of southwest Bahia. As the buses traversed the dirt roads, people were perching on seats from which the fabric had long ago vanished, speeding past thornbushes. They were leaving jobs as construction workers and nannies, as street merchants and factory hands. A large number came off the enormous new mechanized plantations, where they had earned salaries for planting coffee or irrigating lettuce. They were going to live as peasant farmers on tiny, parched plots, more than a hundred kilometers from the local city, in villages with inconsistent electricity and no running water. They would gather firewood for cooking; they would carry water on their heads in pails.

Martinho came back to the village after he had spent a night tied up by the thieves who were robbing the chemical factory where he worked. Laura came when she quit her job as a chef and converted to evangelicalism. Seu Jairo came with determination. "I don't ever want to work for anyone anymore," he declared. "No way."[5]

To move to Rio Branco or Maracujá in the early 2000s meant walking away from growth.[6] It meant leaving jobs for which pay was rising rapidly. Migrants who moved to the villages would live on vastly less than what they had been earning in their previous employment, often a quarter of their former wages. Why would people depart from a booming labor market? What kind of life could they expect in the place where they were going?

These are questions about how to see growth from the perspective of people who leave it behind. They are the questions that Alexandra found herself facing when her mother called her from the village.

The boom did not last. By 2015, global demand for Brazil's iron ore and soybeans was collapsing, and the nation entered a devastating recession. By 2016, Felipe was telling me that he now hauled fewer bottles of beer and cognac each month when he restocked the village bar that he operated in a cinderblock room attached to his home, a few doors down from Alexandra's parents' house. The economy was so bad, Felipe groused, that people had stopped drinking.

A bad economy could be a good reason to return to the countryside. In the villages, farmers could plant their own pink beans to eat and no one charged rent. Interestingly, though, many of Felipe's neighbors had left the wage labor market *before* the recession. It was as if they foresaw the downturn, or, perhaps, it was as if they never really trusted growth in the first place. They had another project in mind.

The Courage to Say No

The day when she had had enough, Tamara told me, was the day when her boss kept her trapped for five hours.

Tamara had been living in the boss's house ever since she started working there as a nanny, three years earlier, at age fifteen.[7] She ran after the children and kept them fed; she played with them in the mornings and watched them in the evenings. On that memorable day, though, Tamara was supposed to be able to leave work by noon. It was the Saturday of one of her few weekends off. Noon came and went, and at 5:00 p.m., Tamara's boss was still nowhere to be seen.

In that moment, Tamara later said, she genuinely didn't know what step to take. She was caged in by her obligation to the children. "How are you going to leave other people's kids in the dust?" Tamara mused. "Because it's not the fault of the child." So, Tamara shaved off the hours of freedom that she could have spent laughing with her own nieces and nephews, and she stayed where she was, duty-bound. But what would she do when the boss walked through the door?

Three years earlier, Tamara had come to that house, and to the megacity of São Paulo itself, because she was running away from a romance. Tamara's mother believed that a young man should go to a young woman's home and ask her parents' permission to date her. There weren't many young men in the village where Tamara lived. She and her family had a neat white house atop a dusty yellow hill covered in cactus, overlooking a river far below. Tamara's mother toiled near an enormous fire where she dried out manioc roots. Her father labored in the fields. There was little time for luxury, and, for a while, Tamara did not need to confront her mother's beliefs about boyfriends.

Then, one day, a young man climbed the slope that led to her family's four brick walls and asked for permission, just as her mother wanted. Tamara accepted the young man's affections, she later told me, so that she could "open a path [*abrir caminho*]." After this first relationship, she figured, she could date other people, and her mother would have no grounds to object.

But everything moved more quickly than Tamara had planned. The next day, the young man returned to the house. This time he was asking for her hand in marriage. Tamara's mother did not disguise her happiness: Tamara was fifteen, and her mother thought this was the right age to find a husband.

Tamara disagreed. Without saying anything to the young man, she left home and traveled a thousand miles to São Paulo.

There, atop a leafy green hill crowded with skyscrapers, overlooking a cathedral far below, Tamara found work. She spoke to a family whose children needed a nanny. She moved in. Tamara liked her boss, the mother of the household, and the boss liked Tamara, who was young and ready for instruction. Tamara could learn how to do chores the way the boss wanted them done. Soon, Tamara chased after babies, kept house, and worked almost all the time.

"I suffered in that house," Tamara remembered. The work felt endlessly exhausting. And it always seemed to go beyond its limits. Her boss would send her to the grandmother's house to toil there, or decide to have a dinner party with a friend and make Tamara watch the children and help with the meal, too. She would ask Tamara to work beyond the hour when work was supposed to stop. Tamara did not date anyone for three years. She didn't have time. "I'm a person with a great sense of shame [*muito envergonhada*]," Tamara explained to me. "I'm not the kind of person—" She paused. "I don't have the courage to say the word no."

"I worked," Tamara reminisced, "but I had the benefits, too!" Her boss was unusual, Tamara told me: "She's not prejudiced. Like, we would go to a restaurant, and I would sit at the table alongside them. I would eat lunch and dinner at the table with them." Things were different for the other nannies whom Tamara knew. They would eat ahead of time, then sit at the table only to give food to the boss's child. They wouldn't even touch a glass of water themselves.

In the village on the hill, some days there had been so little food in Tamara's house that her father would set aside every morsel for the children. On those days, Tamara watched him leave for work, knowing that he would go hungry. Now, in São Paulo, she was learning about chopsticks in a Japanese restaurant. She got invited to accompany her bosses on a yacht. They asked her to travel with them to Disney World in Florida.

Over time, however, Tamara's frustration grew and grew. She heard other nannies talk about going to their own families' birthday parties. Tamara did have relatives in the metropolis, but birthday parties were usually out of reach. She didn't get enough time off.

Then came the Saturday when her boss delayed and delayed, and Tamara only managed to stop work after 5:00 p.m. She was eighteen, in the place where she had been working since she was fifteen. After she left the house that day, walking down São Paulo's wealthiest streets, she knew that she wanted never to go back to that job.

What Do People Say about Why They Leave Growth Behind?

Tamara and Alexandra: their reasons seemed different. Scholars might say that Tamara was *pushed* out of the city by a bad job, while Alexandra was *pulled* out by the draw of kinship when her mother called and asked her to come take care of the children. Yet, in some sense, Tamara and Alexandra were both deciding what kind of life they wanted to live and the kind of system in which they wanted to live it. They were making statements about the meaning of growth.

Is it possible to reject growth? For that matter, what does "growth" mean? This book brings the dilemmas of migrant Brazilians into dialogue with the fierce social science debate over growth. I consider the reasons and dreams, the life plans and the family disputes in which people come to understand growth as a proposition that can be turned down.

When I bluntly asked migrants why they were moving to the countryside, they usually told me that they came to the village because they loved it. Their particular journeys might have been sparked by a misfortune, like Alexandra's phone call. But migrants tended to describe their ultimate reasoning in terms of something they cherished.

These migration stories were far from the dismal yarn in which impoverished workers, deprived of all aspiration, find themselves tragically pushed into the countryside and out of modernity. Just the opposite. These were stories about dreams. During one of the bus rides, a seventy-nine-year-old man told me about the place from which many migrants returned: São Paulo, the wealthiest state in Brazil. "There, it's oppressed," he explained pityingly. "Nobody trusts anybody." When people came back from São Paulo, he noted, they found something better. "In Bahia, there's freedom."

Dona Cássia spoke about this freedom, too. "Now here," she told me—just after detailing the poverty and deprivation her family faced in the village—"it's a lovely land for living in [*Agora aqui é um amor de terra para viver*]."

"Pardon me?" I asked her, with surprise.

"We—" she began. "Even in the friendship of the people, there's friendship with God. Here, nobody bothers anybody. Nobody persecutes anybody. Here, we do how—however much we can or we want to. You know?"

The residents of Maracujá and Rio Branco should not be seen simply as perpetual rebels against growth. As I show in chapter 2, people in the villages often said that they had benefited tremendously from economic growth: from new vaccines, for example, and electricity and pay phones. What made the villages special was that villagers built a space of autonomy that enabled them to participate in only certain elements of the growth project, at certain times. They acted as those using the world market, but not using it fully. In the face of the imperative to grow, they managed to develop an attitude of freedom.

The village farmers cultivated freedom as the opposite of dispossession. In the capitalist world, dispossession is one of the oldest stories. Today's workers, or their grandparents, or their great-great-grandparents, once watched an army occupy their pasture, or an official impose a hut tax, or lawyers and police steal the farm. In some cases, enslavers ripped them from their societies. They were hit with the blow of primitive accumulation. Now, they must do wage labor because they have been robbed of the means of subsistence and cannot survive without the boss's pay.

What small farmers demonstrate, at Maracujá and Rio Branco, is that dispossession can be reversed.[8] People who start out possessing only the most marginal land, or no land at all, can carefully, thoughtfully create a place where

INTRODUCTION

they are free to live without wage labor. If you have access to such a place, participating in growth becomes an option, not an obligation.

It is important to note that, in addition to freedom, migrants often cited two other reasons for leaving growth behind. They talked about their wish to feel close to kin, and they described their fears of violence in the city.

Unsurprisingly, many people said they were following the same kinship trail as Alexandra. She had moved to the city to help her sister with a baby, and now her mother was asking her to come back. Migrants created their kin network, in part, as a result of the decisions they made about growth.

In a discussion of Brazilian labor migration, it would be wrong to omit the violence that migrants have to face. Maura, who lived in a village not far from Alexandra's parents, came back to the countryside after her father was murdered. She told me she could not stand the thought of the men who had killed him. She was not the only one to suffer this way.

This book will not do justice to the complex and crucial task of assessing violence in Brazil. Others have written powerfully on the subject.[9] Let me make clear, at least, that migrants did often tell me that they left the urban labor market because they were afraid of attacks by thieves or, less frequently, by the police. Other migrants took a different position: sometimes, I heard villagers say that organized criminals were their friends and best protectors in the city.

Summary of the Argument

As the plain around Maracujá village grew dark one evening, Marcos, who lived next to Alexandra's parents, told me about the day he had just spent toiling alone in the coffee field. "I sat down there and I ended up thinking," Marcos brooded. "What is it that I am going to do with my life?"

Marcos was in his early twenties. Just a few months before, he had been washing enormous vats at a yogurt factory in the city. Now he was back in the village and wondering about the future. "Am I going to go to school? Am I going to leave here to work? How will it be? And all of that—it ends up jumbling a person's head."

Marcos was a participant—an ambivalent one—in the raging worldwide debate about economic growth. On one side stand those who feel inspired by growth. They watch growth draw people out of poverty and improve life expectancy; they see growth create human ties across borders.[10] For these debaters, Marcos's return to the village is a disappointment. "In any country," *The Economist* writes, some parts of the economy (such as manufacturing) are more productive than others (such as agriculture). But this gap is unusually large in developing countries [. . .] In Latin America and the Middle East [from 2013 to 2015], the contribution [of labor mobility to labor productivity] was negative: workers moved the wrong way, to where they were less productive. (2020: 70)

Marcos, by this standard, is one of the people in Latin America who moved the wrong way. Why did he do that?

Others, however, would cheer for Marcos. They understand economic growth as a deception, a project that wreaks ecological devastation and launches people on a meaningless drive to acquire goods. This line of argument can be traced at least to Aristotle, and recently it has found eloquent expression in the writings of degrowth theorists, who hope to build a society without economic growth.[11] On this view, Marcos made a powerful gesture for justice when he moved back to the village. What gave him the strength to swim against the tide?

This book does not render a verdict in favor of growth or against it. The notion of "economic growth," as I see it, is so broad that it cannot be simply embraced or rejected. Instead, this book attempts to ask *how* people in two villages came to distance themselves from the growth imperative.[12]

Here is an opening gambit. We can imagine economic growth as a form of enthusiasm—an enthusiasm about cooperation. Growth is a new sense of intensity in cooperating with your co-workers and your bosses, with your neighbors and with people across oceans from you. In the coffee fields he knew from childhood, Marcos toiled alone, and in the yogurt factory, he came to depend on perhaps dozens of other people who labored alongside him, hundreds of suppliers, and thousands of customers. One of the side effects of growth, then, is a sense of autonomy lost.

"Cooperation," "enthusiasm," "intensity": let's consider these terms. First, cooperation. My use of the word may sound startling or strange to readers. In fact, I hope it does. Many English speakers imagine cooperation as a sterling virtue. So do some farmers at Maracujá and Rio Branco, who sometimes yearn for cooperative farming practices like shared fields and joint marketing. Sometimes, but not always.

Is cooperation always the right way to work? Here, I do not want to suggest that cooperation is always oppressive or that co-ops are necessarily misguided. But I do want to appreciate noncooperation. Think of the feat that migrants already achieve in the *initial* act of returning to these independent-minded villages—right away, before anybody tries to develop any new rural cooperative relations. The initial act expresses a noncooperative politics. My aim is to show that noncooperation in rural Brazil can encode a view about freedom, distance, and the power to become ungoverned. By taking this politics seriously, we may come to a deeper appreciation of uncooperative people and listen better to their reasons.

The sort of cooperation I am referring to is *labor* cooperation. This includes unpaid labor inside the household (Waring 1988). Here, I am repeating a theme from Smith and Durkheim and also Marx, who devoted the middle portion of *Capital*'s first volume to an analysis of collective labor. (His chapter 13 is entitled "Cooperation," a term that refers to cooperating both with co-workers and with the boss.) Labor cooperation, of course, is not the only kind. Beyond the realm of daily work, villagers cooperate gracefully when they stage prayer nights, protest marches, and birthday parties. Villagers also hold periodic collaborative work days, as we will see. These village cooperative events, tellingly, occur as occasional interruptions in the regular regime of solitary labor. In other words, when migrants move back to the village, they are leaving behind a labor market where cooperation was mundane toil and going to a place where cooperation feels like a special event.

"Mundane," "special": we are now discussing the "public feelings" that growth creates, to cite Hirsch's insightful term (2022: 11). This is the topic covered by my other two keywords, "enthusiasm" and "intensity." Already I have suggested that economic growth is a new *enthusiasm and intensity about cooperating with those around you*. Note that the people who feel the enthusiasm are not necessarily the same people who feel the intensity. The stockbroker senses exuberance when growth takes off. For the rural day laborer, this same energy may appear as something much less optimistic: an intense extra load of coffee beans that she must harvest in order to pay the rent. Brazil's history of enslavement offers a stark example of the divide between enthusiasm and intensity. A sugarcane boom could mean ebullience among the enslavers and heavier toil for enslaved people.

Brazil's millennial growth spurt, in the early 2000s, was unusual because the enthusiasm became so widespread, crossing the lines of class. The poor were increasing their incomes faster than the rich, and many working-class Brazilians expressed great optimism about growth.

Not everyone felt this way, however. Those exceptions—the workers who, in a moment of general economic enthusiasm, did not cooperate—are the people at the heart of the story I tell here. When people are surrounded by the imperative to grow, how do they turn in the opposite direction and make autonomy happen? From what do they become autonomous? As I attempt to answer these questions, I sketch out the two main arguments of the book. The first is about freedom, the second is about permanence. Together, they build toward a broader anthropological theory of accumulation.

First, *economic growth involves submission to command*. Migrants enter a growth boom by agreeing to accept a boss's commands, and that submission becomes the foundation that allows them to cooperate with other workers. In the yogurt factory, Marcos and his co-workers collaborated with each other by all following (to some degree) the boss's system of commands. Marcos' boss was not just accumulating yogurt and profit; the boss was accumulating cooperation.

Over time, people like Marcos may leave growth behind for a very clear reason: they don't like being commanded. But what turns a phrase into a command? The first part of this book, chapters 1–4, considers how a command sounds, which words render it persuasive, and how it might be refused. Commands, I propose, can make labor abstract. To turn away from growth is to undo the abstraction and to seek, in its place, a substantive vision of freedom.

My second argument inquires into the aspirations that people bring into—and then out of—an economic boom. I argue that *we can see social class as a relation to labor. This relation includes a dream about exiting labor to find permanence.* The second part of the book, chapters 5 and 6, takes a close look at people who are trying to realize this dream by acquiring assets, with each acquisition a bit more permanent than the last. On a construction site, a migrant acquires first a cellphone and then a motorcycle; in a village, first a bean field and then a pig. I call each sequence of acquisitions an *asset chain*. An asset chain encodes a specific vision of objects and of the time it takes to attain them—a "class sensorial," to use Moisés Kopper's term, "a topography of images and affects through which class mobility is experienced and located in time and space" (2019: 83). Through these images and affects, an asset chain creates a class position.

I suggest that an asset chain has its anchor and endpoint in an object I call a *premio*. A premio is an asset that promises to allow a worker to leave behind the sort of labor they have known. A farmer might find their premio in a sturdy herd of cattle large enough to sustain itself for years. A factory laborer might aim for the money to open up a hair salon. Premios, I argue, amount to a dream of permanence, a permanence that the worker finds by escaping the familiar workplace. When migrants exit growth, sometimes it is because they are seeking a permanence that growth has not offered them. The regnant growth model has not given them a realistic path toward a premio. So they

INTRODUCTION

switch asset chains, embarking on a peasant project that provides them with steps toward something that can last.

The two parts of this manuscript come together to sketch an outline of an anthropological project that is still incipient, the *anthropology of accumulation*. This anthropology asks: across the range of human societies, how is it that people multiply the resources they consider important?

Such an analysis requires the insights generated by the extensive literature on value. Anthropologists seem to agree, minimally, that value is a ranking of objects and that this ranking renders the objects commensurable.[13] To investigate *value* is to focus closely on the moment of commensuration. In contrast, to explore *accumulation* is to look more broadly at the process through which these objects, once commensurate, circulate and expand.[14]

One way to accumulate is to make others submit to your command, and then use this submission to organize their labor, in an effort to bring even more people under your command: in other words, to accumulate cooperation. That is the mechanism that ran Marcos's yogurt factory, the approach that helped drive Brazil's economic growth in the early 2000s.

But economic growth is not the only way to accumulate. During those same years, some workers were pouring their resources into very different regimes of accumulation. Tamara sent her nanny earnings back to the village and acquired a house so far from the nearest road that it would be difficult for her ever to sell it. Alexandra's neighbors avidly bought cows that were "clandestine"— unregistered with the state vaccine registry—and therefore forbidden in the urban marketplace and useful only for local consumption. Purchases like these actually transferred wealth away from the world market. They were hardly investments in Brazil's growth economy. But they were forms of accumulation. In this book I attend to both sorts of accumulation, those inside the growth process and those beyond it, and attempt to locate the intersection that connects them.

When Marcos left his job at the yogurt factory, Brazil was already nearing the end of the growth episode that opened the millennium. Soon after Marcos ceased polishing the giant vats, the nation would fall into the recession that drained the demand for beer out of Felipe's bar. It was nothing new. For five hundred years, Brazilians have known an economy designed to export natural resources in waves of boom and bust, from the sugarcane cycle of the seventeenth century to the soybean craze of the 2010s. Given that context, people live out growth not as steady progress but as a series of oscillations, of enthusiasms indulged and then rejected. This book focuses on the second movement: the backward turn that makes autonomy possible as one response alongside—not separate from—the world market.

Two Villages at the Edge of the Plantations: Research Setting

While passing through the fields of cactus on a scrub brush plain, you might find a valley deep with trees. If you face away from the valley's edge and look back toward the plain, you will sense the warmth of cookfires. You will hear the sound of distant radios in small white houses. This is the Maracujá Land Settlement, where Alexandra and Marcos grew up. A dirt road leaves Maracujá. After 15 kilometers of brushwood and several flocks of green parakeets, the road arrives at Rio Branco. There, the earth is harder packed, and it has patches of mica flakes that look like spills of tinsel or diamonds. Otherwise, though, the two villages today seem quite similar, like a couple who have come to resemble each other over time.

They have indeed grown closer. Maracujá and Rio Branco face comparable climatic and economic constraints, and they are now home to similar miniature farms, but they have contrasting pasts. Rio Branco has been inhabited by small farmers probably since the late nineteenth century. Maracujá was founded in 1996 through a landless people's occupation on a coffee plantation. The two communities today are spaces of autonomy etched out of the terrain at the edges of the great landholdings.

In 2012, when fieldwork began in earnest, Rio Branco had been in existence for nearly a century. The community consisted of thirty-five neat adobe houses, each one near a field, spaced out along a network of narrow dirt paths that ran on for several kilometers. In all, 103 people lived there. The paths converged to a soccer field, meticulously scrubbed of all vegetation by the young people who gathered to play in the evenings. Seu Gaspar, who lived at one end of the soccer field, had extended his porch so that he could put out metal chairs and sell liquor to the spectators. His competition was his sister, Dona Eva, who built a one-room bar a few feet away. Behind Seu Gaspar stood the tin-roofed schoolhouse that doubled as a Catholic chapel, and in front of him was the Protestant church. In the absence of a priest, Nelson ran the Catholic celebration each Sunday. His father, Seu Catulo, was the Protestant pastor. The two of them scheduled services at times that did not conflict with each other.

Maracujá, the land occupation community, initially looked more imposing: its 120 houses stood in four tight lines, making a sizeable rectangle at the high point on a gently curving plain. The houses were white with blue shutters. All of them had been built by the government land reform agency to lodge the landless farmers, who were still sleeping in tents two years after the agency expropriated the coffee plantation in the late 1990s. But the dry earth in the village fields proved challenging, as did a series of leadership disputes,

INTRODUCTION

and thus many farmers left. By 2011, there were 62 households in Maracujá, with 205 inhabitants. The empty houses stored people's beans or housed their visiting cousins (and anthropologists). Otherwise, Maracujá had the same features as Rio Branco: a giant soccer field, bars in people's houses, a school, and a Catholic and a Protestant church. At Maracujá, though, the Protestant building had been located at the very edge of town, so that its amplified late-night services would not bother those farmers who rose Monday before dawn.

Both Maracujá and Rio Branco were crisscrossed by extensive kin networks. The basic unit of residence and economy, however, was the household. In both villages, some households consisted of single adults; more were nuclear families, sometimes including a collateral relative or a third generation. When they encountered people from outside their own households, villagers practiced what was perhaps their highest virtue: hospitality. Families strove to welcome each other, outdoing themselves with decorated cakes and coffee or tea made to the visitors' tastes. Even more extravagant was the gift of hospitality time. Virtually any person showing up at a door, at any time of day, would cause the adults of the house to drop their activities—laundry in the suds or food on the fire—and sit down for a chat.

By the standards of the region, the two villages were considered difficult places to earn a living. Their semiarid land yielded harvests that varied dramatically with the rainfall, and even in good years, the distance from the city made it hard to sell agricultural products. Nonetheless, nearly every household had access to at least one field, and nearly everyone planted crops or raised livestock, at least for subsistence. Villagers sowed manioc, beans, corn, and squash; grew coffee, sugarcane, passion fruit, and *Bixa orellana* shrubs for urucum (a red dye); planted watermelons and pineapples; and raised cattle, chickens, pigs, guinea fowl, turkey, and ducks. During the coffee harvest season, villagers often traveled to the nearby plantations, where they could earn pay by the liter for the coffee berries they harvested off the bristling trees.

Counting all sources together, incomes at the villages were far below the national average. Household per capita income tended to cluster between half and four times the World Bank–endorsed poverty standard of $2.00 US per day (see graphs on pp. 14–15). The distribution in each village included a few wealthier households—although from a quick visit to the villages, it would be hard to distinguish those from the rest. Farmers took to heart the often repeated maxim, *Don't think that you're better than the others*, and even the most prosperous tended to live in conditions similar to those of their neighbors.

The agricultural calendar in the villages had two poles: the heavy *rains of the waters (chuvas das águas)* in September or October, and the lighter *rains of the fogs (chuvas das neblinas)* in March, both high seasons for planting. The periods without rain were marked by festivals, of which the two greatest were Christmas and the June Festivals. The latter were in some sense the opposite of Carnival—rural rather than urban, cold weather rather than hot, based in the home rather than the street. During the June Festivals, which span the feasts of St. John the Baptist, St. Anthony, and St. Peter, urban family members flooded in from throughout Brazil, sleeping on village couches and floors. The feasts called for enormous bonfires, peasant garb, dances all night long, and full days devoted to hospitality.

Both Maracujá and Rio Branco enjoyed relatively autonomous self-government. Police, soldiers, and government officials were almost never seen. Teachers, doctors, health agents, and priests began appearing, for the most part, only in the 1980s. As a result, people in the villages were quite used to managing their own affairs. At Maracujá, the landless movement had set up an elaborate series of regular community meetings, run by village officers chosen on a two-year cycle. The meetings tended to spark verbal conflicts, and they addressed major issues, including the entrance into the community of new landless people who had declared interest in farming a field there.

Rio Branco had much less turnover and a much more peaceful government. Nelson, the village's community health agent, would occasionally convene meetings in the tin-roofed school to discuss the shared water pump or other question of common interest. More commonly, though, problems could be managed through a series of visits and chats among all those involved.

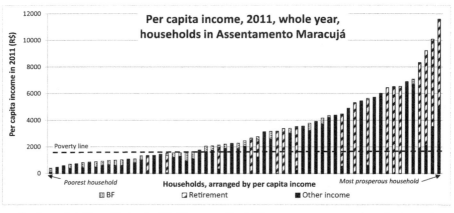

Graphs reprinted from Morton (2018b). The poverty line is R$140 per person per month, a criterion used by the Bolsa Família program in 2011 and roughly corresponding to US$2 per person per day. Graphs represent income in Brazilian reais. The 2011 exchange rate was approximately 2 reais to 1 US dollar. Data from survey conducted by author; see Morton (2015a: appendix) for method.

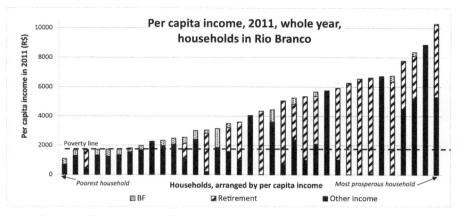

Graphs reprinted from Morton (2018b). The poverty line is R$140 per person per month, a criterion used by the Bolsa Família program in 2011 and roughly corresponding to US$2 per person per day. Graphs represent income in Brazilian reais. The 2011 exchange rate was approximately 2 reais to 1 US dollar. Data from survey conducted by author; see Morton (2015a: appendix) for method.

One of the key acts, in both villages, was leaving. Working-age adults remained alert to labor opportunities in the cities or on large plantations, and often, villagers created migratory chains: one worker would find a successful job in a new city, then bring a friend, and then another, until the village had established an outpost in an urban neighborhood somewhere. Teenagers usually longed to travel to these places. Going to labor, though, required a significant investment. It took money, knowledge, and connections to buy a bus ticket, pay rent, purchase food, and find a job. Once the outlay had been made, some villagers would establish permanent residence in the city, adding themselves to Brazil's booming urban working class. Others, however, would come back.

Methods

I first came to Maracujá in 2005 as an idealistic visitor. Although I had never been to South America, I had heard about Brazil's landless movement, the MST.[15] The MST is composed of small farmers and rural workers who organize themselves to occupy thousands of large plantations. These peasants—that is the word they emphatically use to describe themselves—famously march to the edge of an unused field and cut the fence that surrounds it. They build tents for themselves out of sticks and black plastic tarp, and they live in the tents until the government compensates the plantation owner and redistributes the land to people in need—or, more frequently, until the police evict the occupiers.

I had heard stories of the MST in a Portuguese class I took in the late 1990s, and I felt shocked. I wondered, could the occupiers ever win? Eventually, in 2005, I managed to find a phone number for the MST headquarters in São Paulo.[16] I called with shaking nerves and a vague notion that I might go volunteer to help the movement.

As it turned out, my call was routed to Esteban, who, I would later learn, had migrated from Mexico to Brazil in the 1980s so he could join the landless movement. No, Esteban told me, the MST was not interested in volunteers.

I felt devastated, but only for a moment.

Esteban continued: although the MST did not accept volunteers, he said, they would be glad to welcome me as a visitor.

Not long afterward, I disembarked from a plane in São Paulo, carrying a backpack that my grandmother had helped me pack and a piece of paper with an address that Esteban had supplied. Within a few days I was staring at a row of houses that stretched along the edge of a former plantation field. This land had been occupied, expropriated,[17] and turned into a land settlement for landless farmers: Maracujá village.

In 2005, I was not a researcher but a hapless guest who could barely communicate with his hosts. On my first night on an MST farm I was rushed into the seat of honor at Dona Josefina and Seu Tarso's tent. Unable to explain that I was vegetarian, I found myself face to face with Dona Josefina's solicitous smile as she handed me a plate piled high with eggs and fried pork intestine. Dona Josefina seemed unreservedly happy to have me in her tiny, unfinished home, even though she did not know me. I ate every bite. For the next few months, family after family of landless farmers received me, with similar smiles, finding me a couch or spare bed and a space at the dinner table. I did not spend a dime for lodging or food.

In 2011, when I began field research in earnest, I noticed that I was not the only new arrival. Migrants were coming to the countryside. Young people were leaving factory jobs; middle-aged women were ditching their agribusiness salaries; aging butchers were retiring. They were joining the MST in order to become small farmers. This reverse migration puzzled me. While I had long understood that some agglomeration of people felt motivated to occupy plantations, it had not occurred to me to ask why—what they were leaving behind and what was motivating them to move. I assumed, for the most part, that the occupiers were driven by utter poverty and desperation. The more I listened, however, the more I noticed that while impoverishment was usually *part* of the story that occupiers told me, impoverishment was rarely the motive they cited to explain the specific moment when they moved back.

INTRODUCTION   17

Instead, they spoke about dreams. "My dream was always to get land to work," Miguel told me. "I'm in love with land," said Fábia.

I began to see the connection between the dramatic land occupation protests and a much more mundane act: simply moving to the villages. From the perspective of a migrant, I began to think, occupying land with the MST was only one of *many* ways that a person might enter small farming. I began to wonder about this act more generally. Perhaps I had never quite realized that the simple gesture of moving to a village also had its politics, just as a land occupation did.[18] But what politics?

I also noticed that people were moving to the village in the middle of an economic boom—turning down a wage increase in order to earn far less money in the countryside. This seemed like the opposite of my original assumption that migrants were acting out of desperate poverty. With that, I came to the problem of this book.

The process of reflection happened gradually, but the research had to be planned on a schedule, before my ideas had settled.[19] After 2005 I made trips back and forth, spending sixteen consecutive months in the two villages in 2011–12. I made return visits in 2013 and 2016.

My presence in the villages was deeply marked by my identity as a white man, unaccompanied by family, coming from a powerful and suspect foreign nation. Perhaps because I was an unmarried man by myself, I was generously received as a guest by couples who treated me as a person far from my family and hence in need of the hospitality that might socialize me into the group. Often I would be welcomed to a couple's home for television-watching, dinner, or a lengthy chat.

This socialization took place inside a specific gender context. At Rio Branco and Maracujá, households were typically anchored by a male-female couple. Heteronormativity was pervasive, if not absolute. Moreover, household tasks seemed to me—at least at first—to be split quite firmly by gender, with men taking responsibility for fields, while women labored inside the home. Although Brazil's cities have long been home to a venerable tradition of nonbinary gender categories, I never heard anyone discuss these categories in the countryside.

Over time, I came to believe that dichotomous gender roles were in fact more fragile and illusory in the villages than I had initially perceived. Women, for example, often harvested and hoed the land clean, just as men did, and female villagers sometimes cooperated with each other to plant their own "women's fields" of beans and other crops. Or consider Suso, the teenaged son in Maria's house, next door to me: I watched him mop the cement floor of the house and slather thick, unscented soap on the evening dishes each night. Actually, village gender roles seemed to be in the midst of a fraught transition. Men and women argued about which money belonged to whom, what food to buy at the market, and who deserved what kinds of freedom. A seventy-three-year-old man summed up the sentiment for me. "The woman used to be a nation that suffered a lot of wild insults from man," he observed, "and today she's just not taking it anymore" (Morton 2013: 49).

Sexuality, too, was less tightly moored to the binary than I initially realized (Green 2001). From time to time, I heard people joke bemusedly about dalliances between local men. These stories were told in tones that ranged from silliness to disdain. But other voices seemed to take the question seriously, like Isabel, from a neighboring village, who declared herself to be lesbian, or like the MST activists who adopted a pro–LGBT rights position. In 2016 I learned that Afonso and Diogo, two teenage boys I knew at a nearby landless settlement, were publicly in a relationship with each other.

This context shaped my socialization in the villages. In a historical moment when gendered realities seemed to be shifting, my arrival gave people the opportunity to enact the conservative tropes that created a unified front in the face of an outsider. It seemed to me that many couples sought to present me with an idealized representation of their household as a cohesive unit, as if the home achieved some kind of semiotic completion when it turned itself outward to a stranger. Family members finished each other's thoughts, divided labor along predictably gendered lines, and scolded each other gently for small shortfalls.

These habits often persisted—although not always—even when I knew a couple quite well. As a man, I found myself politely excused from some areas of household life. I was almost never expected to participate in the production of the household through chores, so I never developed the knowledge that might have resulted from a closer familiarity with domestic work. I have a limited comprehension of important facets of my female interlocutors' daily lives. Because my very presence as a single male outsider provided the occasion for the household to depict itself as a tranquil whole, and because there were levels of understanding I did not achieve with my female interlocutors, my view of social life in the villages is, I think, biased toward harmony. My guess is that I detect structure and regularity more than contradiction and power.

During fieldwork, my primary research approach involved participant observation bolstered by open-ended interviews, which meant endless hours attending church, visiting houses, listening to stories, and scribbling down gossip. The project also included two, more quantitative aspects. I conducted a census of all households, using questions based on the PNAD (Pesquisa

Nacional por Amostra de Domicílios, a nationally representative household survey carried out annually by IBGE, Brazil's statistical service). My census attempted to measure total income and the value of all assets in 2011. It also included a series of open questions—including, perhaps most significantly, inquiries about each person's work history.

Once the census was complete, I chose nine "focus households"—selected for their diversity in age, income, and household composition—and began to conduct weekly interviews that recorded their expenses and income flows.[20] The quantitative elements of the project were probably important less for the numbers they produced and more for the relationships they inspired, since the structured census protocol gave me a reason, even when I felt exhausted, to go to every household—and, in many cases, to keep going back.

Long Histories of Growth

When I chatted idly with farmers at Maracujá and Rio Branco, under smoke-stained kitchen roof tiles or over glass cups of hot black coffee, one word that I frequently heard uttered was *world*. "The world" was a place distant from the village, somewhere different from the ground on which we stood, "out there in that big world" (*lá naquele mundão*).[21] "You can run around the whole world," Sérgio mused, remembering his own days as a worker in the city. "But you have to come back to that little destination from which you left." Hence my choice of title, *Return from the World*.

What was this world, I wondered. How had people come to understand the villages as somehow separate from "the world"? These are questions that frame the history of the villages inside a longer history.

The coastline a few hundred miles from Maracujá and Rio Branco was colonized in the sixteenth century by Portuguese plantation owners. They turned northeastern Brazil into one of the wealthiest and most dynamic centers of the global economy in the early modern era. Indigenous people living in the region were massacred. From the sixteenth to the nineteenth century, millions of African people were enslaved, and very often worked to death, on sugar estates. Processing plants were built around giant machines that ran day and night. The owners received financing from foreign investment capital. The product traveled thousands of miles to reach consumers across the oceans. In other words, Brazil's sugar installations were, in an important sense, among the world's first capitalist factories.[22] They were fueled by the destruction of African and Indigenous life and freedom. Inside their confines, dozens and sometimes hundreds of people worked together, cooperating to crystallize sweetness under the force of central command.

Since the earliest days of Brazilian colonialism, however, there have been some workers who have made efforts to leave this cooperation behind. They have run away, refused to labor, moved inland with the cattle, saved up money to buy land, hidden in the forests, or revolted. As they exited the center of the world market, these sugar exiles often founded villages based on subsistence agriculture, much like the place where Alexandra grew up. Such farming hamlets may look ancient or traditional, but they are just the opposite: the genocide of the sixteenth century virtually wiped out the region's earlier cultivation systems. As Sidney Mintz (1973), Michel Rolph Trouillot (1992), and Eric Wolf (1955, 1957) have noted, the region's current small farming communities were established *after* plantation agriculture, often by people *escaping* plantation agriculture. This is a postcapitalist peasantry.

Katherine McKittrick describes its potentials. "The forced planting of blacks in the Americas," she observes, "is coupled with an awareness of how the land and nourishment can sustain alternative worldviews and challenge practices of dehumanization" (2013: 11). She notes, "These alternative worldviews were not sealed off from or simply produced in opposition to the plantation; rather, they were linked to the geographies of the plantation economy and the brutalities of slavery." When small farmers moved beyond the edge of the world market, they remained distant, not separate, from its bloodstained cycles.

Brazil's economy since the sixteenth century has been propelled by the export of primary commodities, one following the other in a wave of booms and busts. Sugarcane was a major new export product in the 1600s, then later gold and diamonds, then coffee, then rubber, then finally, in the first decades of the twenty-first century, iron ore and soy. Each swell is pushed forward by workers who enter the global workforce. Each also involves a reverse flow of workers who leave—and who sometimes do so during the moment of expansion, because generations of experience have taught Brazilians that growth is an unreliable proposition and even if one manages to eke some gain out of it, that gain must be consolidated somewhere safe. The movement of migrants into and out of the world market makes a rhythm, a "permanently unbalanced oscillation" (Mintz 1973: 100). At one end of the oscillation, departing workers build for themselves zones that they render distant from the global economy. They return from the world.

Enslavement, Race, and Growth

For farmers at Maracujá and Rio Branco, growth happened as an unavoidably racialized process. They found themselves marked with signs of Blackness as soon as they reached the big cities in Brazil's Southeast and began to search

INTRODUCTION

for work. Race was made patent in the names they were called, in the attitudes of their bosses, and in the ideas about enslavement that sometimes surfaced for open debate. Often, I did not grasp these facts.

When I asked my interlocutors about the past, they tended not to discuss enslavement with me. "In that time," I inquired of Dona Zaida, "was there anyone who still remembered the era of—of—of the slaves? The time of slavery?" Dona Zaida had been born around 1930, forty-two years after the end of legal enslavement in Brazil.

"In my time," Dona Zaida replied, "those that I knew, none of them knew that slavery." She continued, "Slavery had passed many years before. In my—people suffered—they worked a lot, but it was already a different situation."

During the day-to-day conversations I heard in the villages, a few people used the language of enslavement during moments of intense bitterness over their work. "Being a household servant is slavery," an exhausted Analis proclaimed to me. "You work the whole day and all you earn is a pittance."

"Does it look like we were born to be slaves?" Maria snapped on another occasion. She was talking with a neighbor about the uncompensated toil that she and her friend undertook on behalf of the village. "We're dark-skinned women [*Somos pretas*]," Maria continued, "but we're not slaves."

Such moments came like rare flashes. Most of the time, so far as I could tell, people did not recall the past by talking about slavery, not when I was present. This omission points toward the importance of ethnography conducted by Black researchers in Brazil.[23] It also highlights the need for more institutional support for Black anthropologists, especially those seeking to do research at the intersection of peasant studies, race, and the history of enslavement in rural Brazil. My status as a white researcher shapes what people tell me and what I allow myself to hear; all of us as knowers are partial in our knowledge. No matter what our perspective, we absolutely cannot listen to contemporary narratives of freedom without bearing in mind the history of slavery and racialization that helped to form them. Scholars other than myself have highlighted the place of enslavement in the development of contemporary notions of freedom, as is clear in the work of France Winddance Twine (1998), Angela Gilliam (1974), Hebe Mattos (1995), Kim Butler (1998), Jonathan DeVore (2014, 2018, 2020), Manuela Carneiro da Cunha (1985), Kesha-Khan Perry (2013), and Walter Fraga Filho (2016), among many others. This book should be read in the light of their insight—and in the hope of future insight from scholars and activists to come.

One unavoidable legacy of enslavement is Brazil's contemporary system of race and racism.[24] Nearly everyone in the region around the villages seemed to identify in some sense as at least in part Black or African. In the neighboring city, a middle-class teacher, a friend of mine, told me as much: *We're all a little Black*. But things were not so simple, as I learned one day on a bus where a man eagerly recounted a story about the history of the men in the family from which my teacher friend was descended. The man explained, *In the old days, they would threaten to kill any Black man who wanted to date one of their daughters*.

Racism, I eventually learned, inflected the process of economic growth in the villages, both because villagers were likely to be racialized as Black when they sought wage labor employment and also, in a more subtle manner, because not every villager was subject to this racialization to the same degree (Fernandes 1964; Andrews 1991). Many migrants told me about the label that was attached to them in the big city: *baiano*. A baiano is a person from the state of Bahia, the state in whose countryside Maracujá and Rio Branco are nestled, a state renowned as a heartland for African presence in Brazil (Collins 2015). In the great cities of the Southeast, a thousand kilometers from Bahia, baianos were associated with Blackness, regardless of how they identified themselves (Enriquez 2022b). Baianos had their own neighborhoods and stores. They were stereotyped into certain occupations and out of others. Some bosses denounced baianos as lazy; other bosses insisted on hiring only baianos because baianos were alleged to be hardworking and willing to accept low wages.

Virtually everyone from Maracujá and Rio Branco, then, had to navigate the anti-Black racism that twisted outsiders' view of their state. But not every villager faced racialization of the same sort. For some, racial discrimination influenced the jobs available to them in the urban economy. For others, this discrimination became a jarring roadblock that kept them out of urban labor altogether. The roadblock is what confronted Suso, a diligent young man from Maracujá who encountered racist violence when he went to the city (see pp. 121–22). In every case, Brazil's economic growth takes on a racialized shape—and it has done so for as long as there has been a Brazil.

Growth Models and Recent History

A few miles from Maracujá, you can find the Rio-Bahia highway. President Lula rode down that highway in 1952, when he was seven-year-old Luiz Inacio da Silva, whizzing past Maracujá Plantation while perched on the back of a truck with his mother. Like the millions of Brazilians who migrated to the cities from the 1950s to the 1970s, they were leaving the countryside to find a better life.

Lula did not forget the lessons of the trip. He was elected on a pro-poor platform as the first-ever Workers Party president in 2002, and this platform

INTRODUCTION

was reaffirmed in 2010 by his hand-picked successor, Dilma Rousseff, who held power until 2016. Dilma and Lula built a growth model that fit inside a broader vision for new social democracy. The poorest Brazilians began to spend more, thus spurring economic growth, thanks to a series of redistributive policies enacted by the government. The two signature policies were, first, a steadily increasing minimum wage, and, second, Bolsa Família, the famous conditional cash transfer. The minimum wage hikes put more money in the pockets of workers in the formal sector. Bolsa Família gave modest sums of money monthly to poor mothers who got their children vaccinated and sent them to school.

In addition, the Workers Party gradually expanded access to the basic services that had long been denied to everyone outside of a city. (The preceding Cardoso administration had also made efforts to improve rural services.) The state sent out teachers, nurses, and even the electricians who installed the first electric wiring in candle-lit hamlets. The difference between city and country started to shrink. Since you could now have school and some medical care in the village, many urbanites began to think more seriously about moving back to rural areas.[25]

All in all, the Workers Party approach created the initial context for this ethnography: a moment of egalitarian, sometimes tumultuous social transformation. From 2003 until 2014, Brazil's GDP grew steadily—with only a brief blip during the global financial crisis of 2008—and this growth was led by working-class Brazilians. Hunger, extreme poverty, and income inequality all dropped at an extraordinary pace (see graphs on pp. 24–25). Miriam Belchior, minister of planning, wisecracked, "We're splitting up the cake at the same time as it's growing" (Branco 2013).

The Workers Party plan was only one of a series of economic approaches that presidents had used to manage growth after World War II. Nor was it the last. After Dilma's impeachment in 2016 (Sosa 2019), social democracy would be replaced by a new conservative drive for smaller government and freer markets. Indeed, the history of Brazil's last half-century can rightly be told as a succession of growth models: from dictatorial nationalism in the 1960s and 1970s to neoliberal social rights in the 1990s, and from new social democracy in the 2000s to austerity after 2016. In each of these models, the Brazilian state tried a different tactic to integrate the nation's labor force, in particular the millions of citizens who stand precipitously at its edge, citizens who have never enjoyed secure and lasting economic citizenship.

That, anyway, is one version of events. To recount Brazil's history this way is to tell a tale grounded in the lives of the migrants, like Lula and his family, who made Brazil into an urban nation. The tale revolves around integration and inclusion. In other words, it scripts Brazil's past century as a drama about trying to belong in the city.

But that script is not the only one. What if, instead, we paid attention to the people who went to the city and then came back? What if we considered independence rather than inclusion, and what if we thought less about integration and more about the development of autonomy? To tell the story along

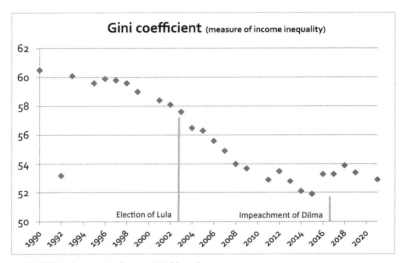

Source: World Development Indicators, World Bank.

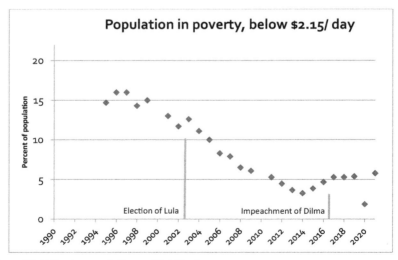

Source: World Development Indicators, World Bank.

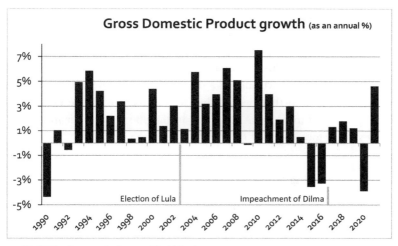

Source: World Development Indicators, World Bank.

these lines is to focus on *urban-to-rural* migration: Latin American history run against the grain.

Such a reverse flow has in fact been a notable feature of Brazil's renewed social democracy. In the dictatorial 1970s, only 11 percent of Brazil's migrants were return migrants (Baeninger 2012). From 1991 to 2010, consistently, about 20 percent of Brazil's migrants were return migrants (Baptista, Campos, and Rigotti 2017: 12). One of the goals of this book is to explore and render plausible the link between democracy and moving back home.

After all, there are specific political conditions that make it possible to exit the heart of a growing world market. If Alexandra could return to her mother's countryside bungalow, it was because she and her mother had occupied that land through the landless movement, the MST. The MST's occupations succeeded because the 1988 Constitution has a clause that allows the government to expropriate large, unproductive plantations and give the land to small farmers. The clause exists because the entire Constitution was rewritten when Brazilians ousted the dictatorship, and the MST spent years protesting to make sure this clause got included. And Alexandra would be able to subsist outside of the wage labor market, in part, through the social programs created after the election of a left-leaning president. In other words, in the moment when Alexandra came home, she was fulfilling a process that had taken decades of democracy to develop, step by step.

Between 2005 and 2010, nearly 1 million Brazilians migrated back to the places where they were born (Baptista, Campos, and Rigotti 2017: 12). Journeys like these suggest a different way of thinking about growth. It becomes possible to depict growth not by imagining an inevitable arrow that points forward, but rather—to recover Mintz's metaphor of the oscillation—by envisioning one swing of a pendulum that could very well swing the other way. We need such a perspective, such a view of the varied possible options, if we hope to understand growth not as a mechanical outcome but as a set of human actions. To gain that perspective, let me tarry with the details of the meaningful world in which Alexandra, on the phone with her mother from the dry village, found herself faced with a dilemma.

Changing Your Objective: Growth in the Oscillation

A year and a half before the phone call, Alexandra arrived in Belo Horizonte. A bus dropped her at a decaying terminal in the middle of a bowl of hills, each hill crested with concrete skyscrapers, while beyond the skyscrapers stretched forests and a wall of red mountains. What made the mountains red was iron.

The iron had drawn in Alexandra's brothers some years before, part of a flood of young people from the village of Maracujá. They worked as subcontracted firefighters for Vale, one of the largest mining conglomerates in the world. Vale guaranteed Brazil's place in the global commodities boom of the early 2000s. The company released a flow of iron ore that poured like a metal river through the shipping lanes of the world's oceans, up to the ports of China. Her brothers labored to make that river run. When they grew tired, they would quit their jobs and return to their parents and wives at Maracujá—only to head back to the city again, usually after a few months.

Alexandra's sister Selma had gone, too, during one of the trips to the city. Selma found work as a servant in the house of a stockbroker's family. When Selma and her husband learned that they were expecting a child, Alexandra felt a sense of obligation to leave the village and to move to Belo Horizonte so she could help her sister. Selma herself offered to pay for something that Alexandra aspired to do: a business management class that culminated in an official diploma. So Alexandra went to the city, not to save up a stock of money, as many people did, but to care for her sister and to take a class.

Alexandra started out in Belo Horizonte by spending five days toiling as a servant alongside her sister. "But there," she explained to me, "I didn't feel myself to be—a domestic worker. I preferred more things." At a bakery, Alexandra overheard strangers saying that one of the employees at the Hotel Paris could not handle the work. "I took the risk," Alexandra remembered. She deposited a fresh résumé and applied for a front-desk job. During her interview, the hotel boss asked her a searching question, which she recalled for me in detail:

"He said—then, what really was my objective there? I said, my objective was to be with my sister and to take a class [. . .] Then he put it just like this: 'Okay, then. You'll work here.'"

Alexandra found other work as well. In the neighborhood where she and her brothers lived, a restaurant owner spotted Alexandra coming and going to the business course, dressed carefully in a student's uniform. The owner had trouble doing figures. She asked Alexandra, *Could you help me?* Soon, Alexandra was starting her days by organizing packed meals for workers to eat at their jobs. She was also growing accustomed to a group of men who filled the restaurant, shut the doors, pulled down the front grating, and brought out suitcases of cash. One day, the men invited Alexandra to lunch at their house. She remembered for me what they told her there: "Hey, Bahia woman, anything that you need—you can count on us. No one messes with you. Not with you and not with anyone from your family."

Alexandra became close to the men, especially one of them, who talked to her about his sadness. He told her never to use drugs. She watched him put toilet paper in his nose on the days when he felt ill from cocaine; she visited his wife at their house. "Over there," Alexandra explained to me, "we made friendships with good people, with honest people, people of good character. But"— she paused as if searching for the word—"people, for example thieves, with those little smoker guys. You know, with everything."

Alexandra did not stop looking for work; she had new possibilities in mind. At the bakery one day, she bought a newspaper along with her bread and milk, and there she found a help-wanted ad from a luxury grocery store. When she interviewed at the store, Alexandra reduced the interviewer to tears with a lengthy description of her children back in the village. She was quickly hired for a job she felt excited to have, and she left her hotel job behind.

Alexandra told me that she felt proud to put on the uniform of the grocery store. She felt glad to send money to her parents every month. She spent her free time at one of the city's shopping malls—even if it was only to ride the elevators up and down, so that every spare cent could go back to the village. She remembered the malnutrition that she herself had suffered in the countryside. When Alexandra was a child, for days at a time there was nothing to eat but pumpkin; on other days, only boiled green bananas. Once, her sister nearly fell off a donkey because she had fainted from malnourishment. Those memories affected Alexandra in Belo Horizonte. As she put it:

> We've been through a lot of hunger. [. . .] And there [in the city]—I was always thinking, 'Gosh, do you think that Mom is eating? Do you think that Dad is

eating?' Early in the morning, I would take coffee with milk in it, with bread, and I always thought, were my children eating? Was my mom eating?

Alexandra's goal began slipping, until it became something new. Now she lived the city in order to earn "that little sacred money [. . .] to send back home. That was what the objective was, there. Not partying and not fun." Her urban life no longer centered on helping her sister and taking a class. The city was for cash.

Alexandra's sister Selma gave birth, then quit her job and returned to the village (losing the suitcase along the road). Alexandra's class moved along to new topics: computer skills, public presentation, accounting. At work, Alexandra was changing as well. She learned to bake panettone; she earned a position as a VIP employee. On Easter she won a coupon that entitled her to four giant candy eggs. She sent them to her children in the village.

Alexandra, now the VIP employee, found herself more comfortable and bolder. During work hours, she would snack on the merchandise. Her bosses scolded her at a store meeting: "Little Bahia girl, you're eating too much! And you even do it in front of the security camera." She told them, "If I'm eating, it's because I'm hungry!" "I always ate live," she recalled, live and in front of the cameras, "for them to see that I was eating, that I was hungry." This was not the hunger she had lived as a child. It was hunger in the middle of a supermarket.

Looking at Growth More Closely: Chapter Summaries

Growth did not simply enable Alexandra to reach her goals; growth changed those very goals.[26] Did Alexandra go to Belo Horizonte to help her sister? to take a business course? to earn money to send home? It was not easy for her to say, and the answer shifted over time.

But if ambivalence echoes inside Alexandra's account, this ambivalence is not hers alone. What is growth really *for*? What does it mean to grow? These scholarly questions are asked by Alexandra and economists alike—and asked, too, by Alexandra's former neighbors at Maracujá and Rio Branco. This book tries to engage with such questions by attending to the small details of migration, step by step. Each chapter in this book discusses one step on a migrant's journey to the villages. Each chapter also covers a question about growth, command, and class.

What turns a sentence into a command? Chapter 1 considers this question by listening to the phone calls that migrants make from the city to the village. Callers can *hear* growth—and its alternatives—not only in the words spoken

INTRODUCTION

over the line, but also in the way those words are spoken, in the speech genres that emerge when people talk into the receiver. Through their phone calls home, migrants hear the difference between a voice that *commands* you (like the voice of the boss in the workplace) and a voice that *offers advice* or *calls on* you to do something (like the voice of a relative on the phone). The friction between these voices can spark a sense of dissonance and nostalgia that impels migrants to imagine a move back to the village.

Chapter 2 inquires into the definition of growth, taking roads as a key example. The chapter explores the roads that have wound their way to and from Maracujá and Rio Branco over the past hundred years—from footpaths and mule tracks to narrow passageways for cars and, finally, a scheduled bus route. By telling the story of a century's worth of roads, the chapter offers a survey of the history of the villages. Farmers recall their varying voyages down these roads, and the voyages become a flashpoint for debating growth. Farmers puzzle over a fundamental economic question: When we talk about growth, what is the thing that is imagined to grow? Is it the flow of goods and services? the store of human knowledge? the strength of institutions? overall human welfare? This chapter listens to the arguments of villagers and academic economists, who engage in strikingly similar disputes over the meaning of growth. The chapter argues that growth can be imagined as a form of intensity, an intense appetite for cooperation. Growth is an enthusiasm that, just like a road, brings people together while it moves forward across distance.

Chapter 3 concerns the bus ride. Passengers usually take twenty-four bumpy, dust-filled hours to ride a bus between the villages and the urban job market. During those hours, migrants change how they talk about themselves. City-bound migrants represent themselves as if they were the bearers of a substance: abstract labor. When migrants travel back from the city, they turn away from growth by inventing novel ideas about their labor. These ideas become manifest in new practices for tracking time. The ideas do not simply require that you be your own boss; they require you to have no boss and to live surrounded by other people who also have no bosses. In the difference between *being your own boss* and *having no bosses*, we can understand the autonomy that blossoms in the villages.

Why would you sell your tubers without weighing them first? Chapter 4 takes a close look at the cargo that flows out from the villages. Village farmers send produce to the world market, but as they do so, they strive to maintain a sense of distance. This distance is powerfully manifested by the practice of *bistunta*, a kind of sale in which the buyer and the seller both agree not to calculate the product's weight until the transaction has finished. By refusing to measure their produce—thus deferring the abstraction—farmers set limits to their engagement with the market.

Chapter 5 traces the circuitous routes that people use to send money out of the city and into the countryside—through purses, third-party bank accounts, loan sharks, and, above all, durable goods. Money, villagers often say, is useless. What matters more is an asset to hold. The chapter outlines a theory of social class that is grounded in assets and the practical movement of money. In charting this motion, I engage with Millar's notion of "plastic economy" (2018: 127). Each migrant traces out a distinctive asset chain: a sequence of special objects to be acquired in order, over a period of years, so as to achieve stability. As a migrant develops a specific representation of things and of time, that migrant acquires a social class position. This position, lived out in the form of the asset chain, offers the migrant a clear response to the question that seems so hard to answer during the haze of a migratory move: what resource matters more than money?

Chapter 6 begins by asking why migrants insist on not speaking about savings. Villagers spend years working in the city to accumulate cash for a new cow, a flock of turkeys—or even a synthesizer. However, at Maracujá and Rio Branco, people do *not* refer to all of these efforts as "saving." "Money's no good for saving," a woman named Marília told me, echoing a sentiment common in the villages, especially after the hyperinflation of the 1980s. Instead of saving, migrants hold on to a family house or a cattle herd. They develop characteristic imaginations about how to preserve some element of surplus from the cycle of labor and accumulation. These imaginations, here referred to as *premios*, are labor's inverse; they are the dream of a realm beyond work, a place to retire to after labors have finished or an heirloom to stay in the kinship line forever. The chapter argues that the dream of a space outside of labor is, itself, a core sign that represents one's engagement with labor. In developing its practices of inalienability, a group takes a fundamental step toward forming itself as a social class, that is, a collective of people who have a shared relation to labor. The villages have become an especially important ground for germinating such inalienable dreams.

From phone call to bus ride, from money to homebuilding, the conclusion draws together the moments that make up a move toward the villages. The conclusion reads these moments as responses to the imperative of command and cooperation. Migrants invent mundane and ingenious logistics to swim against a tide of rising wages, and in inventing these logistics—in forcing the unbalanced oscillation—migrants reveal something of the truth about growth.

*

After the Saturday when her boss kept her for five extra hours, Tamara never did return. She left the job and the city, climbing onto the overnight bus that would take her back to the village that perched on the edge of the yellow hill.

During her three years in São Paulo, Tamara had gotten a few calls from the boyfriend who once asked her mother for her hand. She figured she would marry him when she returned to the village.

On a Thursday, she arrived, walking through the steep and dusty streets once more, heading up to the door of the boyfriend's house. They spoke. He agreed to spend Saturday with her.

But when Saturday showed up, the boyfriend did not. Tamara waited and waited. Someone was throwing a party in the village hills that night, and she could hear the sounds. And finally, she grew tired of the waiting and made her way to the party. There, amid the music, she found an acquaintance named Martim. Tamara remembered Martim from three years before, when she knew him as her friend's boyfriend. Now he was single and nineteen. They chatted; they held each other. The next day, Tamara's old boyfriend came by to talk. She told him it was too late.

Tamara, within the course of a few days, had found the courage to say no first to her boss, then to her old boyfriend. That night, she held Martim in her arms once more. Twelve years later, in the same yellow hills, between the adobe walls of the house where she and Martim lived with their four children, I recorded this story.

*

After her mother called her, Alexandra spoke to her supervisors at the luxury grocery store. They did not want her to leave. Standing in the business school where she almost had a diploma, Alexandra needed to make a decision.

Between the bus schedule and the maze of diploma requirements, Alexandra faced the pressure of something that was pushing against economic growth. She mused about what her objective really had been—and what it was. She had gone to the city to help her sister's baby and to take a course, not to earn money.

> When you leave to go work, you have to have an objective. "I'm going, and I'll work, and I'll get some money together," and that stuff. I did not go for that. But I, I—got the opportunity of employment.

That opportunity had changed the possibilities she faced. It changed her objective. When her sister returned to the village with the baby, Alexandra stayed in the city and stayed working.

She considered what she might be able to get in the city. "I don't know," she pondered.

> I might even not get it, you know? That thing, a, a life that's more—whatever, you know, for, for my children. But—[. . .] We, me and my brother, we would already be financing a house! Because it's like this. With my salary—[. . .] with proof of our jobs, then that would be, like, really big. Because anyone who works in that grocery store is a privileged person.

Why had she come to work in the city, after all? She turned it all over in her head, and then, she said, she made a decision.

> Nothing more valuable. I said it just like this: "I didn't come here to earn money. I didn't come here to do that. I came to be close to my sister. To something that's my family. Now I am going there."

She quit her job, said goodbye to the school, and got on the bus.

1

The Phone Call Home

Forms of Speech in the Growth Process

> On arriving I called home. Before I could speak, I began to weep as I heard the far-away sound of mama's voice. I tried to find the words, to slow down, to tell her how it felt to be a stranger, to speak my uncertainty and longing. She told me this is the lot I had chosen. I must live with it. After her words there was only silence. She had hung up on me—let me go into this world where I am a stranger still.
> BELL HOOKS, *Where We Stand: Class Matters* (2000: 33)

One day at Maracujá, not far from the green coffee berries growing fat on Marcos's tiny field, I asked Marcos why he had returned. Beyond us, a dirt road twisted past old beehives and then it sank until it fell out of sight in the yellow of the dry valley. A few tile roofs peeked out, perched atop adobe walls. The scent of cookfire seeped into the air. It was 2012, and Marcos was twenty-two.

Four years before, he had been living in a factory neighborhood of Belo Horizonte, in a house he shared with Alexandra's brothers. Marcos and the brothers worked together at a giant mining company. Their job was to extinguish the forest fires that broke out around iron ore mines. Now Marcos sat with me by his field, remembering the trees in flames, the biweekly paychecks, the new clothes on payday, the trips to the nightclubs. He said, "It was totally great."

Marcos remembered, too, the phone calls to his family. Every time he called, he would hear, over the noises of the long-distance connection, the sound of his parents crying. "I couldn't stand those *saudades*—missing them desperately," Marcos explained to me. "And I ended up coming back here."

*

Valentina told me that she heard tears during her phone calls, too. The tears were her own. When she moved to the city of Conquista, she could barely speak with her parents because she would start crying as soon as their voices came on the line. All she could manage to get out was the traditional request for a parent's blessing. "'A blessing, Mom! A blessing, Mommy!' [. . .] "And then," Valentina recalled, "a crazy cry-fest [*um chororó danado*]. [...] For me to get used to it, I think it took a year."

*

Diego, in São Paulo, walked every day from the dormitory on his construction site to a pay phone so that he could call his mother and weep. "Over there," he explained to me, "I felt like no one."

Diego, however, got something besides a blessing. Between the tears, Diego's mother dispensed financial advice. He should take his pay, she instructed, and deposit it in her bank account, so he could save it bit by bit.

Diego's mother already knew the money's purpose. When Diego was a child, his parents would hear him singing to himself while he toiled in the field alongside them. Even then, he imagined himself in front of a crowd, behind the keyboard of an electronic synthesizer. "I thought that right there was beautiful," Diego told me. "I started to get obsessed for real. [...] You see that object, and you spend day and night dreaming of it. And really, it's something you can reach." Diego would not come back from São Paulo without buying a synthesizer.

Diego recalled for me what happened once he realized, after months of work on the construction site, that he had saved almost enough for the synthesizer. He went to the telephone. "I called Mom and said, 'Mom, I'm eight hundred reais short of four thousand.'" Hearing the news, his mother picked out the best cow in the family's herd. She sold it and sent the money to Diego in the city—still not enough for the synthesizer, but at least a step forward. "That's how bad," Diego remembered, "the *saudade* was."

*

When migrants told me about their travels, one particular device lurked on the sidelines of the story, never at the center of attention, but rarely missing from the plot. This was the telephone. Subject to the challenges of faulty wires, unreliable reception, drained batteries, and exhausted phone cards, the telephone call was also subject to the tears and joys of kinship drama. Telephone calls served as the supreme setting for unfolding what Marcos and Diego referred to as *saudades*, an emotion that observers sometimes describe as a paradigmatic Luso-Brazilian sentiment (Rebhun 1999: 20), a terrible longing that feels so painful precisely because it contains inside it the happiness of remembering that which is missed. A migrant's journey back to the village often began with a sad, difficult, or hopeful phone call.

This chapter listens for the telephone. It interprets the phone call as a mundane practice that migrants employ to send cash, spread gossip, or sense love. Most frequently, because of the cost involved, migrants in the city called people in the village rather than the other way around. From this practice of city-to-village calling, I derived the titles for this chapter's two parts: "Incoming Call," about the practice of picking up the phone in the villages, and "Outgoing Call," about what happens in the city when a migrant dials home.

Phone calls serve as a key sign of economic growth. Phone technology did not exist in the villages a few decades ago. Today, phone calls bring migrants and family members into more intense relations of cooperation with one another. Growth, in this case, is not only a matter of delivering new machines called telephones; growth is also about the quotidian habits and rhythms that people create as they use the phone to give a new shape to their days.

But when migrants told me stories about phone calls, these stories did not usually glorify growth. On the contrary: in story after story, what precipitated the return trip to the village—what prompted a worker to leave wage labor—was a telephone call. How was it, exactly, that migrants and their families turned the phone call into a persuasive argument *against* growth?

The argument becomes persuasive, in part, because a phone call allows a migrant to hear discrepant voices: ways of speaking and personas that do not fit into her workaday world.[1] During their phone calls home, migrants listen to the difference between the village and the urban wage labor market. This difference lives not only in the message spoken, but also in how that message is framed. I identify two speech-acts that rural family members use when talking to migrants on the phone: *dar conselhos* (giving advice) and *chamar* (calling on someone to do something). *Conselhos* and *chamadas* have hortatory force, yet they do not sound at all like *mandar* (commanding), the forceful speech that comes from the boss at a migrant's job. When bosses issue commands, these commands create the foundation that allows migrants to cooperate with each other at work. *Conselhos* and *chamadas* point toward an alternative, less intrusive mode of cooperation.

Inside the migrant's daily urban soundscape, authoritative speech from the boss made a dissonant counterpoint to authoritative speech from the villages. This counterpoint conveyed a politics. In each phone call, if you listened right, you might hear an analysis of the kinds of authority that accompany economic growth. You might hear a debate about exactly how much growth a person should accept. The analysis and debate were encoded in the different voices that people used as they talked to each other on the line. In boom-time Brazil, as it turns out, growth involved learning a certain kind of speech—and so did leaving growth behind.

Part 1. Incoming Call

A BRIEF HISTORY OF THE TELEPHONE AT MARACUJÁ AND RIO BRANCO

Evening after evening, for a week, Alexandra's family spent hours standing close, but not too close, to the pay phone. One night I stood next to them. Dusk had already fallen, and in front of us, a quiet line of people formed around the pay phone dome. Someone was on a call. On one side of the caller were the school's cement classrooms; on the other, the fields where donkeys had been untied to wander in the night. The people waiting in line were clustered almost directly in front of the nest of barbed wire that the telephone company installed around the multistory antenna, which broadcast the phone's signal to the company's network in the city.

The line at the pay phone was a mundane occurrence, but Alexandra's family were not standing in line. They were waiting, anxiously, for the phone to ring. A few days earlier, Alexandra's brother Natan had been rushed to the city with a fierce pain in his belly. Just as Alexandra had once moved to Belo Horizonte to take care of her sister Selma, Selma now sprang to help her brother. She prevailed upon her boss, a city doctor whose child she nannied, to find an appointment time for Natan. And the doctor did. With Natan now away for treatment, the family gathered stoically by the pay phone, in the evenings, in case a call came through.

Pay phones in Brazil are referred to as "giant ears" (*orelhões*). By 2016, orelhões had fallen into disuse in cities, but they remained important in the countryside, even though it was dauntingly difficult to get a call to connect correctly. An orelhão usually hung on a metal post inside a curving blue plastic dome. The dome provided some measure of quiet for the person who stood inside and spoke on the phone. It was not very effective for privacy, however, as I learned one day in 2012, when I sang the words of a Brazilian children's song while I was talking on the phone to my romantic partner. The area around the phone, I had thought, was empty. But the next day, a village leader came up to me, pointed a finger in my face, sang the song, and burst out laughing.

If other people and I brushed up against pieces of each other's lives, it was because pay phones were semipublic places in the villages. Invariably located in a small dirt patch near a knot of houses, rural pay phones served as collective hubs for connecting a village to places beyond it. This infrastructure was built through a protracted political history.

Until the 1990s, Rio Branco and Maracujá lacked telephones. Instead of using phones, migrants and villagers would send oral messages back and forth through the chain of friends who cycled between metropolis and countryside.

Sometimes, migrants and villagers wrote letters to each other. But a letter had to overcome many obstacles. A sender might need to find someone to help write the letter, and a recipient might need to find someone to help read it. Even getting the letter to the mailbox was a challenge, since the villages had (and still have) no mail service.

The region's first telephones came as the fruit of activism. Once the MST had set up landless settlements in the area, in the mid-1990s, the settlement residents began organizing themselves to demand services—and one such service was telephones. The first pay phones were installed at the centers of the land settlements. These phones had an effect well beyond the settlements, because landless activists welcomed the neighboring small farmers to use the new technology as well.

Throughout the early 2000s, phone service expanded slowly. A few households at Maracujá managed to purchase landlines that were connected to the same big antenna that transmitted the signal from the pay phones. Rio Branco eventually came within reach of a cell tower signal, although as of 2016 this signal was so weak that residents had to purchase expensive amplifying antennas for their households.

The pay phones broke down on a regular basis, leading to irate or supplicatory calls, placed on neighbors' telephones, from the villages to the central telephone company. Sometimes, though, self-help worked better than petition. Once, when a pay phone at Maracujá wasn't functioning, a villager discovered that if you took a wooden stick from a tree and inserted it 5 inches into a small hole behind the cradle, you could get the phone to connect.

Pay phones represented undeniable economic progress. They were signs of growth, if by growth one simply meant an increase in machine commodities. But phones corresponded to growth in another sense as well. Telephones tied villagers into a tighter kind of collaboration with a wider group of people: with the migrant family members whose calls rang in the center of the village, with the phone company technicians on whom the villagers now depended, and with the statewide activists who successfully demanded the infrastructure. This change also happened in an even tinier and more local sense. As they developed practices for answering the telephone, villagers created new forms of cooperation with *each other*.[2] To describe this cooperation, it is first necessary to make a detour and consider the rhythms of an average day at Maracujá and Rio Branco, where work tends to take place as a solitary deed.

Phone call practices are a miniature example that turns out to reveal, in these fiercely freeholding villages, the tense negotiation between collaboration and autarky that surrounds every productive act.

WHAT A PHONE CALL INTERRUPTS: EVERYDAY PATTERNS

A phone call in the villages usually arrives as a disruption in the daily routine. At both Maracujá and Rio Branco, nearly everyone is awake shortly after dawn, but this is rarely a time for phone calls. Instead, a few people set radios blaring loudly enough for the neighbors to hear. Women heat coffee in aluminum pots balanced over a wood fire or a gas flame. After drinking black coffee with sugar—and, in more prosperous homes, perhaps a bit of bread brought in from the city—the children with morning classes go to school.

Men also usually leave the house for the morning. Some days, this means walking to one's own field, perhaps to clear land with a hoe, repair a fence, or manage livestock. Other days, a man might work for pay on someone else's land. At both Maracujá and Rio Branco, some men also participate in a men's voluntary rotating labor exchange (*mutirão*) one day each week. They devote that day to working together on the field of the farmer whose turn it is.

Women engage in a wider variety of morning tasks than men do. Some women spend mornings working in their own fields. Women are also hired as day laborers in the villages, especially during the harvest, and for specific tasks, like removing the skin from manioc roots; they are paid systematically less than men for such work: in 2012, the going day-wage was R$25 for men and R$15 for women. Women at Maracujá are well known for having their own women's weekly labor exchange, or mutirão, better and more consistent than the men's. In addition to all these forms of work on the small farms of the villages, during the coffee harvest season many women, along with some men, travel great distances each day to work on the plantations.

Some women spend the morning earning money outside of the fields. Dona Eva awakened near dawn each day to mix butter with manioc flour, roll it into balls in the palm of her hand, and roast the balls on thick metal pans inside a firewood oven. After a few minutes of heating, she took out translucent pastries and slipped them into plastic bags that she sealed with the flame of a candle. So light and airy that they were known as *voadores*, or "fliers," these pastries became famous in the region. Dona Eva sold them on Saturdays at a fair at a nearby city. Many women, like Dona Eva, toil during the morning to prepare and market goods and services. Some freeze popsicles, run dry goods stores out of their living rooms, or grow patches of greens for sale to neighbors. Others earn money by washing clothes for other households or taking care of elderly people who live nearby. Women, no matter what work they are doing, often care for their own small children at the same time as they labor at other tasks.

Beyond paid employment, villagers also speak of a core set of morning household tasks, referred to as *faxina*, that women are widely expected to perform at home. Faxina is standard across households at Maracujá and Rio Branco. It includes straightening up in the house, mopping floors with a rag soaked in a bucket, sweeping in a pattern in front of and behind the house so that orderly lines are visible in the soil of the yard, and, several times a month, layering green or red wax dye onto a house's cement floors. These tasks are accompanied by clothes washing, washing the dishes from the night before, and preparing food for lunch and dinner. Maracujá and Rio Branco have no running water. To carry out faxina, women are faced with the heavy burden of fetching water from cisterns outdoors. Because of the dry climate and the unpaved roads, faxina involves a constant struggle against dust, which blows in at the edges of the shutters on the glassless windows or through the gaps between the roof tiles, settling in a dark-golden layer over everything in the house.

Women often told me that they preferred to finish as much faxina as possible in the morning. The goal is to leave a clean house with three standard pots of food neatly arranged on the stove: one with simmered pink beans, one with meat (on the days when a family can afford it), and one with rice flavored by soybean oil and garlic. Next to the pots sit several serving spoons and a container of rough manioc flour (*farinha*). Squash, potatoes, lettuce, tomatoes, or home-squeezed fruit juice might adorn the table in more prosperous moments. At lunchtime, unless they are far away for work, children and adults reunite at this freshly ordered house. They eat the largest meal of the day, gathering at the stove to serve themselves with the spoons and cover their plates with the thick, creamy-tasting manioc flour.

After lunch, family members often take brief naps, sometimes near the television, especially on the hottest days. Then children with afternoon classes go to school, while adults turn their attention to the same tasks as in the morning, devoting themselves to agriculture or housecleaning, although often with greater care to avoid heat exhaustion. Once the early evening sets in, the trails and dirt roads around the villages begin to fill with people who return from the fields in the last light of the day.

Evening is the paradigmatic sociable time in the villages. People tend to eat a cursory dinner out of the same pots, which have remained on the stove throughout the day. Evenings do not revolve around one's own household, however, but around others: neighbors, on whose couch one might watch a telenovela; visitors, who might be entertained with a guitar and rounds of coffee; co-religionists, with whom one might gather to pray a novena on wooden pews or to sing the words of an evangelical hymn over a prerecorded mp3 track. In the evenings, families often throw open the shutters of their houses, spilling the light from their few electric bulbs onto the dirt of the street, making themselves accessible to greetings shouted in by passers-by. The villages' home-based bars also open their doors and become centers for (mostly male) storytelling. Churches hold services that run late into the night. Children and young people meet to play soccer and joke together in the middle of each village.

This, the course of a whole day, is the rhythm that a phone call disrupts. It is a rhythm timed by solitude, the solitude of everyday work. Evenings at Maracujá and Rio Branco feel sociable because evening breaks the solitary pattern that dominates the day. In the fields, in the houses, both women and men spend much of the workday entirely alone or alone with small children—alone while you hoe your own field, alone while you water your own kitchen garden, alone while you dye green the stony floor of your own home. Work is basically a solitary activity.

When villagers migrate, they typically dive into a very different labor process. There is little solitude to be found in clothing factories, agribusiness farms, supermarkets, and construction sites.[3] Here, every small gesture of labor may require collaboration with co-workers, and employment hums with the managed, surveilled sociality of shared work. The person who manages this collaborative action is usually a boss holding a paycheck. For migrants in such a context, economic growth means moving away from solitary work and toward more intensive cooperation.

But it would be a mistake to diagnose historical progress here. The villagers are not Europe's ancient peasants, and they have not been working alone since the Middle Ages. In fact, many of the farmers at Maracujá and Rio Branco lived in their youth as *moradores*—resident laborers on the region's giant plantations. Since the era of enslavement (and up to the present), such plantation laborers have spent their days in large-scale collective work directed by the plantation owner. Plantation labor is not solitary.

The plantation system produced a constant conflict between cooperation and autonomy. While they toiled under the owner's command, many of these workers also engaged, as Sigaud (1976, 2007) and Palmeira (1976) document, in continual little maneuvers so they could spend more of their evenings and days off working by themselves, on their own personal fields. Maracujá and Rio Branco today feel like places where workers won these struggles—where workers won the right to be left alone. Indeed, they did win this right: such is, in a very real sense, the history of these villages. They are communities created by plantation laborers who sought to leave wage labor behind so they could work by themselves, for themselves.

The solitude in the daily work process, then, is no accident. Villagers have built this solitude, quite carefully, in contradistinction to the alternatives around them.[4] It is solitude in comparison to migratory work in the cities and solitude in comparison to residential work on a plantation. Solitary labor blooms in the wreckage of previous growth models.

Given the imperatives of solitude and independence, the daily challenge at Maracujá and Rio Branco is how to persuade the people around you to break through the aloneness and engage in shared activity—how to create social energy. In agriculture, farmers often need each other's collaboration, but the mechanisms for organizing it are fragile. Voluntary shared labor arrangements (such as mutirão) often fall apart. Hired day laborers are expensive, fickle, and frequently suspicious of a type of work they find undignified.

Outside of agriculture, the same problem appears in other forms. Religious groups and social movements strive mightily to overcome solitude, aiming to generate waves of excitement for revivals or rallies. Villagers even face this challenge when they plan a party. They take care to spread the word about an upcoming birthday or a baby shower and worry constantly about attendance.

In the ordering of daily action, from cooking pink beans to planning a church service, people at Rio Branco and Maracujá negotiate an abiding tension between autarky and collaboration. Growth means pushing the balance toward more intense collaboration. And during the most recent growth wave, for the first time in the villages, collaboration was debated through the telephone.

HOW TO TAKE A PHONE CALL IN THE VILLAGES

When a pay phone rings in the villages, everyone within earshot is faced with an instant dilemma. Should you answer? Adults look at each other uncomfortably; some pretend not to hear. The call is possibly—probably—not for you. The caller may ask you to take a message, track someone down, or say if a person is or isn't around. To answer means, unpredictably and somewhat irrevocably, to get involved in other people's lives.

Surprisingly, people do tend to answer. Phone calls, in fact, can become the center of a mundane network, stretching across households, that links phone-answerers, message-takers, overhearers, and rumor-spreaders. Phone calls are unifying events. The long, monotone ring from inside the plastic dome easily achieves what bosses, pastors, and activists struggle to accomplish: it unleashes a small wave of collective action.

The best responders to the telephone, by far, are children between the ages of six and twelve. When the pay phone rings, a cluster of them tend to rush out from inside their houses to try to pick it up first. The child asks the caller a single question, at rapid speed and with no preface, *To whom do you want to speak?* (*Você quer falar com quem?*) The child usually instructs the caller to hang up rather than waiting. Then the child goes to fetch the intended recipient of the call, who stops whatever they are doing and stands by the pay phone until the caller calls back. Often enough, the child is unable to find the recipient. This can lead to extended complications: children leaving messages with someone else, children forgetting to leave messages, passers-by picking up the phone when the caller calls back, further messages getting left, and thus, not infrequently, the mobilization of a whole swath of the village in attempting to connect the call.

Maracujá, in 2012, had two pay phones. Rio Branco had none; the nearest was located in a neighboring land settlement. But Rio Branco was close enough to a cellular signal that many households could often (although not always) get reception if they purchased special amplifying antennas. Nonetheless, incoming calls at Rio Branco have a public quality, just as they do at Maracujá. Given the problems with reception and the possibility that the intended recipient may not be home, callers often end up dialing several different houses and leaving messages with neighbors.

At Rio Branco and Maracujá, a call is thus public business. When thirteen-year-old Karina traveled to São Paulo for a visit with her sister, she called on the pay phone and asked to speak to her boyfriend Suso back at Maracujá. She did not ask to speak to her mother. Her mother heard the news and complained loudly enough that the gossip reached even my ears.

On another day, I found Analis in happy anticipation inside her tiny brick house. "The kids are in São Paulo," she explained. "Right now, at six pm, one—one is going to call me."

Analis knew this because of her neighbor Zaira, who, unlike Analis, had both electricity and a phone at home. "Zaira came to tell me. She said that one of them called." Analis's voice strengthened. "And I asked God. 'God, I want to talk to my children. Lord, figure out some way for my children to talk to me' [*o Senhor dá um jeito para meus filhos falar comigo*]. [. . .] God worked. So you have to thank God very much. Even out here—getting rain on your back, toiling at heavy labor."

"Mm-hm," I murmured.

"But you've got to thank God just like that."

Phone calls in the village are a focal point of energy, a compelling reason to reach across the fence and get involved with your neighbor. From the metropolis to the dusty pay phone dome, via generous neighbors and angry mothers, phone calls create something greater than a connection between a caller and a receiver. A single phone call knits many people together into a network of excitement. In other words, phone calls nourish the social spirit of growth: they make people enthusiastic about cooperating with each other.

Phone calls appear in the villages as one small instance of what we might think of as the beloved face of growth. Around the same time as the arrival of the phones, villages began to see itinerant doctors and new rural schools, clean water pumps and debit cards that delivered the monthly Bolsa Família cash to mothers of children. Everyone in the villages seemed to feel glad for these changes (see chapter 2). They were growth at its best.

The beloved face of growth came mostly, but not entirely, through government intervention. As farmers enjoyed their pay phones (and schools and water pumps), the Workers Party celebrated. For some policymakers on the "developmentalist" left, perhaps, the villagers' enthusiasm proved a point: pro-poor economic growth really was the best solution for rural Brazilians. Everyone liked a phone.

But the conversation does not end so simply. People did feel enthusiasm for phones—but people also turned phones to their own purposes (Sahlins 1994). At Maracujá and Rio Branco, farmers seemed to appreciate both the power to grow and the power to set a limit on how far growth could go.

DECOMMODIFYING THE PHONE CALL

People at Maracujá and Rio Branco are enthusiastic about phones. Villagers channel this enthusiasm into a flood of new practices that involve *sharing* phones and *leveling* economic differences. If you have money, you are obligated to help others use the phone. We might think of these new practices as efforts to decommodify the phone call.

At the interface with the telephone company, phone calls are undeniably a commodity. You pay a monthly landline bill, you cover the fee for the prepaid minutes that you add to a cell, or you push cash over the wooden counter at a tiny general store in exchange for a pay phone card. Yet in each of these cases, people subsequently make the purchased item available to others for free.

When I arrived at Maracujá and learned about people's landline connections, I expected to find small entrepreneurs charging for the use of their landlines. This kind of business has been documented elsewhere (Karim 2011: 96). But, as best I could discover, such transactions do not take place in the villages. People do ask their neighbors with landlines for permission to use the phone. But this permission is asked for and granted as a favor, at no charge. Similarly, people share cellphones at Rio Branco. A neighbor's cell might be borrowed for rapid calls, especially on a day when the unreliable cellphone signal seems not to be working at one's own house.

Phone cards circulate in the same decommodified economy of neighborly generosity and obligation. These thin plastic cards, when slid into the slot in the front of a pay phone, allow you to speak for a certain number of prepaid minutes. At Maracujá, people who need to make a call will frequently ask to use someone else's phone card. The phone card is often requested just for the purpose of giving a brief *toque*, a few rings or perhaps a short call to tell the recipient to call back at the pay phone number. Phone services thus become at least partially socialized wealth.

So phone calls generate enthusiasm about cooperating, but that enthusiasm is translated into sharing and leveling—into the idiom of local politeness. Villagers decommodify the phone call, and in this way they guarantee that cooperation does not condense into the form of capital accumulated in a few hands. A village entrepreneur *could* centralize and streamline the cooperation process; an aspiring magnate could build a small business by selling calls from a landline or minutes off a phone card. But nobody actually does this. Growth does not turn into a self-driven cycle of capital expansion. Instead, villagers undertake *growth through the gift*. With no accumulation and no drive for further profits, the enthusiasm about cooperation reaches its limits. The growth in cooperation happens, modestly, and then it goes no further.

In the development of telephone etiquette, something real and fragile is at stake, one of those easy-to-miss common motions in which people build a shared sensibility. As they help each other's calls connect, villagers cut across the lines of solitude that keep them separated from each other during their working day. They undo some of the isolation of their toil in their kitchens or fields. Growth, in other words, takes place not only with the installation of the telephones; it also occurs when people invent new ways to answer the phone. And growth is slowed and tamed—we might say growth is made democratic— when villagers insist on turning phone calls into something other than a commodity.

Part 2. Outgoing Call

LOVE BY TELEPHONE

Valentina and Patrício had a cellphone relationship. When they met, they had both been through pay phone relationships. Valentina, teenaged and devoted, had spent lovelorn years using a landline to stay close to Oscar, a young man from her village. She kissed Oscar on the night of the final day of 2001, and then he left for São Paulo. Oscar and Valentina dated for the next three years by telephone. In those three years, they saw each other for two months. The relationship eventually ended, and it was only years later that she would meet Patrício

Patrício, on his side, spotted Valentina for the first time while he was riding a horse to the pay phone so that *he* could call *his* girlfriend. Those were the days before Rio Branco had a cellphone signal, so Rio Branco's residents were used to traveling the hilly road to the nearby MST land settlement to make their calls. When Patrício reached the bottom of the hill, there was Valentina, surrounded by the children from the local school, planting a garden. Patrício would later learn that Valentina came from a different village and that she had been sent to the land settlement to work as a teacher. What he realized right away, he told me, was that he liked her.

Patrício's girlfriend lived in a small neighboring city. Patrício knew that there was an upcoming party planned at Rio Branco, and he realized that Valentina was likely to attend. He also knew that he had already invited his girlfriend. So Patrício devised a strategy. He told his girlfriend that he would fetch her on a motorcycle and bring her to the party, but when the day of the party arrived, he did not go pick her up, thus leaving himself free to flirt with the new teacher.

To Patrício's disappointment, the girlfriend found her own ride to Rio Branco that day. And so he spent the night with her in his arms, dancing, out of obligation. While he swayed with his girlfriend, however, he was looking over at Valentina. Valentina noticed. In fact, she told me, she had been noticing even before the party, ever since the day when she glanced up from gardening to see a young man, gorgeously mounted on horseback, near the pay phone.

I heard about all of this many years later. I was sitting at a little kitchen table with Patrício and Valentina, surrounded by the gray cement walls of the home they had not quite finished building. Valentina's nieces played close to the mango tree, and the chickens gathered by the kitchen door. To one side stood the new refrigerator that Valentina and Patrício had managed to buy; beyond it, an old, soundless television that they had not yet been able to replace. Rather than watching television, they invited me to look at the large-format pictures in their wedding album, and we flipped through photos and stories.

After the pay phone intrigues and the party, Valentina and Patrício ultimately began a relationship on St. John's Day, around the bonfire. She met his family and became a regular visitor at his mother's house. They shared the hilly landscape with each other, and they walked past the flowering trees together. But still, Patrício told me, this was nothing special: "Valentina, just another one [*Valentina, só mais uma*]." The situation changed only in 2010, when he received an offer to go to São Paulo to work in a clothing factory. He accepted.

Valentina came as far as the city of Conquista with Patrício to see him off, in the bus station where he would catch the twenty-four-hour coach to São Paulo. For a time, the two of them waited together next to the glossy interstate buses, under the corrugated-metal roof that straddled the dry plain, with Patrício's village already 100 kilometers behind them on one side and Valentina's family over the mountain that reached up on the other side. Then Patrício went into the bus station's luxury waiting room, the *sala VIP*, and Valentina decided not to follow him for a final goodbye. She left. As she headed up the avenue and toward the mountain, she began to reflect. "I said to myself, 'My God, I'm not going to see—you know? Not any time soon, you know? I don't know when.'

"And then that saudade came on me, that squeeze in the heart, do you understand?" Valentina turned around and went back up the avenue to the bus station again.

(At this point in the recollection, Valentina and Patrício both burst out laughing, and I joined them.)

"When—when I got back to the luxury waiting room, and I looked around, there was no one there. They'd already gone. The [coach] bus had already left, you know? [. . .] So I hadn't stayed with him to be able to see him get on the bus, right?

"Then there came upon me an even greater sadness, you know? Very, very great. [. . .] And I said to myself, 'My love already—already got on the bus, you know? Now it's all finished. Now it's just—'"

(Here Valentina interrupted her story to laugh a little.)

" 'Now we're only going to talk on the phone or when he gets back, right?' "

Valentina knew that Patrício did not have a cellphone.

Over the next few days, Valentina developed a plan. She found some friends of Patrício's who were traveling to São Paulo soon. She also found a box to send with them. She filled the box with manioc biscuits and other reminders of the things that he loved from his hometown. Finally, to put in the box, she wrote a letter to Patrício.

Years later, as I sat with them near the wedding album and the soundless television, Patrício rummaged through some belongings and pulled out the letter. It was on green paper, written in purple ink, the handwriting clear and scholastic, the handwriting of a teacher. Valentina had folded the missive carefully and drawn a heart at the bottom. "Oh my God!" I shouted when I saw it in his hands. "I'm not going to read a letter that's, like, so . . ."

"No!" Patrício responded in a booming voice. "You can read it!" Valentina began to laugh.

The letter read:

To my love, with much tenderness.

Hello love. I hope that the memories of our love are stronger every day in your memory and in your heart. May this immense distance that separates us be only a mere geographic distance because you live in me even more strongly.

I think of you at every moment and in every place where I am. And if I end up by myself somewhere, I find myself speaking out loud to you, seeming like a crazy person. I knew that this distance would be painful, and I only realized that it wasn't easy to return to being with you on the weekend, like usual, when I went back to the bus station to see you one more time and I didn't find you. Then I was invaded by a horrible feeling of loneliness.

But it's all right, you know? I try to wrap myself up completely in work so that time passes more quickly. It's just that I'm not going to be able to manage if I spend so much time without talking to you. Today, Thursday, the 21st of October, makes one week without news from you. It seems an eternity. But thank God, this will end.

Patrício interrupted the reading to explain something. As she prepared the box with the manioc biscuits and the reminders of home, Valentina visited the *paraguai*, the flea market known for its counterfeit imports, and she purchased one more gift—a cellphone.

Valentina's letter continued:

I'm sending you the cellphone. I bought it at the paraguai. So it won't last long if you use it to watch TV and listen to the radio a lot.

It has a memory card—the black chip on the side—and space for two SIM cards. I already put in a SIM card from Vivo Corporation. The SIM card is already registered. But don't buy any prepaid minutes for it because it's only for you to receive calls from here.

You need to buy a SIM card from TIM Corporation from this area code, understand, love? Because the one that you took with you won't allow us to benefit from the sale price. So go register it and whenever you want to call, always dial the 041 prefix and then Dad's cellphone number.

Now I will wait for your call with much saudades. All of us miss you very much. This weekend I'm going to your parents' house. It rained a lot. I love you very, very, very much. Kisses, kisses, kisses, kisses.

Valentina Moreira. October 21, 2010.

Once the package arrived, Patrício and Valentina began talking every night, after work, on the flea market cellphone. Within two months, he was back in the village of his birth.

ADVICE AND CALLING: AUTHORITATIVE SPEECH ACTS OVER THE PHONE

Valentina and Patrício depend on the cellphone. The practice of their love is wrapped up in the practicalities of phone usage: which company's plan to purchase, what area code to choose, how to take advantage of a sale. As the letter outlines these practicalities, Valentina adopts an authoritative tone, accentuated with verbs in the imperative mood. The letter calls for pragmatic action. In some important sense, however, the letter's call differs from the voice of the boss at the clothing factory where Patrício worked. The letter relies on a different mode of authority.

When migrants unfold a missive or cradle a cellphone, often what they often hear, coming from the countryside, is a *conselho* or a *chamada*, "advice" or "a call to do something." These are two specific speech acts, each with its own weight. Mothers and boyfriends, siblings and neighbors advise migrants to work hard, to use one bank rather than another, to stay at a job, or to leave things in God's hands. Family and friends may also, more pressingly, call on a migrant to return to observe a festival or take care of a child. Conselhos and chamadas are not suggestions to be taken lightly. They have power, and they can feel compelling. Indeed, Patrício told me that he reread Valentina's letter almost every night.

Conselhos and chamadas acquire their sense within the context of a migrant's new place of residence. Migrants in the city are confronted with a challenging and often discriminatory set of barriers. Fortunately, in the face of these obstacles, migrants also have access to a link to home. Placing a call is much easier in the city than in the countryside. One of a migrant's first purchases is often a SIM card, sometimes bought even before the phone itself, since a sympathetic city friend with a phone can allow the migrant to "change cards" (*trocar chips*), inserting the migrant's own card into the phone in order to make a call that will be automatically charged to the migrant's account.

With unstable housing, uncertain employment, and unsteady SIM cards, migrants have good reason to search for an anchor in their phone calls home. This anchor often takes shape through a particular mode of authoritative discourse: conselhos.

CONSELHOS: AUTHORITY THROUGH DECONTEXTUALIZATION

One evening, I watched a young man in a pink shirt duck inside the pay phone dome outside the school at Maracujá. A quarter-moon rose over him, but he was lit mostly by the orange glow of a village street lamp. Sounds of day had mostly subsided, and voices murmured around the houses where villagers sold beer, popsicles, or laundry soap to their neighbors through an open window or across a makeshift counter in a living room. The young man at the pay phone seemed sober and intent. "Let God work in his life," I heard him say into the receiver.

"Give it all you've got [*Bota para pocar*]," a woman enthused as I walked by the pay phone on a different occasion. Her voice sounded warm, and I sensed energy in her words. I surmised that she was offering advice to someone.

Giving advice (*dar conselhos*) is no casual gesture in the countryside. People give each other advice about matters ranging from agriculture to faith, from house construction to romance. Advice-giving is a speech act that villagers themselves name explicitly and about which they have an elaborate metadiscourse. *I gave her advice [dei conselhos] not to sell the pig*, a villager might report to a third person, thus holding the recipient of the advice accountable for taking it seriously.

When migrants travel outside of the village, advice travels with them, too. Alexandra remembered some advice that her brother offered during her first trip to Belo Horizonte. In the street near where she was staying, she had just witnessed a drug dealer being beaten over the head with a bicycle. She recalled for me her brother's words to her: "Simple: 'You saw it there, it's over.' You didn't have to—get in the middle. Nobody would mess with you if you did not mess with anyone [*Ninguém mexia em você se você não mexesse com ninguém*]."

These words of advice abstracted a difficult situation into a general principle expressed in the Portuguese imperfect tense and the language of absolutes, *nobody* and *anyone*. I heard abstraction even more clearly when Melchior described to me the letters he received from his adoptive mother while he toiled in the city.

MELCHIOR: She would ask for us to—have good judgment, be careful in life, and—that advice that a mother gives, you know? She was always, like, very rigid with—that honesty stuff, you know?
DUFF: Mm-hm.

M: [. . .] To take no wrong turns [*literally,* "*not to step on the ball*"], to walk straight, not—not—to want [*pause*] to make anyone into a ladder so that we could keep going onward in life, you know?
D: Mm-hm.
M: For us to—accept what God had blessed us—us with, there. A little—a little or a lot, right? That we should accept it in the same way and thank God. If I managed to get one real [*equivalent to US$0.50*], she would ask me to thank God for that real. If I earned a thousand reais, to thank God also for the thousand reais, you know? So she would give that kind of advice, and she would write back to me.

Mulling over Melchior's mother's words, I was reminded of the phrase spoken into Maracujá's pay phone by the man in the pink shirt: *Let God work in his life.*

Advice, in such instances, has a distanced and tranquil feeling, generated through the use of short phrases and, sometimes, parallelism between the phrases. These phrases invoke absolute principles: *us, anyone,* and *God.* Personal names are not used, and neither are references to specific places or moments. Thus shorn of contextual details, advice acquires a nomic quality and appears to float outside of the particularities of space, time, and person (Silverstein 1993). It is spoken in brief, memorable sentences that can be repeated and reentextualized in other situations. Advice is portable, which gives it the power to traverse the boundary between village and migratory worksite, carrying meaning across a radical change in settings. The phone call home serves as an especially apt milieu for advice-giving.

CHAMAR: AUTHORITY THAT CALLS PEOPLE CLOSER

Migrant phone calls also host a more urgent type of speech-act: *chamar.*[5] *Chamar* literally means "to call on someone [to do something]," and it involves inviting another person to engage in an action, such as attending a party, working at a job, going to church, or returning to the village.[6] Such actions are often cast as a means by which the addressee grows closer to the speaker.

Perhaps the simplest prototype of chamar is a waving gesture that occurs frequently at Maracujá and Rio Branco. When an adult wishes to speak to another adult who is within the line of sight, the first adult will look at the addressee, beckon inward with the fingers of a downturned hand, and sometimes say, "*Faz favor*" (*Come here please*; literally, *Do a favor*). The first time such a gesture was directed at me, I felt indignant, since, in my own upbringing, I had been taught that it was polite to approach your addressee rather than making your addressee approach you. Chamar seemed hopelessly hierarchical to me. What I learned only slowly, over time, was that the gesture's hierarchical quality was fully enveloped by the more powerful theme of inviting another person to come closer to yourself; the joy of closeness overwhelmed any hint of disrespect.

Chamar, as a speech act, extends far beyond the hand gesture. In migrants' phone calls home, chamar can have an especially poignant quality. Already in my introduction I have cited the words that Alexandra's mother, over the phone, used to call her home: "Oh, Alexa, you come back, because—I'm sick. I'm not, I'm not managing to do anything anymore. Come and take care of the kids. And Anastacia, she's starting to cause me trouble. So you've got to come back."

In her letter to Patrício, Valentina was similarly assertive, although about a more minor issue.

> Today, Thursday, the 21st of October, makes one week without news from you. It seems an eternity. But thank God, this will end.

And then:

> You need to buy a SIM card from TIM Corporation from this area code, understand, love?

Speakers carry out their acts of chamar with a tone of unambiguous confidence. *Thank God*, Valentina writes, as if foreseeing the inevitable, *this will end*. Alexandra's mother concludes, *You've got to come*. In these phrases, chamar operates less as a plea for compliance and more as a description of the future that must exist. There is not a hint of preparation for resistance on the addressee's part.

Chamar, in all these cases, involves giving direction while giving reasons—just as, after waving at someone to come over, the person doing the waving must explain the purpose as soon as the addressee arrives. These reasons are not small matters. Chamar rests on moral and aesthetic claims about how the world should be, claims about the imperative of taking care of children or the beauty of one's love.

Thus, chamar is an invitation into one or another future, and the ultimate reason for the listener to come along is not fear of punishment, but rather a presumed shared belief in the worthiness or joyfulness of the result. Often, this belief is not actually shared yet. Alexandra was not sure that she wanted to come home. Patrício, at the time of the letter's writing, still considered Valentina to be just another girlfriend. The magic of chamar, however, is that the speaker acts as if the addressee *does* share the belief, and this act becomes persuasive.

When a migrant calls or writes home, often they hear a voice speaking back to them in the language of advice or chamada. Sometimes the voice offers a tranquil and abstract axiom. Other times the voice, confident and imperative, issues an invitation. In either case, though, the migrant is listening to a form of authority, a mode of authoritative discourse. Advice and chamada, traveling across the long space of separation, echoing on the phone call after a factory shift or reread in the letter before bedtime, become part of the ecology of voices that surround migrants in their workaday lives. Part of that ecology, but not all of it: there are other voices as well. On the work site, a different sort of authoritative speech prevails.

COMMANDS: COOPERATION THROUGH MONOPHONIC AUTHORITY

Not long after Diego spoke with his mother on the pay phone about selling the cow and gathering the money for the synthesizer, he heard his boss give a command. Diego's task on the construction site, that day in São Paulo, was to dig holes for a garage at a condominium. At noon, he took his lunch break.

"I'm there with a plate in my hand," Diego recalled for me, "eating lunch—then—" he paused. "The boss came up to me and said, 'Man, I want you to go spread out that pile of dirt that you made over there in front of the car of the—the condominium owner there. And—I want you to spread it out.'

"I said, 'Hey, dude. I'm on my lunch hour, fuck. I'm eating lunch.' [. . .]

"Then, 'I want you to go there now.'

"I said, 'I'm not going now.' [. . .] Then, when it was two o'clock, when I went to clock in, to return after the lunch break, then the boss called me. He said, 'You don't have to clock in. Because there's a boss on the construction site to give commands.'

"I went and I talked back to him. I said, 'You command. You give commands on the proper schedule and with courtesy. I'm not your son. I'm nothing of yours.' So then he fired me."

Within days, Diego had caught an overnight bus back to the place where he *was* someone's son, back to the village and to his mother, whose advice he had been hearing over the crackle of her long-distance calls.

Diego's story contained a trope that I had heard before. After receiving a phone call or a letter from home, a migrant would blaze into conflict with a boss, then leave for the village immediately thereafter. It was as if the voice from the village, with its advice and chamadas, refused to harmonize with the speech-act most characteristic of the boss, that is, the command.

Hierarchy is built into the double meaning of the verb *mandar*, which means both "to give a specific command" and "to be the person in charge."

THE PHONE CALL HOME   55

When Diego tells his boss, "You command [*você manda*]," Diego could be stating that the boss is currently issuing a particular command, or Diego could be acknowledging, more broadly, that the boss is the one who has authority on the worksite. The verb *to command* in English has exactly the same dual sense. Thus, *mandar* fits neatly into Graeber's theory of hierarchy, which postulates that hierarchical authority derives from the "law of precedent," the principle that when a person carries out an action repeatedly, that action comes to define the person's permanent identity (Graeber 2011: chap. 5). If you give commands often enough, then you must be the one in charge.[7]

People living in the villages are familiar with the dangers of hierarchical command. Interestingly, this bitterness about command was shared both by villagers at Maracujá, who belonged to the landless movement, and by those at Rio Branco, who did not. In her home at Rio Branco, Dona Zaida recalled for me her father and his toil, during the early twentieth century. He resided not at Rio Branco, but nearby. "He lived on the plantation of the rich people," she explained. "So he was commanded by the rich people [*era mandado dos ricos*]. The rich people did what they wanted."

By mid-century, the same was true at Maracujá, on a grand scale. In the era when Maracujá belonged to a network of coffee plantations, hundreds of temporary workers would gather there each year to harvest coffee under the watchful eye of the boss. Command, as a speech-act, made up part of the soundscape of everyday work. Daniel lived on Maracujá plantation as a child, and he remembered those sounds. The plantation owner was "a little old guy, short, white. A pain in the ass!" Daniel told me. "'Go work, kid!' Yeah, he couldn't bear it, us standing around for one minute, he would already come up and command [*mandar*] us to work."

When the landless movement occupied the plantation in the 1990s, Maracujá became what Rio Branco had been since the late nineteenth century: a zone free from big bosses. Daniel, who was at Maracujá Plantation working on the day when the occupiers marched onto the field, discovered in less than a week that he loved the movement. "The landless appeared," he mused to me, seventeen years after the occupation, "and now I live the good life."

"Mm-hm," I prompted, curious to hear more.

"I work—for myself—but I don't end up being commanded [*mandado*] by anyone." A few minutes later, he referred again to the same speech-act. "I've got my things and I don't have to be commanded by anyone!"

Indeed, at Maracujá and Rio Branco today, villagers take pains to avoid giving or receiving commands within employment relations. When one farmer hires another farmer for day labor, the employer tends to refrain from referring to the employee as a *diarista*, or "day laborer," sometimes resorting to the more euphemistic *camarada* (literally, "comrade" or "buddy"). Villagers undertake awkward measures to avoid making it clear who is hiring whom.

By contrast, people in the villages, especially men, seem to relish telling tales about work commands in other places. Some of the edgiest stories in the villages involve the problems that arise when a migrant goes to toil for a big company and ends up in a position to command a co-worker.

Carlos's brother Didier, for example, was an employee at a corporation in São Paulo. After the company's forklift driver injured his back, the boss offered Didier the chance to take his place. Driving the forklift, however, also meant giving orders to other workers. Carlos told me what happened when Didier hoisted some items on the forklift, only to realize that his co-workers were playing with their cellphones, ignoring his commands. Didier looked at his new subordinates and proclaimed:

"Is there nothing for you guys to do? Hey—go there, over that way. Hey. Look at these things over here. Hey. Pick up those things over there."

"But," Carlos explained to me, "everyone was there with their arms crossed."

Another employee went and told the boss, "Didier commanded the guys to do something. The guys didn't do it at all!" The boss called all of the workers together and delivered a harangue: "Didn't Didier command you to do this thing here? [*pause*] Why aren't you doing it? [*pause*] [. . .] The word here belongs to Didier. Whatever he commands you to do, you do. Here, m—my word and his word are worth the same."

In Carlos's telling of the tale, the crucial feature of his brother's promotion is changed speech—specifically, the ability to command.

Command also stood at the heart of a work tale that I heard while sitting with a group of Maracujá's older men. As the heat of the day shone down from the sky, we were crouched on a porch along the village's main dirt road, waiting for a cooler moment to get to our tasks. Isaias sat not far from the battered freezer where he stored the pork that he sold to other villagers after weighing it on a rusted metal scale. With no customers in sight, Isaias opted to regale us with a story from his previous job, in the mining industry.

Isaias found favor with his boss. "One day," Isaias recounted, "he talked to me. He said, 'Hey. I'm going to turn over the work to you. You be in charge of the guys. You work, too, but—you're going to take charge.' So I took charge. It was about fifty-something men."

Supervision came along with conflict. Isaias, newly empowered, ordered an employee to work in a particularly sunny spot. The employee moved somewhere else so he could labor in the shade instead. Isaias confronted him.

"I went up and I talked to him. I said, 'Oh, dude. Your work is over there. It's not here, no way. Here belongs to this guy, that guy, and the other guy. [*pause*] Yours is over there.'

"Then he stayed where he was. A really long time.

"I said, 'Oh, dude. Come down from that task there. And go to the dormitory. Get your bag of belongings.'"

Isaias's boss was displeased when he heard about Isaias's disciplinary approach. But, as Isaias told us that day near the battered freezer, "If you take charge of a job [. . .] and then the guy disobeys, you have to fire him. Because if you don't command, he will command you tomorrow or the next day."

In these tales of supervision, command plays a central role. The command, as a speech-act, takes on particular qualities here. But how could you recognize a command? What was it, exactly, that made a particular phrase into a command?

THE QUALITIES OF COMMAND

Inside migrant discourse, commands had four key characteristics. First, they came in short, imperative sentences. Second, they set up a spatial frame that was centered on the boss, *not* on the person hearing the command. Third, they emphasized immediacy. And fourth, they were devoid of reasons. Each of these qualities deserves closer examination.[8]

Among migrants, commands stood out right away because of their first characteristic: they were short, simple sentences built around an imperative verb. "Come down from that task there" (Isaias); "Look at these things over here" (Carlos).

On second glance, those sentences also feature the second characteristic of the command: they create a particular kind of spatial frame. The sentences are deictically dense. That is to say, they are full of deictics, or words whose meaning is specific to the location of the speaker and the listener. "Here," "there," and "to your left" are all examples of spatial deictics. The meaning of these words changes if the speaker (or sometimes the listener) changes location. If you stand in a church and say, "It's cold here," then *here* might mean *in the church*, but if you utter the same phrase while standing in a field, then *here* might mean *in the field*.

In a command, the speaker presumes that the listener will have to adopt the speaker's own deictic coordinates. "Here" means the boss's "here." When a boss issues a command, that command tends *not* to be built around phrases that imagine the listener's perspective. The listener's perspective could be accommodated, for example, through phrases like *Pick up the rock in front of you* or *Reach for the nearest spoon you can find*. But such phrases do not fit inside Isaias's and Carlos's stories of command. Instead, the boss commands the listener to *go there, over that way* or to *come down from that task there*. To interpret such a command, the people being commanded need to imagine that they are in the same place as the boss. They need to take on the boss's perspective.

The phrasing of commands thus differs strikingly from the phrasing of conselhos. Conselhos are carefully cleaned of contextual details, leaving no deictics at all, or only the most generic ones. In this way, conselhos acquire their timeless and abstract sense. "Nobody would mess with you if you did not mess with anyone" (Alexandra); "Have good judgment, be careful in life [...] accept what God had blessed us with" (Melchior). And so *Have good judgment* is advice, but *Look at those things over there* is a command—different statements that rest on utterly different forms of authority.

The third characteristic of commands is their heightened feeling of immediacy. Diego's boss ordered him, "I want you to go there now." Commands live inside this kind of time, the time of *right away*, and bosses tend to treat commands as words that will directly change the world. Because of their temporality, commands do not resemble chamadas, the speech-acts in which one person calls on another to do something. Chamar, like commanding, often relies on imperative verbs. But a chamada, unlike a command, invokes a vision of the future. To issue a chamada is to claim that at some distant point in time, not right away, things will become better than they are now. "Today, Thursday, the 21st of October, makes one week without news from you. It seems an eternity. But thank God, this will end" (Valentina). A chamada predicts an event that will happen—*this will end*—while a command attempts to make an event happen now.

Fourth, commands do not come accompanied by reasons. Commands, in this regard, are nothing like chamadas. Chamadas are wordy, because chamar involves giving reasons why the listener should act. For example, consider the phrase that Alexandra's mother spoke to her: "You come back, because—I'm sick. I'm not, I'm not managing to do anything anymore. Come take care of the children." The word *because* is crucial here. Chamar runs on an articulated vision of a better or a worse world; a chamada takes a richly substantive position about how the future should look. A command, in contrast, justifies itself simply by its own logic. It works through the circular presumption that someone must issue commands, therefore commands have to be issued. Consider how Isaias, when pushed to offer a reason, uses the same word, *because*: "Because if you don't command, he will command you tomorrow or the next day." Diego's boss spoke similarly: "Because there's a boss on the construction site to give commands." The speech of command is self-referential and admits no reasons outside of itself.[9] To ask why one should obey is already to challenge the authority that underlies the command.

If we listen carefully to people's words, we can hear the tiny steps that turn independent work, guided by instructions or advice or chamadas, into standard and homogeneous labor, run by commands. We can detect the speech-act that alienates people from their labor.[10] We come closer to understanding abstract labor as a feeling—a feeling generated against the backdrop of other possible modes of authority.

It would be wrong to say that commands always lead to abstract labor, and it would be even more wrong to think that commands are only uttered by city bosses. On the contrary: family members, for example, often speak to each other in the voice of command. Murilo remembered for me, with bitterness, the way his father used to talk to him: "You only pick up this thing here when I command you to." Or again: "You sit here. When your mother calls, you come." These are sentences that ring with the key characteristics of command.

Command echoed even more loudly one bright morning at Maracujá, when I stopped inside the tile-roofed farmhouse of Seu Valentim, a man in his seventies, and found him hurrying to transform the milk from his cows into requeijão cheese. Seu Valentim was using a manual milk separator, very old and imported from Germany, its metal pieces painted bright red. Toiling alongside Seu Valentim was Zé, a taciturn teenager who had come to live with him. Seu Valentim let flow a constant stream of commands. "Put that spoon over there, young man. And come here. Take this cheese. Put it inside." "Put the spoon there—hey. You see? You're smearing everything on the bag." Seu Valentim also veered into advice: "Learn to work, young man. For you to become an actual real man. Because you're not a proper man, no way."

The boy mostly stayed silent, but at one point, he objected somewhat warily to an order. Seu Valentim reply was decisive: "Do you want to know more than me, and I've spent seventy-nine years doing this?" Then Seu Valentim seemed possibly to regret the harshness in those words. Breathing quickly from the effort of the cheese-making, he softened his tone and spoke the boy's name. "Zé, bring me—this pan here, if you could, please, young man."

As Seu Valentim demonstrated that day, commands were definitely spoken in the villages. Commands had a special role in rural households, where children often worked for their parents or other relatives, as Zé worked for Seu Valentim. But these family work arrangements had a famously fractious quality. Villagers often told stories about sons who left their family's farms, in anger, to try farming on their own. Even when a household toiled together in tranquility, people expected that the children would eventually transition to adulthood by establishing their own independent fields. Command, in other words, marked a temporary juvenile state in the work life of a young villager. To receive a command was a sign of immaturity, as Seu Valentim emphasized when he cited his age to Zé. Recall Diego's retort to the São Paulo construction boss who issued an insulting command: *I'm not your son. I'm nothing of yours.*

In the villages, you could outgrow command; in the wage labor force, command became a lasting feature of your world. Perhaps this is why, despite the ubiquity of commands inside village households, people seemed to regard the villages as a space relatively insulated from that sort of language. Laura, who had once earned her living as a São Paulo chef, summed up the situation for me one day: "Work in the city, you're going to be commanded [*Você vai ser mandado*]."

"Mm-hm," I encouraged.

"And in the countryside, you're the one who commands at work."

One day, I listened to Dona Eva give her son Patrício advice about commanding. Patrício, after several trips to work with a construction company in São Paulo, seemed likely to get promoted to a supervisory position, and Dona Eva had wisdom to offer him. "Commanding isn't easy," she said. "There are peons who accept. There are peons who don't accept." Dona Eva paused. "And today everyone has to be commanded. [. . .] It's one person commanding the other."

Today everyone has to be commanded. Dona Eva's aphorism conveyed to me something of the total aspiration of command rhetoric, something of the sense that Brazil's contemporary growth process, as a whole, depended on more and more people entering into relations of command. But Dona Eva also spoke the sneaky word *today*. *Today* implied that command had not always been the only speech-act capable of organizing cooperative work. There might even come a different tomorrow. Patrício seemed to know about the possibility of this tomorrow, a time after the time of commanding and being commanded. If he had made several trips to toil in São Paulo, it was because, more than once, listening to his flea market cellphone and reading the letter written by Valentina, Patrício had turned away from wage labor and taken the long bus ride home.

CONCLUSION

Face to face with her boss, Kátia decided she had nothing to hold back. It was already difficult for her to manage the unruly customers who wandered into the lunch counter where she took orders and rushed plates to tables, deep in the industrial suburbs of São Paulo. Her boss made matters worse with his constant reprimands.

Now the boss had caught wind of a rumor: some of the workers were meeting in secret. They were plotting, he had heard, to go over his head, and they wanted to demand a wage increase directly from the restaurant's owner. Kátia did not dissimulate. She told her boss that the organized group really did exist. Moreover, she herself was "right in the middle of it [*Eu estava no meio*]."

This, at least, is how Kátia recounted the story for me one afternoon as we crouched on a log at the edge of the dusty soccer field at Maracujá. Kátia, age nineteen, had just returned from more than a year in São Paulo, and she was telling me her adventures and misadventures. From time to time, the two of us looked up to see farmers and their children scurrying by their whitewashed houses. Red plastic tables sat in front of Russo's window, as if to provide a reminder of the gulf that divided a relaxed home bar in the village from a stressful lunch counter in the city.

Kátia found her boss almost unbearable. Even customers told her that he treated her disrespectfully. "He didn't have the good sense to call [*chamar*] a co-worker—um, an employee and complain in a place that was, like, set apart," Kátia remembered, framing her description through the familiar contrast between chamar and command. "He complained in front of customers."

Eventually Kátia had learned strategically to ignore her boss's complaints, a move that, strangely enough, increased his respect for her. The two of them established rapport. But that day, when he spoke to her about the wage demand that she had been planning after hours with her co-workers, Kátia let him know where she stood. She wanted a raise.

The boss responded to Kátia gently. This wasn't the way to do things, he told her. The workers would need to have patience.

At this point in her storytelling to me, with the two of us sitting uncomfortably on the log in the rural afternoon light, Kátia paused her narrative about the boss. Seemingly without reason, she brought up a different topic: the phone call. She told me that from São Paulo she had been calling Maracujá. There, in the village, her four younger sisters lived together in a cramped house with their mother. Their older sister Dalia, by now married, had the house next door and wired all of the electricity through her own line so that she could pay for the rest of her family. Sometimes their father left for long trips to work; sometimes he fell on his way home, drunk. When Kátia had lived in the village, she had been the daughter kind enough to clean the blood off him, respectfully address him as "Sir," and meet his boozy demand for a kiss on the cheek. Nowadays, when Kátia called from São Paulo, the news from Maracujá seemed always to be bad. She felt worried.

As Kátia disputed over wages at the lunch counter, the phone call news began to float into view. She explained to her boss that she missed her family, and, in addition to a raise, she wanted to go see them.

Her boss told her that he understood. "Let's make an arrangement," he suggested. Kátia would return to Maracujá to visit her family. When she came back to São Paulo, the boss would end her informal work status and register her as a legally recognized employee of the lunch counter.

No one got a raise. Kátia caught the bus back to Maracujá. She stayed there and did not return to the lunch counter.

*

Why did Kátia remember the phone call just then? As she described the crucial turn in her conversation with her boss—the moment when she converted her wage demand into a demand to go home—why did she suddenly tell me about the telephone?

A phone call juxtaposes voices. As a speech genre, the call creates a distinction between two sides, the two ends of the line. Phone calls thus set up an apt narrative frame for growth: in migrants' calls, growth appears as the straight arrow moving from one end of the line to the other, from the village to the city. But if a call can carry the voices of growth in one direction, the other direction is open as well. When Kátia considered how much money she would be willing to accept in exchange for submission to her boss, the telephone appeared, as a sign of her other option.

I have argued that economic growth can be imagined as an intensification in cooperation, a new spirit of enthusiasm about working together. Brazil's dominant growth model, like many others, organizes cooperation among workers through the practice of group compliance with command. People do not enter growth automatically; they have to learn to talk about it, to expect it, and to respond to it in predictable ways. They have to become familiar with its language. This language comes to life, every day, when migrants from Maracujá and Rio Branco accept the unremarkable authority of specific words spoken by particular people in a specific way. Short sentences, built around imperative verbs, shorn of reasons, heavy with deictics, and requiring the listener to adopt the spatial perspective of the boss: these turn into the semiotic markers of legitimacy.

To the extent that a growth model relies on command, it imposes on its participants the costs of submission. Such growth is unable to satisfy a certain wish to have space for what Daniel described as "not having to be commanded by anyone." Adam Smith seemed to recognize growth pitfalls of this sort, especially in the striking passage where he suggested that growth requires "the habit of subordination" (1786: book 4, chap. 7) and indicted the factory system for depriving workers of a broader sense of their own capacity (book 5, chap. 1, part 3, article 2, paragraph 178). Coase, too, understood the downside of command. He referred to supervisors so unwilling to be commanded by anyone else that they were prepared to accept lower earnings than their own workers (Coase 1937: 390n2). These bosses would pay for the right to give orders rather than receive them. This, as Coase knew, was no recipe for promoting growth.

What Smith and Coase may not have discussed is that such a wish—the wish to live without command—does not necessarily hang on like an atavistic survival from a premodern mode of production. The wish can develop *after* one's engagement with the labor market. This is a familiar history in Latin America, where generations of workers have been coerced or cajoled into the heart of world commerce, then expelled from that heart when a commodity boom reached its end. For more than a hundred years, people have found ways to travel to Maracujá and Rio Branco because that dry and hilly land, at the limit of the plantations, is propitious for the cultivation of different kinds of speech and the different modes of cooperation that this speech creates.

Telephones arrived in Maracujá and Rio Branco as the fruit of growth. Yet the machines themselves made it possible for migrants to represent an alternative to growth—and sometimes, in a flash of anger or possibility, to pursue that alternative. The telephone demonstrates that the results of growth can be turned against growth. In the same manner, the process of submitting to command can inspire migrants to imagine autonomy. Autonomy, here, is not a primordial state; workers arrive at autonomy through a dialectical reversal of submission. When farmers told me why they came to Maracujá and Rio Branco, very frequently they used the phrase "not to work for anyone" (*não trabalhar por ninguém*). Tellingly, the phrasing is negative. Command sparks, as its opposite, a vision of autonomy, just as the telephone sparks a vision of a life, close to one's neighbors, where telephones are no longer necessary.

It would be a mistake to conclude that villagers reject growth. Everyone likes the telephone, and everyone likes the other features of the beloved face of growth: the doctor visits, the water pumps, and the new schools, for example. But people seek to tame these features, to turn them to particular ends, to insert them in a broader egalitarian ethos. The phone cards must be shared, and in the same way, the water pump must be organized through a community meeting and the school van driver must respond to the voices of parents (see chapter 2). Farmers at Maracujá and Rio Branco, like people everywhere, accept only certain kinds and only a certain amount of economic growth. The villages are places where farmers have won for themselves the strategic distance that allows them to take some features of growth and leave other features behind.

As they chat with their city relatives over the tenuous phone line, farmers may speak in voices that present the villages as a zone for building an alternative to growth. The villages, in this sense, join the tradition of the quilombo, the Indigenous preserve, the brecha camponesa fields where enslaved people planted for themselves (DeVore 2020), and the subsistence farms that parceiros nurtured on abandoned plantations (Cândido 1964). These are zones of freedom. Zones like these create difficulties for the politicians of Brazil's developmentalist left, enamored of big dam projects, train lines, and a rising minimum wage. Such progressives face an ongoing challenge: how to balance the real accomplishments of economic growth with the real achievements of people who create alternatives to that growth.

Migrants use the telephone to create signs against growth. Perhaps one of the crucial characteristics of a democratic growth process is that it enables these signs, encourages them, and promotes them. Growth is authoritarian when it takes place as an imperative, resting on the logic that people *must* grow, *must* cooperate. Growth becomes democratic when it occurs in a landscape full of alternative spaces and secondary options: social programs that make it possible to survive outside of the labor market, land reforms that open the peasant route, and telephones with links to a different kind of territory. Indeed, growth is only democratic if it renders other options *more* viable—if growth means, among other things, an increase in the number and richness of alternatives to growth. And in their own way, these alternatives might spark a kind of cooperation not easily found in the wage labor market. On a city street, after all, no one picks up a ringing pay phone.

2

The Roads

Histories of Growth as Histories of Cooperation

> The division of labor presumes that the worker, far from being hemmed in by his task, does not lose sight of his collaborators, that he acts upon them and reacts to them [. . .] The economists would not have left this essential characteristic of the division of labor unclarified and as a result would not have lain it open to [. . .] undeserved reproach, if they had not reduced it to being only a way of increasing the efficiency of the social forces, but had seen it above all as a source of solidarity.
> ÉMILE DURKHEIM, *The Division of Labor in Society* (2014: 308)

History in the Villages

No one in 2012 could remember the names of the first inhabitants of Rio Branco or tell me the story of their arrival. Some villagers had heard rumors of a graveyard, several kilometers away, left by Indigenous Brazilians. Who came after the people who built the graveyard? Dona Rosalinda, age ninety-three, directed me to a pile of adobe bricks that were once a house inhabited by her husband's grandfather. He might have belonged to a group of migrants who started the village in its current form. If so, then Rio Branco was probably founded sometime between 1860 and 1900.

I mentioned this estimate one day to Mariele, a historian with two postgraduate specialization degrees who lives in the village next to Maracujá and teaches at the nearby high school. She is married to Dona Rosalinda's grandson. When I began talking about the nineteenth century, Mariele grew animated. The period from 1860 to 1900: she pointed out that this date range overlapped with the year of the abolition of slavery in Brazil, 1888. Maybe, she suggested, the founding villagers were enslaved people who gained emancipation. Maybe they left behind the plantations of the costal export economy and traveled inland in search of a place that no one commanded.[1]

What were the roads they used to get there? What remains today of those roads, the trails that connect the world market to the backlands? This chapter traces the roads, both concrete and metaphorical, that pave the way to growth at Maracujá and Rio Branco—and the way back from growth as well. When I speak of roads, I am referring to the region's actual network of footpaths and dirt highways, which have proliferated over the past century. But

I am also thinking more metaphorically about "growth paths," that is, theoretical models that show how an economy grows. My major argument in this chapter involves the link between growth and cooperation. We can imagine economic growth, I have suggested, as a wave of enthusiasm about cooperating more intensely with other people. To give life to this argument, first I narrate the history of the twentieth century in the villages. I tell this history by recounting the story of new roads built and by tracking the new modes of cooperation that villagers developed (but also, at certain moments, rejected) along those roads.

In the latter part of this chapter, I consider five different growth theories. These theories can be found in the work of academic economists, and the same five theories also shine in the meditations of villagers who stopped to chat with me beside a cookfire or on a living room couch. The theories are stories that aim to explain how people created growth over the turbulent twentieth century. But, I suggest, the theories also should account for the reasons why people stepped *away* from growth and traveled the other way down the road, the way that leads toward autonomy.

DONKEY PATHS, 1900–1960 IN THE VILLAGES

Dona Zaida remembered for me the route that her male relatives took, in her childhood, when it was time to sell their merchandise. At midnight, they would load a donkey with their wares: lassos and bridles they had woven out of cowhide. The men would walk all night beside the donkey, straining to reach the road by early morning. Sometime around dawn, by the roadside, they would catch a ride to the city of Conquista, where they sold their goods in the urban bustle. They also shopped there for bulk foods.

At evening time the men found rides back to the same roadside spot. Then they set out on foot once more, carrying the food they had purchased for their family. They trudged through the darkness. By the time they finished their six-hour walk home, it would be midnight again. Sometimes, Dona Zaida remembered, she would already be asleep. Other times she would stay awake imagining her traveling relatives. The trip was terrifying: "mothers would start to cry when their boy children would say that they were going to Conquista."

Dona Zaida and her family were *moradores*, resident farmers who inhabited the region's vast plantations. Moradores did not own land; they toiled for the plantation-owner and received small personal plots on a provisional basis. Not far from the moradores, the denizens of Rio Branco lived as small farmers and had legal titles to their land. Moradores and small farmers shared similar lives, sometimes sustaining friendships and marrying each other, but the conditions of their labor followed different logics.

Plantations ran by the rhythms of the world market. By contrast, the farmers at Rio Branco practiced subsistence agriculture. Moradores and small farmers thus developed two distinct modes of cooperation, that is, two different patterns for collaborating with their co-workers.

Moradores labored together under the central authority of a plantation owner or supervisor, who assigned and monitored a task for each morador. It was the plantation owner who set the terms of cooperation between workers. Mathias, for instance, remembered for me how Paco, master of an estate, spotted Mathias's own potential in youth and sent him to train as a tractor driver, while other workers on the plantation harvested crops by hand. Some plantation owners managed these relationships effectively and assembled vast crews of workers to toil together over the years. Paco's plantation included a whole village of moradores, who worshipped at the chapel he built, sought him out for medicine when they became sick, and sometimes even lived out their retirement years on the plantation. Paco, Mathias said, "was the one who taught me how to work [. . .] I respected him like my own father."

But the backland small farmers, at Rio Branco, practiced an utterly different type of cooperation. Each household planted crops independently on their own land. Between households, cooperation happened sporadically, when villagers came together for occasional shared projects. For instance, they collaborated to dam up several small reservoirs, safeguarding the water that nourished their fields of manioc, beans, corn, and rice. Rio Branco's residents managed their pastures, too, through a loose form of sharing. The villagers reared goats and sheep for meat, sometimes cattle in prosperous times, and, by local convention, any of these animals could cross onto anyone's territory. The herds roamed free across the unfenced land.

Rio Branco's farmers thus cooperated with each other much less intensely than their neighbors on the plantations. Much of the time, people at Rio Branco worked alone.

Rio Branco's farmers did not live out their loose mode of cooperation just in their agricultural practices. They manifested it in all areas of social life, from kinship to housing to leisure. The village was a patchwork of independent homesteads, each anchored by a focal couple.

Farmers created their households, much as they sowed their fields, with an austere autonomy. Few supplies needed to be brought in from outside. The houses themselves bore witness to this. During the early twentieth century, Rio Branco's residents constructed houses by tying together a framework of sticks and filling it in with mud (*enximento*). Family members toiled to bundle coconut fronds into bunches thick enough to form a watertight roof. Floors might be made by sprinkling the dirt with water and then pounding it until it felt smooth and glassy. (Occasionally, people still build enximento houses today.) To sleep, children would lie down on a cowhide in front of a fire; adults would sleep on a mattress stuffed with banana leaves. Villagers gathered around these same fires to pray the Lord's Prayer. In front of the fire, they would tell exaggerated stories called *causos*, or they would dance barefoot until dawn to the music of a three-person band with an accordionist, a drummer, and a triangle player.

Rio Branco's residents were distant from the city, but they belonged to a single economy with it. Like Dona Zaida's relatives, they sometimes traveled the backlands routes to take their agricultural goods to the market towns, and they brought back metal hoes, pots for cooking, and photographs of themselves. Although many people in the villages seem not to have known how to read or write, they recognized the importance of land titles, and they aligned even their kinship practices to urban standards, aspiring to get married or have their children baptized in a chapel with a priest. And priests were not the only itinerants making occasional trips between the city and the hinterland. The villages were visited from time to time by *mascates*, wandering merchants on muleback who braved the narrow dirt pathways in order to bring products from far away. A mascate would untie some ropes and open his wooden case to show you his wares without even bothering to take the case off the mule.

During the first part of the twentieth century, Seu Nato, a local notable with some inherited land, managed to accumulate a vast area for ranching. It stretched for more than 400 alqueires (4,000 hectares) along the edge of Rio Branco, including the territory that would later become Maracujá. This land was initially devoted to cattle. At mid-century, Seu Nato's vast lands were broken up into several large estates, each inherited by one of his children.

Along the lengthy donkey path that linked Rio Branco to the city, Seu Nato's authority traveled smoothly, linking the urban political elite to the rural plantation. But Dona Zaida reminded me how rough that passage could be for ordinary villagers. Sometime around 1960, after three months' suffering from constant pain, she heard that a doctor had arrived in a neighboring city. "People," she remembered asking skeptically, "how can this man figure out an illness that a person feels?"

"Well," she was told, "there's this man who's figuring it out."

On Good Friday, a group of villagers tied Dona Zaida to a bed—"as if it were a person who had died and they were taking to be buried." They set out at midnight with the bed hoisted on sticks on their shoulders. By seven in the morning, they left her under the doctor's care.

The roads, in 1960, amounted to little more than pathways in such rough condition that a sick person had to be carried out. But the news of the new doctor had managed to travel in. The backlands were distant from, but still connected to, the rhythms of the world market.

CAR TRACKS, 1960–90 IN THE VILLAGES

Sometime at mid-century, Martinho's father rallied a group of men, some volunteers and some paid by him, and they cut an ox path up to the edge of Nato's plantations. Then Martinho's father drove a car down the path to restock the merchandise at the small general store that he ran. This was the first automobile ever to enter Rio Branco. Martinho's father, in fulfillment of a promise he had made, brought along a priest and had a Mass said there in celebration.

Roads were reaching closer and closer to Rio Branco. Brazil's GDP, by the late 1960s, was expanding spectacularly. As the backlands filled with new thoroughfares, local plantation owners and small farmers both entered into the national growth boom—but in entirely different ways. Plantation owners hired more and more people to toil under central command. Rio Branco's small farmers, in contrast, reinforced even more firmly the walls that separated one independent working household from the next.

The region's plantation owners contributed to the national growth spurt by making an epochal transition. They steered their plantations away from cattle and toward coffee. In the 1960s and 1970s, one of Nato's heirs embraced the new trend and ordered the planting of a long swath of coffee trees on one part of the old estate, the section now called Maracujá. These trees required a large migrant labor force during harvest season, and so, each year, Maracujá would swell in size, becoming the home of hundreds of workers.

As plantation after plantation in the region filled with coffee trees, plantation owners needed many workers—but only during the harvest. The owners began replacing their resident moradores with seasonal toilers. These migrant laborers became a new social group. They spent the off-season living in small towns that sprang up on the edges of the plantations, towns that looked nothing like Rio Branco. Each one rose rapidly from the coffee estates, unfolded for a few densely packed blocks of concrete and brick, then just as quickly disappeared into the straight-planted green rows. Compared to Rio Branco, the towns grew denser and larger—perhaps one thousand inhabitants each—because these inhabitants possessed their own houses, but rarely their own fields (Costa Sena 2007: 16).

While their neighbors toiled in transient jobs, Rio Branco's residents held onto the fields they owned. More and more workers in the region now had nowhere to grow manioc, the staple grain. So, increasingly, Rio Branco's farmers turned to planting manioc, which sank deep in the village's dry soil. Unlike the plantation owners, the denizens of Rio Branco did not develop a centralized system for their new crop. Instead, they built little shacks, separately, in many back yards around the village. Inside these "manioc houses," farmers pushed the ripened manioc roots into heavy presses to squeeze out water. Women and men from a household worked together to break the woody root fiber to bits against a scraping wheel. Then they poured the bits onto giant metal plates perched over fires and used a wooden rod to rake the flakes dry, leaving a crispy white meal. After the meal cooled, each household hauled its own sacks to sell in the towns. This was decentralized production.

As the demand for manioc increased, around the 1960s and 1970s, Rio Branco underwent a protracted internal struggle. Some villagers began erecting giant fences. In earlier days, with cattle and sheep wandering freely on village lands, farmers had built only tight stick fences to keep animals out of the small areas where they grew their crops. But with the rising value of manioc, some villagers began arguing that each herder needed to confine her own livestock to her own grazinglands. Then the farmers could plant crops anywhere outside of these pastures.[2]

The enclosure issue led to disputes that are still remembered with bitterness. Ultimately, the enclosers won. The situation turned inside out: instead of cultivators needing to fence in their crops, herders now needed to fence in their animals. Thus, to stop livestock from roaming free across the region, the herders began fencing large sections of territory with barbed wire and reserving that territory for their animals. Before, on the village lands, no one had paid much attention to individual land ownership. It gained sudden importance because of the fences.

New barriers at the village, new migrant labor on the estates: these were the effects of the 1970s growth boom in the region, and they pointed in different directions. On the plantations, growth involved more collaboration between the hundreds of workers now hired for transient work in the fields. Rio Branco's villagers, by contrast, built the separate manioc houses and the fences that, in some sense, allowed farmers to collaborate *less* with each other.

But even at Rio Branco, less collaboration inside the village could mean more collaboration with people outside of the village. Along the region's new dirt roads, cargoes of coffee and manioc were flowing together to the city, ultimately sweeping both village and plantation into more intense networks of cooperation with outside merchants, markets, and consumers.

The roads were changing Rio Branco in other ways, too. A school was built and, starting in the 1980s, a teacher offered classes through fourth grade. A priest began to visit regularly and say Mass every month. Adventurous young people journeyed for spells of labor in São Paulo, a journey so uncertain that their families would set off fireworks to let the whole village know when they returned. The small-time mascate traders began criss-crossing the region in tremendously dirty trucks; in place of their muleback boxes, mascates now had truckbeds that they piled high with pans and furniture for sale, charging about twice the urban price, accepting payment in monthly installments that were guaranteed by nothing other than the local reputation of the buyer.

The government finally put through a dirt road directly to Rio Branco, although the road remained incomplete because it lacked a bridge over a seasonal stream. Eventually, City Hall agreed to send a periodic bus line down the dirt road, but only if someone would build a bridge strong enough to make the stream passable in all sorts of weather. So every Saturday the villagers organized themselves to toil for free, working with supplies that the municipality had given them, sinking stones into the mud. They finally finished the bridge, and in 1988 the bus did start running. There was so little other traffic that when rain fell, the villagers had to weed the dirt road to keep it open. Dona Eva recalled for me the old-fashioned word that she once used to refer to the bus: "marineta." Laughingly, she imitated her youthful self. "Are you going to catch the marineta?" By 2012, this term sounded incomprehensibly archaic to me.

BUS ROUTES: 1990–2006 IN THE VILLAGES

A bus was regularly traveling down the dirt road to the small farms at Rio Branco by the 1990s. At Maracujá, however, the plantation workers remained distant from the bus route. Then the landless movement arrived.

Although Maracujá lacked a bus, in other ways the plantation seemed like a force for modernization in the region. Maracujá boasted endless lines of coffee trees and a large wage labor force. A visitor in 1990 would perhaps have assumed that such highly cooperative plantations were the wave of the future and that, within a few years, Rio Branco would inevitably turn toward centralized production techniques like those used at Maracujá. In fact, just the opposite occurred. Within fifteen years, the entire region would look much less like the big coffee plantations and much more like Rio Branco. The reason for this change, in large part, was Brazil's landless movement, the MST.

The MST has an extraordinary history of land occupations, the first of which occurred in southern Brazil in 1984, the final year of the country's dictatorship. Landless activists began to mobilize in southwestern Bahia in 1987. By the early 1990s, a local group of landless farmers had staged repeated occupations without success. Their efforts came to a head in 1994 at Mocambo, a plantation in the rainy zone more than a hundred kilometers from Rio Branco. Exhausted and dispirited after repeated evictions, the farmers were living in a camp they had set up along the side of the highway that led to Mocambo. Repeated disputes with the landlord had already erupted. On October 29, the landlord's gunmen began shooting into the camp. Eleven farmers were wounded. Two farmers, Maria Zilda and Manoel Bomfim, were killed. Ariosvaldo José dos Santos, known as Negão, was badly injured in the shooting. In the ensuing melee, as the combatants fought each other with farming tools, some of the landlord's companions were also wounded ("Trabalhadores Rurais são assassinados por jagunços em Vitória da Conquista - BA," 1994).

The deaths shocked the region. Bahia had a reputation for peaceful land occupations, and, to my knowledge, no further MST activists, landlords, or bystanders would be killed in land conflicts in southwestern Bahia until the assassination of Fábio Santos, a brilliant speaker and Catholic organizer who was executed by a death squad on April 2, 2013. (Only a few years after Fábio, in 2018, Márcio Matos was murdered.)[3]

After the deaths of Maria Zilda and Manoel Bomfim, the federal government swiftly expropriated Mocambo. The plantation was too small to accommodate all the landless farmers in the camp, so a group reorganized themselves for a further occupation. They had heard rumors about another promising plantation: Maracujá.

Maracujá made an appealing target. It was enormous and its coffee trees were in poor shape, increasing the likelihood that federal inspectors would certify that the plantation met the constitutional requirement that it be "unproductive" in order to be eligible for expropriation. The heir who owned it had taken up residence in the city and seemed inattentive. In 1996, the landless activists filled a giant truck, drove down the unfinished dirt road up to the plantation's gate, and announced their occupation.

Their initial audience was Daniel, a morador. He and his family were maintaining the owner's herd of cattle. The activists took care to explain that they felt no animosity toward the moradores, and one leader had enough gallantry to proclaim that Daniel's elderly mother was under the MST's protection. The friendliness worked: as the landless occupiers built their shack village out of sticks and black plastic sheeting, the moradores began cooperating with them. Within three days, Daniel and his relatives joined the occupation.

The landless occupiers were a mixed group. Many had been drawn to the movement through the careful preliminary organizing of MST activists. During a series of meetings, the activists reached out to day laborers living in the area's agricultural towns, the very people who had been moved off the plantations when coffee arrived some thirty years before. Moradores joined the movement, too. So did frustrated city-dwellers. Many of these urbanites had been raised in the countryside and left it behind. Now they hoped to return to agriculture—but this time without a boss.

The occupation dragged on for months. With little to eat, isolated and far from the city, the occupiers could sometimes count only on the support of an Italian nun who trekked out to bring them supplies and encouragement. But their calculation had been largely correct. The heir had little will to fight, and he ultimately reached a settlement with the federal government, received his compensation for the value of the land, and handed over the plantation. Maracujá Land Settlement was born.

This dramatic, peaceful success helped to escalate what Loera (2010) has called "the spiral of encampments." Seeing Maracujá as an example, hundreds of other landless families flocked to the MST, and the movement began progressively occupying the neighboring plantations. Within a decade, all the heirs of Nato had ceded their land to INCRA, the federal land reform agency. The plantation empire Nato had built at the beginning of the twentieth century had become an unbroken chain of MST villages. Nor were his descendants necessarily angry about it. Many years later, an MST teacher was making small talk with a man at a gym in Conquista. When the teacher mentioned that he taught at Maracujá, the man grew wistful and said, *I used to own all of that.* He was one of Velho Nato's heirs. *At first we were upset,* the heir remembered. *But those were failed coffee plantations. And the government compensated us very well.*

The MST farmers arrived with high hopes for building a collective production system that they could operate together. In the late 1990s they tried a number of ventures, ranging from shared fields to an apiary. These had disappointing results, and a bruising internal leadership conflict worsened the situation. Arisovaldo, the farmer wounded in the shooting at Mocambo, was settled on the land at Maracujá but died there, possibly because of his injuries. After a few years, Maracujá's residents adopted the same sort of low-cooperation techniques that had long predominated at Rio Branco. Each household farmed largely by itself. The MST activists turned themselves into individual ranchers with tiny herds, planters of small manioc fields, and nurturers of one or two fruit trees.

At Rio Branco, the villagers watched the land occupations with suspicion. MST activists, however, knew how to make friends. The movement regularly held protests to demand that political leaders supply the landless settlements with various supports, including schools and telephones, electricity, adult literacy programs, farm credits, and community health workers. The MST did not forget to request the same benefits for their new neighbors at Rio Branco. Maracujá received its first bus line to travel down the dusty road, and Rio Branco's bus service was improved, with the word *marineta* now nearly forgotten and replaced by the standard Portuguese *ônibus*. A warm relationship soon developed as Rio Branco received government services it had never anticipated; in 2006, electricity finally arrived. But by then, the alliance had already taken on a more classic form: across the divide that separated the century-old village from the new landless occupations, couple after couple fell in love and got married.

When We Talk about Growth, What Is the Thing That We Imagine to Be Growing?

Thus far, as I have told the history of Maracujá and Rio Branco, I have spoken somewhat loosely about "growth." I have described it as an increase in the intensity of cooperation. But this is clearly not the only way to imagine economic growth. When villagers mused about the past, they offered many other explanations, arguing among themselves as they puzzled out the strange and wild transformations they had witnessed in their own lives. Growth was a forward motion, some kind of advancement along a path, as real as the roads that now connected the region. But it was not easy to say what kind of motion this was.

So what did "growth" mean? In the histories that villagers recounted, I heard more than one answer.

*

In the old days, Seu Túlio said, there were caiman alligators and they lived in the pond at the edge of Rio Branco. One kind was black, and the other had a snout that turned yellow during mating season. When the caimans were hungry, they would tromp up to the village and steal away piglets.

I heard Seu Túlio talk about the caimans while he held court in the coolness of his village living room, an old man seated inside a ring of younger relatives. Outside, the sun beat down heavily on the fruit trees that he had planted near his door long ago. Someone asked him, *What made things different back then?* "The people had faith in God!" he answered.

His wife looked on sharply. "They still do," she retorted. The real change, she concluded, was something different: "Today the people have another type of studying."

Some months later, I lay in bed after the cookfire had gone out at the end of a day, and I listened while a different couple stayed up to chat. Seu Andres, age fifty-nine, was speaking harshly. He had no patience, he told his wife, for "the things of the old times, of the backwardness." Why, for example, would anyone today run a manioc flour mill with no power motor?

Later, his wife, Dona Eva, told me about the old times:

> We were born and raised without school. We didn't have here—there was no road, there was no, no bus. [. . .] We lived here inside the brush, here, you know. There were just the houses for us to be in. [. . .] Who said there was anything about washing your head? Or taking a bath, or store-bought soap? There was that stuff for the rich, but there wasn't for us poor people, not at all! And then [. . .] this time started coming, and it started getting better, and it started coming, and it started getting better.

Dona Zaida had a more succinct analysis. "It seems that people's natures have changed."[4]

So much had changed in the villages, in so short a time. When workers finished connecting Rio Branco's first electric wire, in 2006, the whole village set off fireworks to celebrate. The wire was the visible sign, the crowning link in a chain of transformations. But what, exactly, was behind the changes? Was it the people's lack of faith, as Seu Túlio said? or their new studies? Was it power motors? or governments? And why did everything seem to change at once?

People at Maracujá and Rio Branco devoted much thought to the problem. Their reflections ran in parallel to the musings of economists. Villagers and economists alike were theorists in this conversation, and they grappled with the core definitional question: what is growth, really? Or, to put matters more specifically: when we talk about "growth," just what is the thing that we imagine to be growing?

It is worth noting that there is something vague, even strange, about the question as I have just posed it. My phrasing conflates at least three questions that are normally kept separate: How do we define growth? What causes or encourages growth? And what is good and what is bad about growth? Here, I embrace the overlap between the definition, causes, and normative assessment of growth by considering theories that help us think about growth in the broadest possible terms.

Already, I have suggested an answer to the question, *what is it that grows?* I argue that we can think of economic growth as an enthusiasm about cooperating with others, a new intensity. Hence the vibrancy of noncooperation, at once a gesture and an attitude, among people who are looking for an exit from a growth system.

But my approach is just one of many. Economists and villagers alike have suggested various visions: growth is an expansion of goods and services, or of knowledge, or of institutions, or of human welfare. No one definition of growth is fully correct or captures everything; all provide different lenses. Let's consider each one in turn.

WHAT GROWS IS GOODS AND SERVICES

"I remember," Daniel told me, thinking back to his youthful evenings on the plantation, "that at the very beginning when electricity came, there was just one guy who had a television."

All of those creams, Dona Mara exclaimed to me on another occasion. She marveled at the different personal care products her granddaughter seemed to need—not just soap, but shampoo, conditioner, and lotion. Thirty or forty years ago, you would make your own soap by boiling down cow bones, extracting the fat, and combining it with ashes from a fire. Everyone agreed: it smelled terrible.

Several years back, Suso trekked with his friends, little brother tagging along, to a temporary fun fair called Expo Conquista. They could barely scrape together the entrance fee. A passerby had mercy on the little brother and offered him a few tickets for the rides, while Suso and his friends sulked around, looking at everything, eating nothing, gripping the bus fare they would need to get home.

"And a year later, I had the same—I had the chance to go again," Suso told me. "This story, the way it is, it really gets to me." He paused. "This time it was different, you know? This time I went with—with means to enter." Suso, who now had a job at a bus company, took his brother for the second year in a row. "I saw him playing. He played on all of the rides, right? He got on every ride that he wanted."

Suso felt the change. "So I halted. There was a minute where I stopped in the middle of that park, just like that. I stayed there for several minutes thanking God. For—well, you know?"

Perhaps what really grows is what first meets the eye: a vast flow of goods and services. This is the definition of growth that inspired the creation of Gross Domestic Product (GDP) as a measure (see Kuznets 1934). Growth means that televisions and shampoo come into existence for the first time, and then growth also means that these products spread widely into the world, where they may reach the lives of people who never would have received such items when they were first invented. Benjamin Friedman is sensitive to both of these movements—innovation and spread—so he defines economic growth as "a rising standard of living for the clear majority of citizens" (2005: 16). Marx put it more bluntly: "the wealth of societies in which the capitalist mode of production prevails appears as an immense collection of commodities" (1976: 125).

Contemporary ecological economists deplore rather than wonder at the proliferation of commodities—but the model is ultimately similar. In Daly's ecological formulation, for instance, what grows is really "throughput," the flow of raw materials from extraction to commodity to waste (1996: 28). To grow is to increase throughput. With growth, by this definition, more and more raw materials are being used per person.

For all these theorists, growth can be immanently sensed in the products for sale. It is possible to apply clear measurements: growth becomes accountable in dollars or pounds of coal. If we are asking, *What is the thing that grows?* perhaps the easiest answer is, *GDP is the thing that grows* (Oulton 2012; Coyle 2014).

But GDP has many critics—starting with Simon Kuznets, inventor of the concept of GDP, who felt that the number should not be used as an indicator of a society's success (1934: 5–7). Environmentalists (Daly 1996; Pollin 2018; Vettese 2018) note that GDP increases when a forest is cut down for lumber but not when it is preserved. Feminists observe that GDP tends to omit people's unpaid efforts to care for others and to foster life, and, in general, GDP systematically excludes tasks undertaken by women more often than those done by men (Donath 2000). (In Marilyn Waring's famous example, a young woman in Tanzania adds nothing to GDP when she spends a twelve-hour day hauling water and cooking for her family, while a male soldier in the United States makes GDP grow when he is paid to sit by a nuclear missile for eight hours in case he is ordered to kill people by launching it (1988: 15–16).) The ecological and feminist critiques are important ones. Let us also note another problem with GDP, the problem of comparability.[5]

GDP is a tool for comparing societies.[6] The more dissimilar societies become, the more the comparison falls apart.[7] GDP may teach us something important about the comparison between people who live in São Paulo and people who live in Cuzco today. It may teach us less about the comparison between today's Brazilians and the Quechua speakers who lived in the Andes in 1491.

Sometimes comparison by number does not capture what is happening. This problem is relevant when we try to account for the growth at Maracujá and Rio Branco, where Daniel can remember the first television set and Mara feels surprised by the profusion of her granddaughter's soaps and lotions. Many of Daniel and Mara's neighbors have come to Maracujá specifically for the purpose of rendering themselves less comparable to the world market, more distant from the places that abound in televisions and personal care products. GDP does not accidentally fail to describe their lives; rather, they carefully make themselves less describable by GDP.

Consider a good Sunday at Maracujá or Rio Branco. Early in the morning, a volunteer crew of young people begin to swing their long hoes, meticulously cleaning the common soccer field. By noon that field fills with the jostling of several local teams and the shouts of delighted fans. Someone keeps a careful eye on the younger children, who run back and forth near the schoolhouse fence. The games end in time for people to wander into their relatives' kitchens and dine on manioc from the field and lettuce from the kitchen garden. Perhaps the village health committee is starting to think about mopping the schoolhouse floor and preparing the single vinyl hospital bed in anticipation of the doctor's monthly visit tomorrow. By nightfall, the devout have packed themselves into one or another of the churches, reading the Word or swaying to a hymn led by a parishioner with a beautiful, sturdy voice.

In the city, each of these tasks might have been carried out by a worker paid for their time: a grounds maintenance gardener, a professional soccer player, a child care provider, a restaurant cook, a doctor's assistant, a choir leader. In the city, GDP would have increased with the payment offered for each task. The village's Sunday did not add one cent to GDP.[8] But was it worthless? People sometimes move back to Maracujá and Rio Branco because they enjoy such a day, with less specialization, less cash, and more manioc grown in one's own field.

It would not quite be right to say that, because the villages lacked many of the market goods and services that GDP can measure, the villages were not experiencing economic growth. So much was changing, and much of it was free—or at least not counted in GDP. Now there were schools and doctors, new ideas and more literacy, longer life expectancy, different ways to plant a manioc root, close bonds to family in cities a thousand miles away. Even soccer was a sign. When villagers started playing amateur soccer—a sport that Brazilians learned from the British—then something new arrived, something connected to the flows of the world market and the rhythms of cooperation, even though village sports, being unpaid, did not increase GDP.

A major change separates Rio Branco in 1950 from Rio Branco today. This change is not just an incremental increase in the commodities available, a little more soap each year. It is a break, a qualitative difference. It is a transformation in ways of living. In some sense, the different ways of living are mutually incomparable. To the extent that they can be compared, they involve not only commodities, but also ideas and wishes, habits of subordination and visions of the good life.

GDP, as a measure of national income, is grounded in the conviction that what really grows is a society's collection of goods and services. This notion has vital importance. But GDP misses something. It focuses attention on products without highlighting the social relations that surround them. Too easily, we can come to treat growth as a fact rather than an action. Marx, who seemed aware of this danger, built a twist into the grammar of his sentence. Under capitalism, he wrote, wealth *appears* as an immense collection of commodities. What if the thing that *really* grows is something deeper?

2. WHAT GROWS IS HUMAN KNOWLEDGE

One day, Dona Zaida, then in her eighties, set out to explain to me why conditions had changed over time in the villages.

"Oh, Duff," she began. "It changed because of the knowledge of men [*sabedoria dos homens*]."

"Hm," I mused.

"Men went on living their lives. And they went on studying, and they went on—understanding how things were, until—things got a little more straightened out."

"Hm!"

"Those plantation owners started leaving. They saw that there were more people who knew more than they did, too."

"Hm!"

"A new crowd from outside started showing up. Coming here. So this started taking away their strength."

"Hm."

"They started understanding how things could be."

"Mm-hm."

"But that was because people from outside kept showing up. And coming in, and getting closer, and explaining to everyone else how things were. And so it changed."

From tractors to pay phones, the evidence of Dona Zaida's "new knowledge" was easy to find in the villages. To make such products—indeed, just to use them—required a wealth of information.

For certain economists, as for Dona Zaida, what really grows is *knowledge*. "Growth in the modern era," Mokyr postulates, "has been increasingly driven by what was known in the age of the Enlightenment as 'useful knowledge'" (2017: 4). Growth tends to happen when the knowers open themselves up to learning from people in different places. As Dona Zaida put it, knowledge grew *because people from outside started showing up*. These outsiders connected Rio Branco to ideas from the rest of the world. What really grows, in this theory of growth, is the stock of human knowledge in general: everything useful that humanity knows.

Other economists disagree. They believe that growth is not simply a matter of increasing useful knowledge in a general sense. What matters is *who has the knowledge*—how it is distributed, which rural roads it travels. Dona Eva, who farmed a small plot at Rio Branco, seemed to believe this as well. When schooling past fourth grade became available in the region, the school's van driver refused to drive down the long dirt road that led to the village, thereby excluding Rio Branco from the new educational opportunity. Dona Eva fought an extended bureaucratic battle, including no fewer than three 100-mile trips to complain to the Secretariat of Education, so that the students of Rio Branco could get a ride to school. Ultimately, she won.

Human capital is knowledge as it is held by actual people and groups of people. If the children of Rio Branco learned basic algebra, they did not increase the stock of useful knowledge in general, because basic algebra was already known by humanity. Instead, they increased the stock of human capital. Robert Lucas cogently argues that human capital, not just useful knowledge, is part of what grows in the usual process of economic growth. This human capital needs to be acquired through a community. Lucas notes that it is very rare for an individual to master advanced physics (to take one example) just by reading books. Instead, knowledge is frequently passed along through dense networks, such as schools and circles of friends. People tend to learn in "groups larger than the immediate family and smaller than the human race as a whole" (2002: 58). Thus, the unit that really *knows* the human capital is neither the person nor the species, but something of more intermediate size, such as the firm, the school, the nation, or the village. When people have the chance to gain human capital—when they are included in one such network—then they affect the direction of growth. If the school van refuses to drive down a certain dirt path, the shape of growth changes.

There are important insights to be gained from the knowledge-based theories of growth. Whether focused on knowledge in general or on human capital in particular, these theories point directly toward a social relationship. They explain how growth happens between people. The weakness of such theories, in my view, is that they presume that there exists a single, easy-to-identify substance called "knowledge." But what if different kinds of knowledge exist? What if they are incompatible with each other? This problem was highlighted for me when I met Leonardo.

On a tall, red slope facing Dona Zaida's hill, Leonardo, in his forties, took cowhides and turned them into gigantic saddlebags called *buracas*. A good buraca felt rigid to the touch and held water without leaking a drop. I was amazed to find that Leonardo's buracas were made only of leather, little bits of leather tied around larger pieces, with not a single metal or plastic component. Leonardo had learned this technique from the farmers before him, and now people at Rio Branco wondered if some child from the new generation would even bother to study it. Did growth mean increasing the store of human knowledge—or did it mean losing some kinds of knowledge in order to replace them with others?[9]

3. WHAT GROWS IS INSTITUTIONS

In those days, Dona Eva reminisced, "there was no such thing as a poor person's opinion. No way. An opinion was for a rich person."

It was 2012, and we were at Rio Branco, seated inside the thick adobe walls of the house that Seu Andres had built for her when she was his young wife. A massive wood-burning cookstove loomed to one side of us. Beyond the stove, a window without glass let in a bit of the sun that shone on the pigpen and on the flowers planted in front of a barbed-wire fence. From the darker recesses of the house, Seu Andres complained, "You've already told that story two times today!"

"Duff's writing it down," Dona Eva shot back, and Seu Andres appeared to take that for an answer.

Dona Eva went on. "Let me tell you something here. My dad had a disagreement with a—a brother-in-law of his. Over what? Over land."

In those days, it seemed, Dona Eva's father put up a fence to separate his land from his brother-in-law's. The morning after the fence was finished, Dona Eva went out, in the early light, to watch the livestock crowded into her father's pasture. A part of the fence was lying on the ground: her uncle had uprooted the section that bordered his territory.

"So what happened?" Dona Eva asked me rhetorically, perhaps relishing my sense of suspense. "Today there's the justice system to deal with these things, you see?"

"Yes, exactly," I answered.

"My dad went to find a rich person."

Dona Eva's father sought out the family of Nato, owner of the giant plantation nearby. Having heard the case, the plantation owner traveled to the city of Conquista. He wanted help from one of his sons-in-law.[10] Together, the owner and the son-in-law returned, met with Dona Eva's father and uncle, and set the boundary between the two plots of land.

"The poor person," Dona Eva concluded, "here, in the old days, was underneath everyone."

Of all of the major economic changes that Dona Eva witnessed between the 1960s and the 2010s, maybe the most foundational were the changes in institutions. She and her neighbors became ever more deeply connected to the predictable order of the nation-state. Starting with the end of the dictatorship (1985) and accelerating with the Workers Party victories in the municipal government (1996) and national presidency (2002), villagers found new doors opening to them. People from Rio Branco began to vote in large numbers. They went to banks. They received personal credit ratings. They turned to the court system, rather than plantation owners, to arbitrate their disputes. They even worshiped differently: Dona Zaida told me that in the old days, people prayed to Saint Lucia, Saint Joseph, and Saint John, but nobody had heard of "these saints of nowadays [*esses santos de agora*]," like Nossa Senhora Aparecida, the patron saint of Brazil (Pimenta 2012; Fernandes 1985).

People in the villages seemed to be building deeper links to the nation. In Douglass North's terms, they were entering new institutions: they were living under new "humanly devised constraints that structure political, economic, and social interaction" (1991: 97). These institutions, when they operated well, could spread information and reduce the risks that arose when collaborating with other people. Precisely because more and more Brazilians began to share these common practices, economic growth became possible. What grows most fundamentally, in this view, is institutions: the laws, habits, and shared understandings that make it feasible to work together in wider circles.

When growth is imagined as a change in institutions, not just an increase in knowledge, the vision becomes even richer and more fully social. Indeed, almost any human process can be described under the rubric of institutions. One of the drawbacks of the institutional approach is that this blooming diversity is organized through the concept of *constraint*: "humanly devised constraint" is the common quality that unites all institutions.[11] Growth is about how to put up fences the right way. Institutions can thus come to seem fundamentally legalistic, and the story of growth is ruptured into two pieces. On the one hand, there is a story about institutions, a set of law-like constraints. On the other hand, there is a different story about production, the activity that happens inside these constraints. But what if we imagined growth by starting with the human act of production rather than with the constraints that hold it back? This is the approach at the heart of a theory of cooperation.

4. WHAT GROWS IS HUMAN WELFARE

"A child would cry from hunger. Then fall asleep. Just a light sleep. Wake up in the night crying to eat." Dona Zaida was telling me about the bitterness of years past. "They'd cry until the day dawned. When the day dawned, you would have to go—hunt for some little thing to give the child to eat."

"Wow," I said.

"A suffering, Duff! The people today are in such richness that children eat whatever they think of eating."

"Hm."

"It's not what the mothers want to give them, no way. It's what they want. If there's a food already prepared right here, you say, 'Hey, child, do you want this food?' 'No, I really don't want that one. I want this other thing. I want this thing. I want that thing.'"

"Hm."

"Oh, my time!" Dona Zaida concluded abstractly. "Oh, my time!"

If the villages now had shampoo and televisions, villagers could also see changes of another sort, changes that improved the fundamental conditions of life. These changes were the beloved face of growth. Progressive politicians made farmers eligible for small retirement pensions. Pregnant women began to claim a maternity payment. A medical team started visiting the villages once a month, while the municipal government employed certain villagers as community health agents. And after the 2002 election of Lula, the Workers Party president, one-quarter of Brazil's families—including a large number in the villages—began to receive money through a yellow plastic debit card. The card came from Bolsa Família, the conditional cash transfer that gave a small monthly payment to mothers each month if their children were vaccinated and went to school.

These programs have transformative effects. An extensive body of research on Bolsa Família demonstrates that it has improved schooling, lowered income inequality, and increased the height of five-year-old boys. Bolsa Família is associated with a 65 percent drop in childhood deaths from malnutrition.[12] Moreover, Bolsa Família and the retirement pensions have allowed small farmers to develop an altogether different relationship to the cash economy and to expect a new minimum standard of decency that determines how a society distributes its resources.[13] Even the poorest now have a reason to believe that they should receive money regularly and use it to support their own survival. As a number of people told me, after Bolsa Família arrived, destitute villagers no longer went from door to door begging for food.

Perhaps this is growth in its truest form. Mahbub ul Haq has argued passionately that "people are both the means and the end of economic development" (1995: 3). On this view, what really grows is human welfare. Economists of this persuasion, led by Haq, have supplemented GDP measures by developing the Human Development Index, which accounts for a nation's level of education and life expectancy as well as its income. On this view, the new shampoos and the televisions are signs of a fundamental change. Growth is only growth if people's lives get better.

But what does it mean to get better? For economists who subscribe to the "capabilities approach," growth is ultimately defined as an increase in each person's power to make choices that matter to that person (Sen 1992, 1999). Note a certain duality in Dona Zaida's story: children stopped going hungry, and at the same time, children began to choose what they ate. Similarly, choice lies at the heart of the capabilities approach. If a farmer who was previously trapped on the farm can now decide whether to become a grocery store clerk or to remain a farmer, then growth has occurred, even if the farmer stays put. The farmer now has a greater "capability set," a broader number of possible ways to be in the world. For these economists, an increase in capabilities does not necessarily correspond to an increase in the number of commodities in a person's life; it corresponds to a strengthening of the person's capacity to live well and achieve their own ends.

The capabilities approach focuses on human flourishing, but its advocates are thinking about something beyond health, education, and other concrete measures of human welfare. For these theorists, growth is not just an increase in people's well-being or satisfaction; it is an improvement in capabilities, what people are "actually *able* to do and to be" (Nussbaum 2000: 63; italics added). In Sen's words, "the capability approach [. . .] [is] geared to the evaluation of living as such rather than merely of the happiness generated by that living (as in the utilitarian approach)" (1988: 20). This argument seems in some senses to have been anticipated by Lewis, who postulated a similar view in 1955: "the advantage of economic growth is not that wealth increases happiness, but that it increases the range of human choice [. . .] The case for economic growth is that it gives man greater control over his environment, and thereby increases his freedom" (1955: 420–21). Hence, Dona Zaida was highlighting more than a tiny detail when she described children who leave behind hunger and begin to try choosing their own food. Perhaps she was presenting precisely what growth means.

Today, Bolsa Família and similar benefits create a floor below which people will not fall (Morton 2019c). Bolsa Família, in particular, serves as de facto social insurance against farming disaster. Farmers who get the monthly money can afford to stay in the countryside even during the punishing droughts.[14] Thus, Bolsa Família helps subsistence agriculture to become a feasible alternative to the labor market. Social democracy redirects some of the fruits of economic growth in order to make it possible for people to step outside of the growth process. As I suggested earlier (see page 64), we should see this as a fundamental criterion: for economic growth to be democratic, it has to *increase* the viability of the alternatives outside of growth.

Haq, Sen, and Nussbaum would surely approve of the increased welfare and improved capabilities that Bolsa Família has fostered. The various welfare and capability theories, however, face a shortcoming in their portrayal of growth. These theories are fundamentally individualist and aggregative. They ground themselves in some property possessed by particular people, such as education, health, or (less tangibly) capability. The theorists add up this property across an entire society to come up with a metric for growth. Thus, these theories, while analytically powerful, say very little about the quality of relationships. The theories trace the characteristics of people rather than the connections between people. According to a theory of cooperation, it is connections that lie at the heart of growth.

AN ALTERNATIVE: WHAT GROWS IS A NEW INTENSITY ABOUT COOPERATING WITH OTHERS

One noisy summer dawn, I gave up on sleep and allowed myself to be drawn into the crowd of men gossiping loudly in front of the blue wooden shutters of my home at Maracujá. I could not understand why they went on chatting far into the morning, long after the time when people would usually head to their solitary fields. Then a small car pulled up, wheels churning the dust between one whitewashed house and the next. Two men bounded out with a sense of purpose. They had a clipboard.

Methodically, but evincing great energy, the men brought the clipboard to person after person in the street. Who, they asked, would like to sign up to pick coffee on an estate located near the rocky coastline, a thousand kilometers away?

The question was an annual ritual. Maracujá's residents had developed a bond with a plantation owner in the state of Espírito Santo, and each year at harvest time, he paid for their bus tickets so they would come and spend fifty-five days pulling his coffee beans, still green, off the long and spiky branches.

The two men circulated the clipboard, and name after name began to fill the paper, each name followed by a government ID number. The younger man was busy dispensing bonhomie to everyone who considered signing the worklist. Zé recounted ruefully that his wife didn't want to go work in the coffee. Wages for women are great, the young man from the car proclaimed. One and a half times the minimum wage if you do house cleaning! His feeling became contagious. *By nightfall*, Zé predicted, *I'll get my wife's name on the list*.

This was the sensibility of growth (Hirsch 2022: 11): the energy on the street that morning, the vibrancy that pulled people away from their personal fields and into a shared overnight bus trip to an extensive plantation. What was driving the growth forward?

Adam Smith offered an answer that began, famously, with the pin factory (1786: book 1, chap. 1). In the past, Smith said, a single worker used to work alone and forge an entire pin, from raw metal to finished product. And then the pin factory was born. In a pin factory of Smith's day, each worker relied intensely on all the others, because each created only one piece of the pin—the head, the body, or the sharpened end. This system made production more efficient, and the output of pins multiplied enormously. Thus, the change in the production process drew people and objects more tightly into networks with each other. A larger number of workers could now be employed at a single site. The enormous new output of pins could reach a wider population of consumers. As with pins, so with coffee beans. After all, Maracujá's farmers also grew coffee individually on their own tiny plots—but they became more efficient coffee producers when they toiled together, a thousand kilometers away, on the great plantation.

One might look at Adam Smith's pin factory and see the huge increase in the number of pins being made. Or one might look at the pin factory and see, first of all, the new relations that were being forged there. Is growth about products, or is it about relationships? In the second view, when economic growth takes place, the thing that is growing is cooperation. Growth is an intensification in cooperation, or, in other words, a novel impulse toward working together on common productive projects. Seeing growth in this way is like taking an x-ray in which a growing economy appears as a mesh of new connections between people (and nonhumans).

In such examples, cooperation becomes more intense—intense in several related senses. Cooperation is more *expansive*, as each worker now relies on a larger number of co-workers, suppliers, and consumers. Cooperation is also more *far-flung*, with these participants connecting across greater geographic and social distance. Cooperation is more *intimate*, since in the minutiae of a worker's everyday work process, she depends more closely on her collaborators and finds it more difficult to work without them. Finally, cooperation is more *all-consuming*, because workers cooperate for more hours of the day and have a harder time imagining an economy outside of such relationships. What makes cooperation more intense is the combination of these changes: more expansive, more far-flung, more intimate, more all-consuming.[15]

Economic growth is thus a collective action problem; each person needs the others to cooperate for growth to occur. Like all collective action problems, economic growth challenges any simple account of individual choice. You cannot enter into a growth project unless I do as well. This problem constrains your choices—and it gives you a reason to reason to influence my choices (or force them) by persuading, cajoling, or coercing me into following you.

On this view, what is fundamental to growth is the enthusiasm for new bonds with other people. This is what Durkheim suggested in the passage cited at the beginning of this chapter: growth is not only about increasing economic efficiency. More importantly, growth is about building solidarity. To think this way is to focus on the sociality of growth.[16] Or in Erik Harms's words, "growth is itself just another word for human activity, an abstraction of a social process; for growth grows out of society itself" (2011: 46).

CONCLUSIONS: GROWTH AND THE PATH THAT LEADS IN TWO DIRECTIONS

What *is* it that grows, then? goods and services? knowledge? institutions? human welfare? cooperation? Ultimately, we are missing the point if we choose only one answer; growth is a process in which many things change at once. Each theory of growth allows us to see a different feature of this change. Here, I have emphasized the cooperation account because it highlights a reality that is patent at Maracujá and Rio Branco: the growth path leads in two directions, toward growth and away from it.

The four initial growth theories tend to represent growth as an undeniable force for good. Who could ever want fewer goods and services, less knowledge, worse institutions, decreased human welfare, or poorer capabilities? In these theories, the problem with growth is always some factor external to growth itself, some tradeoff that has to be made (more pollution, less leisure, stricter laws) in order to obtain the unquestionable benefit that is growth. Degrowth theories (at least in certain cases) follow the same logical structure, but they tell the story backward, portraying growth as an unequivocal problem. What all of these perspectives obscure is the possibility that growth might be a dilemma.

The dilemma lies at the heart of the cooperation approach to growth. On this view, growth intrinsically raises the question of *how intensely to cooperate with other people*, a question that has no easy answer. This means that growth itself—not simply the external factors associated with growth—can provoke ambivalence.

One of the benefits of the cooperation approach is that it takes this ambivalence seriously. When Alexandra (see the introduction) struggled with her mother's call to leave the business school and return to the countryside, she had to decide how much she would cooperate and with whom. Alexandra's ambivalence about exiting the big city was not a brief pause as she weighed her options. The ambivalence was genuine, a real experience in which she needed time not to calculate her preferences, but to create them anew.

In most theories of growth, there is really only one way forward, only one direction that anyone would want to take along the path: the direction of growth. (Or, for dissidents, the direction of degrowth.) Every other consideration amounts to an obstacle on the path. The obstacles might possibly require a change in the speed of growth—hence the calls for "slow growth"—but never in its direction.

By contrast, the cooperation approach allows us to see growth as a serious question. We can imagine why people might want to step away from growth. Maracujá and Rio Branco are places where people certainly experience economic growth—think of the electric wires installed and the new schools opened. But these villages are also places where people can say no to growth—think of the factory jobs abandoned and the rising wages turned down. When we conceive of growth in such a context, we envision a road with real options that leads in both directions.

The road that leads in both directions: this metaphor has special meaning in the history of Maracujá and Rio Branco. The villages might sometimes look like pristine zones outside of modernity, places belatedly drawn onto the growth path. But such an image deceives. Both villages are havens built by people who knew growth too well and who walked backward out of the world market. People came to the region in order to reject sugarcane and enslavement, iron ore mines and coffee harvests. Thus, the past in the villages is not a pure state of nature. It is the remains of some previous growth cycle. These remains occasionally show up, appropriately enough, in the words that people use to describe vehicles on roads.

Take the mascates, those small-time truck traders who went house to house, extending credit based on personal connections. As it turns out, the word *mascate* derives from the city of Muscat, in Oman, famed for its merchants in the Indian Ocean commerce. The village mascate is not a local oddity, but the inheritor of a cosmopolitan trade practice that filtered through the Portuguese colonial project and installed itself halfway around the world from the Indian Ocean, in the drylands of Bahia.

Or *marineta*, the word that Dona Eva used to describe the bus. The term is hardly a village localism: it was applied in 1926 to the first city buses in the state capital of Salvador. The word *marineta* (or *marniete*) commemorated a famous visitor to Brazil at the time, the Italian poet Filippo Marinetti, founder of Futurism, lover of machines and speed (Bergman 2017: 421). At Rio Branco and Maracujá, his name persisted as the trace of something gone by.

Maracujá and Rio Branco do not sit at the primitive, unspoiled starting-point of the growth path. Just the opposite. These are places that have Futurism as their past. Their language preserves the memory of the heedless velocities that one's ancestors, during some previous outburst of growth enthusiasm, left behind.

*

Four years after I spotted the car and the clipboard on the morning streets of Maracujá, I finally found out how the village had become bonded to a plantation owner a thousand miles away. It was because of Josue. Soft-spoken, chronically thin, and given to wandering, Josue himself was born on the rocky coast near the plantation, and during one of his journeys, he passed through Maracujá. He decided that he liked the place and simply moved in. From time to time he returned to his homeland for little spells of work. He would invite a few people to come along with him, then more. Then the cycle spun out of his hands. "At some point," Josue told me, "I wasn't even going there anymore. The people that I took began to take other people." Now, Josue said, more than a thousand workers from the region made the trek every year.

Josue's journey set a pattern, a single relationship copied into a lattice of a thousand. It was the very portrait of growth. But why had Josue himself stopped traveling? Josue now lived in a nearly empty house at the edge of Maracujá. When I saw him there in 2016, he rushed to take me down the dirt road, just a few minutes' walk, to his plot of land, a splash of green hidden behind gray scrub brush. Josue had coaxed several dozen citrus trees to survive in the dry ground; he had learned to graft them and to guide their growth upward. Josue grabbed armfuls of oranges, insisting that I taste, apologizing for imperfections that only he perceived. Why did Josue's orchard cure his wandering in a way that the plantation could not? For what reason had he once migrated into the world market, and for what reason had he left it behind? These were questions that uncovered something about growth by considering its opposite.

Josue with his oranges.

3

The Bus Ride

Making and Unmaking Abstract Labor

> Capital cannot do without labor, nor labor without capital.
> POPE LEO XIII, "Rerum Novarum" (1891: para. 19)

The jungle of stone was what Carlos called São Paulo.[1] He left it repeatedly. To exit the largest city in the southern hemisphere, Carlos preferred to catch the 2:00 p.m. departure out of a cavernous bus terminal with gray floors. He stood in a line full of people and baggage, then presented his paper ticket to a driver in a short-sleeve uniform with a tie, then settled into the air conditioning that he would breathe for the next twenty-four hours. Carlos was willing to pay a bit more for a bus with air conditioning.

When the coach bus pulled into the city of Conquista at 2:00 p.m. the following afternoon, Carlos would find a taxi to carry him to a little street at the edge of a park that was always busy with street vendors. There he would wait outside a barbershop, smelling exhaust and tropical fruit, until the driver of the decrepit rural bus started up the engine. He would climb on board and fit his thin body into the seat where he would ride without air conditioning for the final three hours of his journey.

Out the open window, the view was scrub brush and horse carts, small forests and smoke rising from brick homes that had been cemented together by the people who lived in them. Sometime around first darkness, Carlos would step off the aging rubber of the bus floor. His feet would land on the empty soccer field at the middle of Rio Branco, and he would be ringed by wooded hills and the shapes of his siblings' and cousins' houses surrounding him on every side.

If São Paulo was the jungle of stone, Carlos knew the stones. At age thirty-three, he had left behind his work in the fields to become a bricklayer in the metropolis. Later, he toiled in a chemical plant that he hated and he repaired an apartment so fancy that two police officers stood guard over him while he worked. Eventually, he specialized in applying a shiny finish to the outside of the city's tallest buildings.

Carlos came back to Rio Branco many times to visit. He usually made friends on the bus ride. During one trip, he found an older woman sitting on one side of him and, on the other, a man with a cellphone. The phone turned out to be loaded with love songs by Amado Batista, a hit musician who had once migrated from a farm to work as a janitor in the city. Carlos, the woman, and the man began listening to Amado Batista when the bus pulled out of São Paulo at 2:00 p.m. They spent the entire day playing song after song, and by 7:00 a.m. the next morning, they were sitting together drinking coffee at a roadside stop on the border of Bahia state. When they said their farewells, the woman and the man both gave Carlos their phone numbers. He never called and at some point he lost the piece of paper. Carlos explained to me that city friendships were different from village friendships.

Carlos hated leaving the village. He remembered for me a thought that ran through his head once on the last day of his visit: "Oh, my God, I've got to go to that São Paulo again." When I first met Carlos, in 2012, he had just moved back to the village in a permanent way. But he was haunted by worry. In São Paulo he left his son, Bruno, living with Bruno's mother. Carlos talked about lawyers and child support payments, arguments and phone calls. During the first year, Carlos traveled back to São Paulo four times to see Bruno. "The only precious thing I have in my life," Carlos told me, "is him."

Carlos said that his trips to Rio Branco had lost part of their sparkle because now he was leaving his son each time he departed. Still, Carlos described something special about the ride to Rio Branco. "Ave Maria! For me, that was my happiness." He said he could feel it when the bus was several hours away. "Thank God," he remembered thinking. "I'm already in my land."

*

By the time the silver, red, and blue bus rumbled into the village, minutes after dawn, Dona Marta had already wrapped up beans with toasted manioc flour. Her son Diego would be able to slip the meal into his bag, alongside the new clothes he had purchased on store credit. Diego was traveling a day and a night to reach his first construction job in São Paulo, and he carried five reais (about $2.50) in his pocket. That was too little to buy lunch.

Dona Marta had raised Diego while she lived in other people's houses, caring for cattle and toiling in tall fields. In these fields she would hear Diego, still a child, singing alone. Over and over again, he explained to his mother and father that he could see himself as a music star, his fingers dancing along an electronic keyboard. Now, on the side of the dirt road with the bus rumbling into view, Diego was headed to São Paulo in search of money to buy his instrument.

Dona Marta was familiar with dreams. At midlife she had turned herself into a leader in the landless movement. She brought Diego and the rest of her family to live in protest tents on the dry, sprawling plantation next to Maracujá. When the federal government finally redistributed the land, Marta and her husband gained a small field and eventually a cement house, and she was chosen as the new community's leader.

Dona Marta dreamed, too, of becoming a baker. She made an oven out of a giant metal barrel built into a wall in her house, with space for firewood beneath the baking racks. When she showed it to me, the oven had not yet outcompeted the industrial kitchens in the nearby city, but it worked.

Diego told me that his mother sympathized with his aspiration. So did his father. They were dreamers, as he was. Dona Marta confessed to her son that she wished she could buy him a keyboard as a gift. Then he could stay in the village.

Instead, when Diego reached age eighteen, his aunt found him a construction job in São Paulo. Diego had no way to get to the city. In the back yard of their whitewashed house, under the open skies of the dry plain, Diego's father was raising a sow for slaughter. Diego remembered for me the words his father spoke to him on that occasion: "What I can do for you is sell—is sell this sow and give you the money for the bus ticket." Diego's father fulfilled the promise. That was how Dona Marta ended up mixing beans and manioc flour for her son, who stood on the side of the dirt road in the first light with the dust from the bus approaching.

*

A migrant's journey to Maracujá or Rio Branco takes place, most simply, as a bus trip, dark wheels rolling over the miles of parched soil that separate the villages from the heart of the world market. Migrants flow out to their workplaces by bus, as Diego did, and they drift back along those same bus routes, as Carlos did and as Diego eventually would do after his phone calls to his mother, already described in chapter 1.

In the context of Brazil's growth process, Maracujá and Rio Branco are remote in a specific sense (Piot 1999; Tsing 1993): they are remote from the urban labor market. Hence, this chapter is not about transportation per se, but instead about transportation as a means for creating (and unmaking) abstract labor. I understand buses as tools that people use for the purpose of managing the distance between themselves and markets. It is a bus ride that converts a migrant into a specific quantity of labor to be sold in the city's labor market.

Diego's bus ticket provides a case in point. If Diego lived on the family farm and took an absent-minded stroll to feed scraps to the sow after dinner, he was not performing labor measured by any market (Morton 2019a). He was raising the livestock that he might end up eating. When the pig was sold and her value converted into a trip to São Paulo, Diego lost his means of subsistence, and in that same moment he turned himself into a worker for hire at the standard wage. No wonder, as he put it to me, that on the bus ride he felt at risk of becoming "an asylum-seeker [*um asilado*]," a person cast out of place.

The conversion can be undone, too, and the tool for undoing it is a bus ride back. Diego did not aim to remain a worker forever. He had a plan to make it possible for himself to live outside the wage labor market by procuring a special asset: a synthesizer keyboard. Then, he hoped, he could return on the same bus line, transformed into a rural rock star.

Robert Solow's pioneering model of economic growth, first developed in 1956, includes two neat variables that each contribute to development: capital and labor (Solow 1956). For "capital" and "labor" to exist as separate categories, however, a prior act of separation has to occur. When he wanders out to feed the back yard pig, Diego is both a capitalist and a laborer, or maybe neither one; it is hard to identify the moments in which he is "working" and the moments in which he is "around the house." The bus trip makes clear the line between them. On the other end of his journey, after he has lost family ownership of the sow, Diego knows the hours of his labor and his leisure.[2]

To speak about this another way, Diego has watched his time turn into abstract labor. But what *is* abstract labor? Labor, for Marx, is in the deepest sense the action of humans on the world: humanity, as a part of nature, temporarily separates itself from nature and changes nature, thereby changing itself as well (Marx 1994; Marx 1976: chap. 7; see Davis 1981). The history of capital is the story of how labor acquires a dual character. On the one hand, labor under capital is *concrete labor*, that is, the sensuous acts of particular people with particular tools. On the other hand, the labor that capital organizes is also *abstract labor*, a generic commodity for sale in standard quantities. Seen from one perspective, Diego's day on a construction site may look like the concrete labor of a dreamy Bahian eighteen-year-old hauling an especially heavy load of cinderblock. Seen from a different perspective, the same day appears, abstractly, as eight hours of unskilled construction work that can predictably build a certain percentage of a house.[3]

When labor becomes abstract, then workers, bosses, and consumers all come to perceive the world differently. They look at each object that a worker is producing, and they see that object in generic terms, as one unit among many: no longer *the beans from Seu Félix's back yard*, but instead *five kilos of regular pink beans.* They look at the worker's effort, and they see a standard span of time: no longer *a hot afternoon in the back yard* but *four hours of labor.*

For this reason, I suggest that we can helpfully think of abstract labor as the production of homogeneous objects in homogeneous time.[4] Workers are producing a standard object, in such an economy, and they are producing it by exerting themselves for a measured unit of time. This formulation implies an argument about what happens on the bus ride: to make labor abstract means to change the relationships between people, time, and objects. In other words, labor inside modernity is first of all a matter of time and things; the domination of the supervisor is secondary.

The abstraction can take place even when no one is anyone else's employee. If labor is about how we engage with time and things, then there can be work without employment, labor without wages, and commands without bosses. For that matter, even without bosses, there can be exploitative work, alienated labor, and oppressive commands. Farmers at Rio Branco and Maracujá confront this challenge every day, as I describe in chapter 4. The villages, which exist very much inside modernity, are home to their own characteristic labor abstractions. But in the village toolsheds, one might also find some useful tools for undoing abstraction.

If labor is about how we engage with time and things, then different timing and different things lead to different kinds of life. Hence this chapter's main argument: people can reverse the process that renders labor abstract. Many scholars have insightfully shown how capital makes the world homogeneous, and this chapter serves as a sequel to their work. It argues that the gears can turn in the opposite direction as well, that the world can become *less* homogeneous. But, just as every opposite contains what it opposes, so Carlos's return journey presupposes the capitalist market from which he returns. If Maracujá and Rio Branco offer some distance from labor's abstraction, the very effort to generate distance, here, is predicated on the tacit acceptance of abstract labor as the standard. Villagers are being heterodox, and they admit it. The villages remain inside a capitalist world system.[5]

In such a system, this chapter looks at how people move around. The chapter traces out the small steps that migrants take to render their labor abstract—and then to undo the rendering. First, I consider the way a migrant sits in a bus seat and the bureaucratic identity that such a seat promotes. Second, I consider the timing of the bus's departure. This timing turns into an example of the sort of time a migrant will encounter in the urban labor market: time beyond one's power to adjust. Third, I assess the role of the bus ride as a separator that makes the boss seem distant, turning bosses, in the language of the villages, into "other people."

The bus ride produces bureaucratic identity, homogeneous time, and separation from the boss. In other words, the bus ride contains the ingredients for abstract labor. In the chapter's final pages, I consider two critiques that migrants launch against abstract labor—one grounded in the notion of *substance* and the other in the notion of the *standard*—and I consider the mode of political action that each critique makes possible.

Laborers can only become laborers thanks to the help of other people, especially the people in their own households. When Dona Marta wrapped up beans and manioc flour for the bus ride, her unpaid effort was one crucial step in the chain of separations that produced Diego's abstract labor—at a bargain rate. Feminized work was making a working class. Thus, from one angle, people who live at Maracujá and Rio Branco are semiproletarians, the extra soldiers in the reserve army of labor.[6]

The semiproletarian story, however, may not fully capture the return side of the migrant's journey. Such a story may miss the joyful energy that workers bring to the project of leaving labor. Hence, this chapter is concerned with *the bus seat*: the small space that one person occupies while they wrestle with the making (and unmaking) of abstract labor.

Being in the Seat

To get from São Paulo to the villages, you needed at least twenty-four hours and two bus rides, the first seated in a fuzzy recliner on a slick coach, the second oftentimes perched on top of pieces of wood and loose springs inside a creaky, repainted vehicle.

Nonetheless, in both rural buses and their fresher long-distance counterparts, the practice of occupying a seat seemed remarkably consistent. A passenger's first gesture, frequently, was to place an item of low value, like a plastic bag, at the center of one's own seat and any companions' seats, thus laying claim to the area while one loaded one's baggage or strolled around outside waiting for the bus to depart. Next, once the engine had begun rumbling, passengers settled into their seats and arranged their possessions in locations that corresponded to priority. Food, pillows, and jackets might be placed near to hand. Less urgent items went far underneath the seat or in the compartment above. By contrast, goods closely linked to one's formal identity, like purses and cellphones, tended to rest directly beside the passenger in the seat. Some passengers—usually the more prosperous—might save seat space for an mp3 player or a small DVD machine, while others hung clothing in the window in order to manage the light. There could also be a bag to hold garbage. Bus riders thus set up a whole liminal system for living. In those moves, inside a compressed place, passengers expressed certain core principles of the urbanism they were either entering or leaving: scarcity of space, the pursuit of one's own preferences, a spirit of provisional temporariness, close surveillance over official identity markers, and the right to a limited but fully individual range of motion. Like all forms of long-distance travel, the bus ride required people to restate who they were, given specific ritual constraints.

You could become something new, during those twenty-four hours in the seat, and one of the new things you could become is a container for labor. Along "the conscious journey of ritual," as DaMatta calls it (1991: 74), a migrant would turn into a wage laborer because of the objects they did *not* bring along. They could not carry with them the tools that would make it possible to subsist outside of the labor market: Diego's father had to kill the pig in order for Diego to get on the bus. Hence the increased salience of personal identifiers, like ID cards and cellphones, usually tucked under the bed in the countryside but now somewhat anxiously monitored right next to oneself on the bus. These identifiers allowed you to demonstrate to a boss that you were you: a name on a résumé, a tax ID number, a cellphone reliably answered, a set of skills verified through the government work documents, all of it tied together to create a stable nexus between the work you did from one day to the next and the paycheck you would receive. Your bureaucratic identity abstracted you. You stepped off the bus not as an owner of tools but as a bearer of labor-hours, stored up inside yourself, and your identity was the guarantee that those labor-hours would flow from you to the boss in a reliable stream.

You might also turn yourself into something besides a laborer during the bus ride, and Carlos reminded me about this. You might become a friend. Once every four hours, at roadside stops, passengers could leave their bus seats. Carlos reminisced with me about these stops. He would stroll over to a table at the nearest lunch counter and drink coffee alongside his fellow passengers. He would ask people where they were from and tell them about his life. "Always," he concluded for me, "you gain a lot of friendships on those buses."

But Carlos noted a peculiarity: people did not pay for each other's coffee. "I never paid for anyone's," he mused. "No one ever paid for me." In the countryside, the primordial welcoming gesture was to invite someone into your house to drink a coffee. In the space of the bus seat, it was not possible to invite a guest, not even metaphorically, not even paying for a fellow rider to gulp the dark brew out of a glass from the dishwasher at a truck stop. As Carlos put it, "No one offers." There was a lesson here, and he summed it up for me: "Over there in the city, nobody gives anything to anybody, no way." Carlos paused, then repeated it for emphasis. "Nobody gives anything to anybody, no way."

During Carlos's long days and nights in a bus seat, he eventually devised a technique that allowed him to perform hospitality in a mobile context. In place of coffee, at the roadside stops, he purchased cheese breads (*pães de queijo*). These tiny white pastries came in small units, each one a dollop of dough the size of an apricot, dappled with drops of pale flour on the outside and airy enough to reveal the molten cheese at its heart. While other passengers downed their private beverages at a lunch counter, Carlos might buy four or five cheese breads. He would climb back to his seat. Then, as the bus lurched forward, he would offer cheese bread to the riders around him.

Coffee was liquid. Cheese breads were solid. They were discrete, individuated, quantized; they were objects easily rendered homogeneous for distribution to a wide group of people. In Carlos's habit of generosity, I see a rearticulation of the hospitality discourse he knew in the villages, now adapted to the standards of a different context. The bus seat was a place where the elements of the social world might be differently arranged and newly signified. But these elements did not necessarily disappear. Like Carlos's persistent concern with hospitality, the elements could remain as signs that pointed out the road back to another way of living.

The Bus Hour, the Plantation Day: Homogeneous Time and Its Undoing

For a migrant's labor to become abstract, that labor needed to be fitted into a special kind of time: homogeneous time. The bus ride itself imposed that timing. To ride the bus back, then, was to undo the abstraction.

One of the few unmovable deadlines at Maracujá and Rio Branco was the hour of the bus's departure. Other schedules could bend. Meals with friends happened at whatever time the friends arrived; work in fields began more or less flexibly; a pastor would start a church service once a crowd gathered, sometimes after the pastor sent a child from door to door to fetch tardy congregants. Villagers rarely expressed irritation over waiting. Wait time was normal and often even pleasant, since it provided an opportunity for jokes and sociability, and it demonstrated respect for the people for whom one was waiting.

It was not so with for the bus. At both Maracujá and Rio Branco, a bus roared into town like clockwork each morning. The stoic bus driver and the usually garrulous ticket-taker, wearing the same uniform, would peer out the window at the lines of people waiting at the established pickup spots. The passengers boarded, and the bus roared away again: there was no rescheduling.

Perhaps the bus served as a first sign of the time-discipline that workers would face at city workplaces. There, the minutes mattered. Orestes remembered for me that he would walk to his urban supermarket job early enough to arrive twenty minutes before he needed to clock in. He wanted to head to the cash register with a calm, collected appearance. It was important both to be timely and to feel timely.

In the villages, it is not a coincidence that the bus—the point of connection with the world market—is the instrument that marks an unalterable time that you are powerless to change. I think of this kind of time as "bus time." Migrants often referred to such time with great resentment. Indeed, they cited time freedom as one of the reasons for returning to the villages.

Seu Jairo remembered eating bananas with manioc at noontime, back in the days when he worked for the bosses in the South, because he had no time to go home for lunch. Ana told me a story about how she injured her hand in a stapler at a clothing factory. Her supervisor pointed out to her that time was measured by the minute. "That second there, that I had injured myself, those hours, if I didn't go back to work, they were going to take it out of my salary." Adelberto, recalling a job where he had to start at 5:00 a.m. and got no break, summed it up: "That's another life, dude."

Bus time was not just about precise timing. Bus time was less a matter of *exact* temporality and more a matter of temporality *beyond your power to change*. Factory laborers learned this lesson when their shifts were modified without warning. The lesson could be even harsher for women who went to the city to work as domestic servants. Often, these domestic workers had great difficulty persuading their bosses to allow them to *stop* working at a fixed hour. Their labor time was disciplined not by their bosses' exactitude, but by their bosses' fuzziness about time. So it was with Tamara (see pp. 3–5), who finally left her nanny job because the boss would not let her end her work day at the agreed-upon time.

Migrants tended to talk about their urban work experience in terms of hours, worrying about start times or complaining about periods spent off the clock. Village work was different. For this reason, migrants often described the village as the place where they enjoyed a form of freedom expressed as a matter of *different hours*.

I heard villagers speak frequently about the freedom of the village hour. In the village, Lara declared, "you're working for yourself. You work at the hour that you want. You stop at the hour you want." On a different occasion, Simão sounded similar. "Here, it's for ourselves. There's no one to say, 'Hey, you arrived late. Don't do that anymore.'"[7]

No one described the village hour as eloquently as Ademir. He had returned to Maracujá after a stint as a firefighter for Vale, the giant mining corporation, where he spent his days battling flames around the mines that sent iron ore to China. Vale, he reflected, "is a company. We can't rest. We have to start at the right hour, and stop at the right hour. Inside here," he noted, turning his attention to the fields around him, "no way. Here we work a little hour, come back inside the house."

"Mm-hm," I answered, eager to hear more.

"In the company, dude? You've got to do a job the right way: valued. And here it's not like that. Here it's—work a little hour, dude, and come back inside the house, and rest. That's why over there the work was heavier."

I heard all this talk about hours as commentary on that quintessential urban contraption, the boss's time clock. More directly, though, Ademir's words reminded me of a song that Cecílio often strummed on his guitar at landless movement protests:

> I don't know the hours
> But I see the light of the dawn
> God and me in the backlands.[8]

Not to know the hours: you could live as if the clock itself had simply melted away. This was one way to describe the dream of freedom that might guide you to a small farm.

The hour, however, was not the only idiom available. If villagers had previous work experience on a large plantation, they tended to speak not about the *hour*, but about the *day*. Time on coffee plantations was measured in days, not hours, with workers receiving a day-wage. The day provoked bitter memories, too. "Every day, you had to work," Daniel reminisced, recalling the landholders who had hired him to plant coffee trees as a child. "Now I'm an owner. [. . .] Work on the day that I want."

Seu Álvaro had started toiling on farms at age ten, after his father died. In 2016, I found him tying together the mesh of a fishing net hung between two trees in the darkening evening, obviously following his own schedule. He described that schedule as Daniel did, as a matter of days. At Maracujá, Seu Álvaro reflected, "nobody bothers you. On the day when you can work, you work [. . .] There's none of that plantation owner business."

As I mulled over these stories, I came to the conclusion that the people around me were defining village time primarily by what it was not. Villagers described village time by contrasting it to the specific unit that had previously rendered their own labor homogeneous. Thus, for migrants who arrived from a city job, the small farm had its distinctive *hour*, unlike the hour on the time clock or the work schedule. For villagers who came off the big plantations, the small farm allowed you to work the *day* that you wanted rather than obeying the plantation master who summoned you every day.

In both cases, I heard villagers doing something more than simply protesting against time discipline in general. They were objecting to the particular term that had been used in the past to abstract *their* labor. They were commenting on the variety of powerlessness they had known.

In moments like these, I slowly came to realize that, for many of my interlocutors, Maracujá and Rio Branco made possible a special type of time. What the villages offered was a change in the quality of time, not a decrease in the intensity of work.[9] This subtlety became clearer to me after I talked to Santiago, who had returned to Maracujá from a stint at a furniture factory. He described the toil in the village as "calmer." I might have heard this as an admission that he worked less hard in the fields than on the factory floor. But no, he said: *city* work "is more—it's lighter, you know? Like, it's not the type of work where you end up in the middle of the thick underbrush and taking the heavy sun." Toil in the field was heavy. I wondered how Santiago could describe village work as both *calmer* and *heavier*. He explained: in the village, "you stop at the hour you want, you start at the hour you want. And—and out there, no. Working for other people, no. You have to fulfill a time schedule."

"In the countryside," Pastor Pedro agreed, "we work too heavy. [. . .] We don't just work eight hours a day, but twelve hours." Pedro was clearly right. In the villages, days tended to run from sunup to sundown, and villagers mocked anyone who stayed in bed after dawn. Nor did the farm allow for regular weekends. Farmers had an expression that seemed to poke fun at urban work rhythms: "The fields," people reminded each other, "don't give you vacation time."

This was a sly, knowing witticism. Villagers had heard of the concept of vacation time. For migrants at Rio Branco and Maracujá, village temporality did not arise simply because of unfamiliarity with metropolitan standards or a "cultural" failure to understand urban calendars and clocks. Migrants knew bus time all too well, and their temporality was a political rejection of that sort of measure. Village timekeeping practices were not an effort to work less hard, nor were these practices motivated by a distaste for exactitude. The problem with migrants' previous jobs was not that, on those jobs, time was exact, but rather that time could not be moved; time served as an instrument of class domination, and it had power over you. At Maracujá or Rio Branco, you could maintain some distance from that powerlessness, but it returned every morning in the form of the implacable bus. Hence the philosophical urgency of speaking about the kind of time that mattered to you.

"Where I used to live," Seu Miguel told me, recalling his past as a farmhand, "it was like this. It was day after day at day labor. The whole time! The freedom that we had there was just a little bit at night."

Seu Miguel had left that life to join the first wave of landless activists occupying Maracujá. Now settled on a piece of land at the expropriated plantation, he felt sympathy for his neighbors who still worked "for the owners out there, the big estate masters. It's like this," he continued, "they—they're captives there, the whole time. If they miss the day of work, [then the bosses] don't want them in the field any longer."

Seu Miguel knew what it meant to miss days of work. Bitten by a sand fly, infected with leishmaniasis, he walked unsteadily and had been hospitalized several times. His wife was finding few jobs to pass through the electric sewing machine that she kept meticulously clean. Finances were difficult. As the three of us talked, we sat between the pastel-painted walls of their living room, not far from the plot that Seu Miguel cultivated for his family. He gestured toward me. If he and I wanted to spend the day at the riverbank tomorrow, he said, we could do it. Seu Miguel summed up the lesson. "There's no money that can pay for our freedom, Duff."

A World without Bosses: Bosses as the Others

Melchior remembered for me the first time he got off the bus from the countryside to São Paulo, accompanied by his brother. He was seventeen and carried his relatives' address scribbled down. He laughed at the memory of the bus station: "Those escalators there, we didn't even know how to put down the first foot, because we were scared of falling, you know? It was rough."

Like Melchior, migrants exit the bus and step right away onto a moving escalator. They must find work quickly, since the bus trip itself has been a major investment and they usually carry only a little money to live on until their first paycheck. They tend to have few links to the urban workforce, so they often take the first job available. To the extent that they are in the city to labor, migrants watch their city time as a whole become abstract, an interchangeable succession of dormitories on construction sites, résumés printed at copy shops, and standard workplace meals packed into metal pails. Migrants are famously vulnerable to labor exploitation in this context. Separated by the bus ride from their previous mode of subsistence, incapable of sustaining themselves without immediate employment, shorn of the personal networks and marks of distinction that might set them apart from other workers, migrants incarnate generic labor power. Yet they have a decisive advantage not shared by their urban-born counterparts. They can ride the bus back. Through one big departure, they can aspire to leave bosses behind altogether.

Urban employees typically split their time into intervals of "labor" and "nonlabor," and this split is produced each day by the daily commute. When

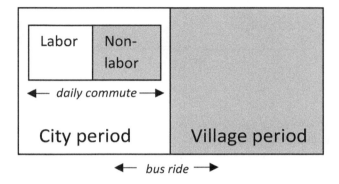

employees arrive at work, they find their hours abstracted into units under someone else's command.[10]

For migrants from the countryside, though, this split is doubled. The initial bus ride divides a migrant's time into two large sections: time in the countryside and time in the city. Thus, the daily alternation between labor and leisure is all fitted into a *city period*, which stands in distinction to a *village period*. A migrant worker may go to work and come home every day in the city, but they could perpetually be preparing to return to the other kind of home—a home in the country—as if their urban life as a whole were always on the clock. Every day in the city already has all of its hours counted.

Young migrants tend to alternate most quickly between city and countryside. It is a mark of maturity to stay longer in the village, to build up one's herd with strong cows, to nurture coffee trees as their green leaves darken, and to anchor a house solidly on one's rural land. In this way, migrants can make the graceful transition toward full-time residence in the countryside. A third cycle thus appears. The alternation between city and village belongs to the *youthful stage*, while migrants get to live in the village full time once they reach the *mature stage*.

A migrant, then, can oscillate on three levels at once. Every day, you sway between labor and rest. From season to season, you move between city and

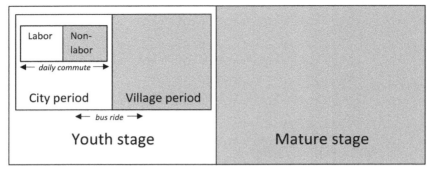

country. In a lifetime, you shift between youth and maturity. These three levels run in parallel. What unites them—what is common to all of the levels—is the line between having a boss and dispensing with the boss. This line is produced through a transportation ritual (often enough, on a bus). When you go home from your job at the end of the workday, perhaps hopping on a local city bus, you leave the boss behind. The tiny bit of freedom in this moment can become a prediction, a sign, of that grander moment when you board a coach headed for the village that has no bosses. The act of stepping on that bus, in turn, gestures toward the moment when you will finally take your last big bus ride, settle on your own land for good, and never have a boss again. The three levels are linked through a relation that Gal and Irvine have dubbed "fractal recursion" (2000), in which a tiny everyday gesture comes to stand in for a much weightier principle, with each evening's clock-out representing the possibility of greater departures. Thus, a migrant's labor becomes abstract through the time clock, but also through the link connecting the time clock to the other schedules organizing a migrant's life. The core axis that arranges this abstraction is the distinction between having and not having a boss.

At Rio Branco and Maracujá, migrants spoke frequently and vehemently about their wish to live without bosses. "Working for other people isn't good," Russo concluded, having returned from a job managing illegal urban cockfights. In the city, he sighed, "there's always that *right hour* to work."

I heard this wish even more loudly from a discontented urbanite named Murilo. Murilo was soft-spoken and self-assured, a tall, thin man who loved reggae, and who was employed as an office clerk and a ticket-taker on the São Paulo buses. He used his Christmas vacation one year to visit his aunt in Bahia. It was there that his aunt's neighbor told him about the landless villages. Fourteen years later, Murilo remembered for me the decision that he made that holiday on the spur of the moment. "I'm going there! If there's no boss to give orders, then I'll go." He went.[11]

As it turned out, urban emigrants were not the only ones to talk this way. When sharecroppers left a plantation to come to Maracujá or Rio Branco, the sharecroppers would explain their departure by invoking the same distaste for supervisors, the same vocabulary of aspiration. The sharecroppers, too, said that they arrived in the hope of finding a *place where no one was boss*.[12]

A job on a plantation meant spending your time in fields that were not your own, often while living in a house owned by the plantation owner. "A whole life working for other people," mused Seu Jairo, who had cared for cacao on the great estates. "I've already suffered too much. I don't want to work for anyone anymore. No way." Dona Anita, age fifty-four, told me something similar when she recalled her years moving from one plantation to another. "I've never stayed quiet and peaceful in one corner," she said. "Always in the other people's place."

Always in the other people's place. At the villages, both urban migrants like Murilo and rural migrants like Dona Anita tended to describe their former bosses with two words: *os outros*.[13] Although I have translated *os outros* as "other people," it more literally means "the others," and it conveys something of the poignancy of living one's life inextricably bound up with outsiders.[14]

"I don't like to work for other people," Analis said to me one night after she finished dinner in her candlelit house. "I like to work for myself." Analis had recently moved back to Rio Branco, and she possessed very little to live on. Her lack of electricity did not dissuade her from sewing her riotously colored pillowcases by hand, and even if they did not earn her much money, she sensed that, in the right marketplace, they might succeed. The one-room shack was surrounded by manioc she had already planted. "I used to ask Him all the time," she explained, "for a way for me to work for myself. And God found me to bring me here."

Three months later, Analis's finances had not much changed, but she remained determined. Although she was earning far less than the minimum wage she might get in the city, she told me that what might persuade her to move wasn't better pay. It was autonomy in the labor process. "For me to work in a city,[15] for example, I would only do that if I had an area of responsibility. [. . .] I don't want to be a servant," Analis announced. "Tied in to work for other people, I don't want that."

In fact, farmers at Maracujá and Rio Branco did often spend at least some of their days working for other people. This was especially true among farmers who had recently arrived in the village or who were too young to have established a mature field and herd. In the season when the coffee beans ripened yellow and red on the trees, Analis herself caught the bus to nearby plantations for harvesting jobs, and some of her neighbors did the same. Others worked inside the village as day laborers or *empreiteiros* (workers contracted by the job) for more established farmers (see chapter 4). But these arrangements had a sporadic and fragile quality. The employers were frequently older villagers who received a retirement pension just generous enough to allow them to hire a farmhand for a few days each month.

Villagers treated contract work and especially day labor as something of an embarrassment both for the employee and for the employer. Employment ran against the grain of the villages' specific egalitarianism. "Whoever talks about day labor," asserted Rodrigo, who regularly worked for his neighbors, "is insulting me."

This sense of insult could sting the person who was doing the hiring, too. Zima, at Maracujá, had a small field of coffee, and she often paid other people in the village to care for the trees or harvest the beans. Nonetheless, she vehemently denied to me that she was a boss. "Here," she explained, "no one has a boss [*Aqui ninguém tem patrão*]."

In an important sense, villagers made Maracujá and Rio Branco into a world without bosses. This was true not because nobody hired anyone else, but rather because nobody identified as a boss. Nobody aspired to become one. To act like a boss was to place oneself outside the norms for decent neighborliness and thus to cease being *one of us*. Bosses were, in the local idiom, *other people*.

The *other* described in this idiom is a powerful other, fitting into a long tradition of social theory about Brazilians who envision otherness as power. The Brazilianist literature overflows with examples of workers who identify with a powerful boss-as-other, or, at least, workers who strategically align themselves with that sort of boss.[16] But for the small farmers of Maracujá and Rio Branco, the story runs in the opposite direction: rather than identifying with the other, they refuse the other. Seen in this light, small farmers at Maracujá and Rio Branco come to resemble the rebels who ran from enslavement to a quilombo in a forest, the sharecroppers who struck out alone, the smallholders who refused taxes even when faced with the army. They are rejecters of the powerful other.

In this sense, migrants came to Maracujá and Rio Branco to live in a world without bosses. This is different from being your own boss. Brazil's cities offer opportunities to become one's own boss: to sell candy on the street, to peddle fruit from a stall, or, with resources and luck, to open a bar or a restaurant that looks out onto a bustling avenue. In such urban settings, one can boss oneself in a world full of bosses. One can manage one's own time, monitor one's minutes, as if one were disciplining an employee. And, if successful, one might become the boss of other people, too.

Maracujá and Rio Branco were different. There, no one would admit to having a boss or to being one. Everyone had no boss. To get on the bus back to the villages, then, was to seek a place where everyone held in common the dream of living without bosses, a place where you would see your own particular kind of freedom reflected in the freedom of the people around you.

Migrants often spoke about living without a boss as a process, an aspiration to be achieved slowly. Living without a boss was thus a vision of the future. Less tradition than horizon,[17] it was a type of life that villagers were in the process of building. I sometimes felt surprised to realize just how long this process could continue without a sense of completion. Seu Álvaro, the man I once saw slowly knotting together a fishing net between two trees, advised me to be persistent: "Hope your whole life and never lose faith in God."

Seu Álvaro had been planting rice, beans, and coffee since the 1940s. He had acquired 16 hectares of land for cotton and then lost the cotton to boll weevils. When I interviewed him, he had spent nearly twenty years on his plot at Maracujá, where he labored each day amid a spiny field of pineapples, a herd of cattle, and a grove of orange trees watered by one of the region's few irrigation systems, which he had installed. He was seventy-six years old. "My dream," he told me, "is to work—" He stopped. "Is to work and still imp—still improve in life so I don't live subject to other people [*os outros*]."

Two Ways to See Abstract Labor as Exploitation: Substance or Standard

Sometimes, migrants described abstract labor as more than just unpleasant. Abstract labor was unfair, the use of a subject as an object:[18] it was exploitation. But what, exactly, made the unfairness?

I heard migrants offer two very distinct answers to that question. In the first answer, migrants depict labor as an intimate, personal substance. Exploitation happens when someone steals this substance from the worker.

At different times, however, migrants talked to me not about substances but about standards. In this second answer, the boss exploits the worker by failing to live up to a fundamental standard that all workers deserve.

Exploitation as *theft of substance* or exploitation as *distance from a standard*: migrants thus opened up two different lines of critique against abstract labor. Each line led toward its own type of remedy. Each had its own metaphors, too. When villagers talked about exploitation as theft of substance, the metaphor I heard most commonly was *sweat*.

Carlos normally looked so jovial when I saw him in the village—the same Carlos who gave out cheese breads to his seatmates—but he seemed to grow a little somber when he talked about the thirteen-year-old child he had left behind with his estranged wife in São Paulo. Carlos said that he needed to gather cash for the bus ticket to see his son. Carlos told me the word that his neighbors used to describe drinking away too much of what you earned: "That's giving sweat to the guy. That's when people say, 'You throw your sweat away, dude.'"

Carlos was not the only one to use this fluid idiom.[19] I heard it from Lara, too, when she recounted the agonizing period when her husband Rodrigo was drinking to excess. In that time, she said, he worked hard, but "he didn't make use of his own sweat."

If Carlos and Rodrigo drank, they were wasting something special. Their sweat incarnated labor, labor understood as a deeply personal substance, a possession vulnerable to dispossession. Carlos came up with another phrase. "Giving your dream to other people," he announced. "It's the same thing as me picking up my dream and giving it to him."

Ana referred to the stolen substance as *happiness*. Returned from a migratory trip, she told me how it had felt to gaze at the piles of clothes that she produced at an urban factory. She sensed a twinge of happiness, she admitted. "But it was a happiness that didn't compensate very much." She continued: "We were doing everything for other people. For the happiness of other people. Because they were the ones who were getting rich, rich. And you—earned minimum wage or less." Then Ana spun a second metaphor to describe the substance that the bosses were taking: "They would suck out all of our capacity."

Ana talked about factory *happiness* and *capacity*. But Analis spent her early mornings at a plantation tearing the hardened coffee beans off their sharp stalks, and she had a more financial name for the substance. "Profit," she pronounced. "Whoever works on other people's land, whatever we make there, it's like the profit is more for the other people."

Analis lived down the hill from Murilo, the Christmastime visitor who quit an office job in São Paulo to live in the hilly fields of the Northeast. Murilo offered yet another word for the substance of labor. "All a boss does," he proclaimed to me, "is take away our relaxation."

I was perplexed. "Re—relaxation?"

"Mm-hm," Murilo affirmed. "Relaxation. A boss leaves us naked if he can. So a boss isn't any good." At the idea of denuded workers, I couldn't help laughing, but Murilo kept going with his analysis. "Yeah. You're going to leave the guy rich, and you end up poor."

Thus, villagers used many substances to explain what labor *was*. Labor was sweat, a dream, or happiness. Labor was capacity or profit. Labor was relaxation in reverse, or labor was clothing removed. These are substances that have a deeply personal quality to them. They seem intimate, idiosyncratic. Even the act of coining each metaphor is idiosyncratic, so much so that people often came up with two metaphors in the same conversation, as if to say, This substance is so much a part of me that I can change its name at will.

But, of course, the substance is not quite inalienably a part of its owner, because the other quality of this substance, its tragic quality, is that it can be taken away. The political problem lies here. The boss, per se, is not the issue. What is troubling is not exactly the fact that a boss seizes the substance; what is troubling is the fact that the substance departs from its primordial owner, the worker. Hence, a night at the bar poses the same moral challenge as a day at the plantation. Both of them separate the laborer from the labor.

On this account, then, exploitation is theft of substance. But this was only the first of two accounts that I heard. For some workers, exploitation meant distance from a standard.

One morning, Kátia caught the bus that left the dry fields, and she rode a day and a night until she arrived in the biggest city in the southern hemisphere. There, tucked in an industrial suburb, she found her job taking orders at a lunch counter. And she came to a realization. She realized that the lunch counter only hired migrants like her, migrants who had come to São Paulo. When locals from the city stopped by looking for work, the supervisors said there weren't any openings. "Why?" Kátia demanded of me. Why not hire city workers? She answered her own question. "Because the bosses knew that they would not think like we did [. . .] They wouldn't think as small as we did."

Kátia was in fact paid far less than the standard for workers born in the city. She was not even legally registered as an employee with work rights. This discovery changed Kátia, she said, slowly, "with the passing of time. With that familiarity with people from São Paulo state, we started—having a better head. [. . .] We started wanting to think bigger. [. . .] I opened my eyes."

Notice how differently Kátia describes her labor. She does not talk about a unique personal substance like sweat or happiness. She speaks in the terms of a singular scale, small and bigger. But on this scale, she never gives a name to the element being measured. Instead, she refers to it as a pure quantity, a way of thinking. Kátia portrays her labor conditions as a relation. This is not simply a relation between Kátia and her boss. It is a relation between Kátia, her boss, and the workers from São Paulo. The relation is built on comparisons. Kátia does not worry about the stealing of her substance. She worries that there is a standard—and she feels excluded from that standard.

One day, a customer asked to cut the line at the lunch counter. Kátia responded with a little speech. "Sir, you'll pardon me, but everyone else got here ahead of you. Everyone knows—who arrived first and who arrived last here. So here, what counts is who arrived first."

What counts is who arrived first: Kátia was giving a homily about standards. The other diners had arrived first at the lunch counter. The local workers had arrived first in the city, before she did. They set the standard. That's what *counts*, she told the customer, or, to translate her Portuguese more literally, that's *what has value* (*aqui, vale quem chega primeiro*). Her workplace lived by the rule of a substance with no name and no qualities. In other words, her labor was measured as value.

Substance? Or standard? Did exploitation mean losing a part of yourself, or did exploitation mean getting less, in comparison to other people? The two different accounts of exploitation implied two different solutions, a difference I heard clearly when I talked to Analis and Kátia.

It was Analis who told me that the substance of labor was called "profit" and that big landowners stole this profit from you when you worked for them. We were talking inside her tiny brick house, lit by candles rather than electricity. Inside were her hand-sewn pillowcases. Outside stretched the hilly red soil where she had dug in dozens of manioc roots and where she let loose a panicky brood of chickens. This was her own field. She mused about it. "The place that really belongs to us—" Analis paused. "If you plant there, right there, it's got a foundation in the ground. Whatever comes from there is yours."

So Analis was an autonomist. But Kátia was not. One day, at the urban lunch counter, Kátia confronted her boss with her analysis of São Paulo workers. "They ask for work here [. . .] and you guys don't give it," she fumed, "because you know that they aren't going to be dummies like we are."

"I believe that unity makes strength," Kátia proclaimed. She began spending her off-hours at the messy house where her co-workers lived as roommates. She talked about higher wages. Kátia exhorted the other lunch counter employees: "I'm only getting into this thing, to ask for the raise, together if it's for everybody there." Swayed by her words, the lunch counter staff assembled and decided that they would go over the head of their boss. They plotted to demand a pay increase directly from the owner.

But before the plot was realized, Kátia's boss found out. He pulled Kátia aside and addressed her alone—the story told in chapter 1 (see pp. 60–62). Ultimately, no one received a raise. Kátia quit the lunch counter and headed back to the countryside. She summed everything up for me while we sat together, a few dusty doors down from her family's rural homestead: "At least," she said, "we tried."

Kátia tried one way; Analis tried another. Kátia planned a strike for higher wages. Analis sought a field where she could keep the fruit of her labor. For Kátia, unity makes strength; for Analis, the answer is to find the place that really belongs to you, so that whatever comes from there is yours. Each mode of action flows from a different theory of exploitation. In one view, exploitation is theft—the theft of a substance unique to you. Thus, you resist by finding an autonomous zone where you hold on to your own toil. In the other view, exploitation is exclusion—exclusion from the standard that others enjoy. Thus, you resist by rearranging your relationships, standing together with your peers and staring down the boss.

Two metaphors for labor, two theories of exploitation, two modes of action. Because Analis describes her labor as a substance containing her subjecthood, she embraces a politics that necessarily makes herself as different as possible from other people. For Kátia, on the other hand, politics requires an invidious comparison with other workers; the rivalry comes baked into the work situation, and indeed this rivalry forms the basis for political intimacy. Thus, two different metaphors for labor lead to two different dilemmas—two very practical dilemmas—for the people who would fight social struggles against dispossession. If labor is substance, then struggle leads to separation from other workers, the lonely autonomy of one's field. If labor is standard, then struggle relies on rivalry between workers, the constant comparison of one's own conditions to someone else's.

Conclusion

William, at age seven, had converted a forgotten corner of my back yard at Maracujá into what he considered a bus. He cobbled the bus together out of pieces of wood, a makeshift steering wheel, and an abandoned tire that appeared to have come from an actual bus. Often I found him and his friend Noel pretending to drive. The bus was the most exciting game in town, for children, the source of enthusiasm, and the ultimate sign of newness: on at least one occasion, William and Noel turned their bus into a spaceship.

Or maybe a better way of putting things is to say that the bus was the source of enthusiasm for children. Adults, after a few migratory trips, seemed to detect another side of the bus. Its arrival time never waited for you. Its ticket-takers required you to clutch your ID—the same ID that you would need to get a job. Its comings and goings were the indicator that you were traveling into or out of the zone where you needed to submit to a boss. The bus did not only look super-modern, like the Hermes of growth; it also looked like the spirit of abstract labor arriving in the villages each morning at 6:00 a.m.

If people caught the bus back to Maracujá and Rio Branco, perhaps this was in part because they did not like the abstraction they found inside economic growth. At the moment when a migrant steps away from the market—at the hour of the bus ride home—the qualities of abstract labor suddenly become visible in a new and harsher light. We can learn something about labor's mundane properties if in that instant we listen carefully to the migrant's complaints and rejections. These give us a sense of what abstraction means to people who live through it.

First, abstract labor often manifests as a sense of being bossed. Analis's words are deep ones: "The place that really belongs to us—" she said, talking about her rough field, and then her sentence trailed off. Analis spoke of *us* and not *me*. Rio Branco was not just a hideout where she had no boss, not just the reverse of the plantations to which she rode the bus before dawn so she could earn a few coins in the coffee harvest. Rio Branco was something more than the opposite of her personal relation to the boss. Rio Branco was a hamlet where her neighbors had no boss, either. She would not become like Kátia at the lunch counter, constantly comparing her wage to someone else's take-home pay. To live in the villages meant to sense the consensus, the shared values, and the common assumptions that pervade a place where no one aspires to be the supervisor. If we pay attention to the difference between *being your own boss* and *living in a place with no bosses*, then we can spot the kind of autonomy that germinates in the villages.

Second, abstract labor calls for homogeneous time. It is above all by learning a different kind of time that prospective workers come to abstract their labor—and also come to dissent from it. Migrants speak eloquently about the problems of time discipline, but their objection is not an objection to the practice of precise timekeeping. It is an objection to the hour or the day, the specific unit that has been used to manage *their* labor. This observation serves as a warning against an overly culturalist analysis that focuses on rural people's failure to adapt to the meticulous modern clock. However true such an analysis might ring in other places and other eras, rural Brazilians today seem to be speaking about something different. Here, labor time chafes when it becomes "the right hour," the tiny unit of time that stays always the same, empty and identical, regardless of who you are or what happens to you. What is wrong with bus time? Not that it is exact, but that it never waits for anyone.

The major lessons of the bus ride are taught in seconds and minutes. However, abstraction can arrive through other vehicles, too. When villagers remain in the village and sell their produce to the world market, their labor still becomes abstract—but in this situation, the key site for abstraction is not time but things. Rather than homogeneous time, homogeneous objects come to the fore. I turn to that possibility in the next chapter.

As I readied myself to return to the United States, Carlos told me that he needed to prepare for a trip, too. He was placing repeated phone calls to São Paulo. Carlos's wife had said that once the school year ended, Carlos could come to São Paulo and take his son on the bus back to Rio Branco. There was sure to be a fight, since Carlos's wife felt angry. Moreover, Carlos was behind on stocking up the money he would need for the bus tickets. At the festival on St. John's Day, he had bought a piglet and R$250 worth of fireworks, and then his wife called and he needed to send her R$400.

Nonetheless, Carlos exuded a happy tranquility. He rushed to tell me how much everyone in the village adored the boy: "Big, little, they all like my kid." Carlos's son was perched at the beginning of adolescence, and if he moved to Rio Branco, then he might avoid entering the urban wage labor market in his teenage years. Maybe Carlos's son would stay in the countryside for good. Maybe this trip would be Carlos's last big bus ride. "When you come back to this place," Carlos said to me, predicting my own return, "Godwilling, he will be around here." Carlos laughed, then rephrased with confidence. "You can believe it. Godwilling, by next year, there's already going to be a way for me to hold on to him."

Seu Álvaro ties a fishing net.

4

The Cargo

Marketplaces, Labor at a Distance, and Distance from Labor

Distance is not the same as separation. If separation means an effort to end a relationship or to avoid one, then, by contrast, distance is a *kind* of relationship. Distance is the space that connects two points. In a distant dynamic, this space is traversed or defended, cultivated or mourned; it becomes salient. Rio Branco and Maracujá have spent more than a century being distant, not separate, from the world market.

This chapter is concerned with the cargo that farmers send from the villages to the market. That distance is traveled, early in the morning, by the piles of pineapples, pink beans, and coffee that villagers shove into the baggage compartment under the bus. When a migrant moves from the city to the countryside, that migrant, as a laborer, no longer commutes to work every morning; that migrant now sends produce rather than labor to the marketplace. This new journey has its own anxieties, abstractions, and aspirations.

One day, I heard those aspirations expressed simply—and joyously—while I sat on a bus traveling between the villages and the city. A man arose and spoke with energy to all his fellow passengers. "I'm not going to work for anyone anymore," he declared. "Not even for myself." I felt especially struck by his second sentence. How could you possibly hope to get free from working for yourself? What would that mean?

When farmers sold their crops to the world market, they were still working for someone, even if the someone was themselves. This chapter asks how they recognized, understood, and managed that toil. A farmer can find that their labor is abstracted by the agricultural marketplace, just as a wage laborer finds that their labor is abstracted in the workplace. For wage laborers, as we saw in the previous chapter, the key site of abstraction is homogeneous time. For small farmers, by contrast, the key site of abstraction is homogeneous objects. The market tracks and standardizes the farmer's things. The market accounts for sacks of coffee, kilos of manioc, and dozens of pineapples—not hours or minutes on the time clock—and the market turns these agricultural items into the entry point for regulating a farmer's everyday actions.

But regulation does not amount to total domination. Farmers devise their own techniques for assessing the fruit of their labor, and these techniques do not always look like the scales at a city market. Rural measurement is the topic of this chapter. By measuring differently, farmers create a small gap—a little breathing room—between their work and the judgment of the world market. Villagers are adept at using this distance as a tool to create autonomy.

I began to spy something of the power of distance when I sank into farmers' couches after sunset, little glasses of coffee in everyone's hands, and heard people gossip about a source of income that I didn't understand: *bistunta*. Tons of manioc and herds of cattle were being sold "in bistunta"—or, as farmers cryptically added, "only in the eye [*só no olho*]." Eventually, I pieced together the details. When middlemen purchasers roared into a village with their big trucks, looking to buy produce in bulk, farmers would sometimes insist on selling to them "in bistunta." This meant that both parties would go look at a field of crops planted in the ground or a cluster of cows at pasture. The parties would settle on a price—without measuring the items being sold.

I wondered, *Why refuse to measure?* Over time, I came to see the middleman's truck as something of an opposite to the bus, a way of crossing the distance differently. Much of this chapter will be concerned with trying to understand why, in this alternative crossing, it makes sense for farmers to turn down measurement.

In this chapter, first, we will look at how farmers act when they are in a commodity marketplace in the city. Why, exactly, do farmers find these marketplaces so objectionable? Next, we will look closely at farmers' techniques for tracking the time they spend working. Finally, we will observe the relationships that farmers build with the middlemen who haul away their coffee or cattle on trucks. Middlemen often buy goods in bistunta—which farmers describe as a hilarious habit. Why does it seem so funny?

In the marketplace in the city, middlemen quote a nonnegotiable price, and farmers hear the unhumorous voice of command. Bistunta is different. A farmer who insists on bistunta is deferring the measurement and inserting a space between herself and the market. She is naming her price rather than having it named for her. In the rural bistunta practices that develop between farmers and middlemen, we can detect something of the heterodoxy—that self-distancing from abstract labor, that careful remoteness—that people cultivate alongside their rows of passion fruit, corn, and manioc.

Part 1. The Baggage Compartment

THE COMPETITIVE MARKET IS A CARTEL

After the morning bus ground to a halt in the villages, with dust still swirling behind its big wheels, farmers would form an intense half-circle around the opened metal doors to the baggage compartment. Arms strained to lift loads of pale manioc flour. Fingers delicately arranged a soft space for bottles full of milk taken straight from the cow. Hands yanked and tied thick sacks, frayed by years of reuse and labeled with the name of some former commodity crop. Before the ticket-taker latched the door of the baggage compartment, farmers bagged and double-bagged everything, hoping to protect today's produce from the dirt that seeped through the rickety undercarriage.

"What we do," Carlos told me, "is send everything to the city." Carlos was exaggerating, but, if not everything, then at least a sizable portion of the villages' produce did travel underneath the bus for a hundred kilometers, jostling and rolling, until it finally reached the big central market in Conquista.

Perched inside a valley covered in apartment buildings, bordered by a small river of sudsy washwater, the Conquista market assembled itself each morning underneath an arching cement roof with no walls. This was a space that overflowed with repetitions. Dozens of wooden stalls offered the same carrots, the same green mangoes, the same cuts of pork, and the same handfuls of reddening spice. Every day, a tide of people swept into the valley: warehouse wholesalers and heavily laden farmers and urbanites buying their dinner. All of them could quickly learn the day's prevailing price for each product, so much per dozen eggs and so much per kilo of cucumber.

Farmers expressed great frustration about the singular quality of this price. "Basically," Félix opined, "there's no option in selling." Félix, with a reliable smile below his silver-rim glasses, normally served as Maracujá's inveterate optimist. He had come to the village in recovery from alcoholism, after years in São Paulo, and he brimmed with plans to expand his cattle herd or plant new fruit trees on his land. But Félix's tone turned uncommonly dark when he told me about the marketplace in Conquista. There, he had to accept the middlemen's prices, because otherwise he would find himself stranded in the city with unsold goods.

I heard similar stories over and over again, most dramatically when I accompanied Seu João Batista to his bean field. Crouching while he grabbed each bean with an expert hand, Seu João Batista was harvesting the beans after letting them dry on the stalk, which meant that he would seal them in plastic soda bottles and eat them himself, bit by bit, as the winter grew colder.

If he had harvested them green, he could have sold them in the market. But Seu João Batista recalled for me a past experience. Once, he took his beans to the city because a man offered to pay R$15 per unit, and then, when Seu João Batista arrived, the same man only gave him R$8. Seu João Batista had to accept the price, because the beans were perishable.

In the central Conquista marketplace, villagers tended to sell to middlemen, since villagers themselves lacked the connections and experience needed to retail all of their product to individual customers in a single day. Middlemen had knowhow. "It's their job to sell and to collect money together," as Seu Benajmin put it, so small farmers would turn over their produce to the middleman "and get the money immediately." Yet despite this immediate cash, something seemed to frustrate farmers when they met with middlemen in the marketplace. The problem went deeper than overly low prices. It had to do with the way that prices were spoken.

Félix, the optimist, recounted a tale about the time he took twenty bags of passion fruit to sell in Conquista:

> One of those middlemen showed up there and chatted with me. I gave him the price, you know? So then he didn't accept the price. And then he left, too, you know? And then everybody, everybody who was there in the marketplace only wanted to give the price that the first one had given. [D: Hmm!] You understand? As if it were a cartel.

For economists, the "law of one price" is a core feature of a competitive marketplace. And indeed, according to economists' other criteria as well, the Conquista market is a very competitive institution, teeming with small vendors, overflowing with standard products, surrounded on the outskirts by daring people who sit on the ground with no more than a bowl of fruit to sell to passersby. Barriers to entry are low. Each day's give-and-take leads to a single price. But for Félix, this single price seemed like the very opposite of competition, a cartel. Why? What did Félix mean?

In Félix's description, the middlemen in the marketplace break the standards that characterize a respectful bargaining session inside the village. The middlemen start out appropriately enough: Félix says that they begin by chatting (*conversar*), just as, in the villages, any decent deal usually starts with talk. After the chat, Félix makes the accepted next move. He gives a price (*dar um preço*). What the middleman does next is what creates the difference between city and village trade.

In a village deal, the prospective purchaser would respond by "giving" (*dar*) a different, lower price, and the seller would give another price in return. Both sides would devote time to this exchange, the exchange of prices. The two dealmakers might offer arguments alongside the prices: *that calf is strong* or *those manioc roots have started to go soft*. Even once the arguments have been exhausted, the exchange of prices could go on. One time I followed a farmer at Maracujá into his neighbor's house and heard the two of them negotiate the sale of a cow. After discussing various considerations, the farmers simply repeated the same two prices rhythmically over and over to each other. "Six hundred." "Eight hundred." "Six hundred." "Eight hundred." "Six hundred." "Eight hundred." The very act of speaking, *giving the price*, reaffirmed the connection between the two farmers and expressed faith in the eventual possibility of a deal.

Félix, with his twenty bags of passion fruit that he had hauled to the big central marketplace, heard something entirely different. The middleman named the only possible price—and then, abruptly, went away.

WHY DON'T FARMERS BECOME MIDDLEMEN?
RACIALIZATION IN THE MARKETPLACE

Farmers often dreamed of cutting out the middleman. Sometimes this dream had a political flavor, as when MST activists strove to mount their own urban market stand. Sometimes the dream felt entirely personal, as it did for young people who wistfully imagined a marketing career. Only a few farmers made this dream into a reality. Although almost anyone could enter the market as a vendor, *staying* in the market for any length of time required knowledge, connections, and acceptance into a city network. When my seventeen-year-old neighbor Suso decided to try, I began to see this network's racial boundaries.

Suso had spent nearly his entire childhood at Maracujá, but that childhood was fading into maturity, and now he envisioned himself as a fruit vendor in the city. Maria, his mother, felt frankly worried. Maria was the daughter of Ariosvaldo, the farmer wounded in the shooting at Mocambo. She was one of the few people in the villages who talked to me often about race. She identified herself unambiguously as Black, and her household was one of the poorest. Suso told me the words she spoke to him before he left: *Be careful in the city. Because you are Black, you will have trouble from the criminals and from the police who think you're a criminal.*

Other villagers did not see matters as Maria did. When I mentioned her fears to two middle-aged women a few feet down the road, they chuckled dismissively. Suso was well known to be one of the most honest, law-abiding, helpful young men in the countryside for miles around. Racism? "Maria's the one who put that stuff in his head," one of them explained.

Soon afterward I traveled to the city myself and found Suso in a busy thoroughfare. He wore plastic sunglasses and smiled broadly. He had hidden most of himself behind a giant pushcart of fresh green umbu fruit, which he and his father were selling to passersby, but he was not too busy to stop for a long and hopeful conversation. He liked the city, he said, and he wanted to stay. Apparently, he had even told Maria that he dreamed of going to college for engineering.

On January 13, 2012, the police picked up a man in possession of drugs and asked him where he had obtained them. *The little Black guy with the umbu fruit*, said the man, falsely. Soon after, the police beat Suso in the street, called him "Black man," and, after making more racist commentary, detained him in the police station.

That day, as Suso later pointed out to me, was Friday the Thirteenth. Nineteen days before, on December 25, Suso had stopped into the tiny Protestant church in the village. There it was prophesied to him that he would find himself in such a difficult situation that God would be the only exit for him, and he would abandon the world. In jail, Suso told me, the prophecy came true.

A well-connected friend in the state capital called lawyers for Suso. It turned out that there was no evidence against him, and several hours later he was freed without charges. He moved back to the village. For every villager, the urban road to growth was racialized; for Suso, racism barred the road with a roadblock. He could not sell in the market. But Suso did not scare easily: as chapter 6 recounts, he eventually returned to the city to become a bus mechanic and an aspiring pastor.

MARKET PRICES ARE COMMANDS

When a middleman declares a price in the Conquista market, that price sounds strikingly like a command. It sounds that way because it fits the four qualities of command described in chapter 1.

First, the price is *short and imperative*. Once it has been spoken, there is no need for further talk.

Second, the speaker presents the price as a *spatial deictic not centered on the hearer*. The price is valid here, and "here" refers to the current location of the speaker, not the hearer. Just as a boss's command requires an employee to adopt the perspective of the boss (see pp. 57–58), so Seu João Batista received an offer of R$15 for beans that was no longer valid by the time he made it to the buyer in the marketplace. A price, in other words, contains assumptions about space. In a commodity market like Conquista's, the meaning of the price depends heavily on those assumptions: "15 reais" means that beans are worth R$15 if they are at the marketplace, not in Seu João Batista's field.[1]

Third, commodity prices are *presentist*. In the Conquista marketplace, prices are always today's prices, valid only for right now, not tomorrow. Their meaning is specific in time as well as space; they rely both on the sense of the present and the sense of presence. Price carries no promises about the future and no suggestions for a better world. In this sense, a commodity price shares something of the immediacy of a boss's command. It lacks the visionary power of *chamar* (chapter 1), which calls the hearer to act out of a hope for a distant result.[2]

Fourth, commodity prices are *devoid of reasons*. Middlemen do not explain or justify prices in the Conquista market, and a price quote is not accompanied by explanations. This terseness seemed to frustrate Félix. In a village negotiation, to cite a price is to start a conversation, with partners proffering arguments and counteroffers. In the commodity market, to cite a price is to end a conversation. The middleman quoted a price to Félix and then walked away, as if distantly echoing the boss who intruded on Diego's lunch at the construction site with an order (see page 54). These are speech-acts that leave no room for questioning. Anyone who asks for a reason is already challenging authority.

Under the concrete arches of the Conquista central market, then, hearing a price is not so different from listening to a directive given by a boss. Both sound like commands. In an important sense, for small farmers at Maracujá and Rio Branco, the commodity market *is* the boss. The market abstracts a farmer's labor just as a supervisor does. If abstract labor means the making of homogeneous objects in homogeneous time, then bosses mostly intervene in a worker's life by homogenizing time, measuring each moment by a standard and thus determining how that moment gets spent. Commodity markets take the other route: they homogenize the worker's object. They rank the work product, sift it, and render it equivalent to innumerable other units of merchandise. Either way, whether through the management of time or the ordering of objects, the worker's labor slips into abstraction.

Portuguese, like other Romance languages, features a fortuitous resource for imagining this overlap between bosses and commodity markets. The Portuguese word for "boss" is *patrão*. It shares a root (the Latin *patronus*) with *padrão*, which means "pattern."[3] The parallel is evocative: a boss is someone who forces you into a pattern. The reverse applies as well: a pattern can be your boss. It is through the patterning power of the commodity market—through its scales, standards, orders, refusals, and silences—that unruly small farmers get fitted into a rule. We might refer to this process as "padronizing." A market padronizes your labor, abstracting it by means of the resolute and implacable vehicle of the price.

The commodity price is so simple, just a single number, one that ends all conversation. In its simplicity, it might be called the ultimate reduced form of command. Stripped of reasons, deictically distant from the hearer, bound to the immediacy of the present, such prices are commands without bosses. The commands that arrive in the form of prices are no less authoritarian than a supervisor's orders, although more mysteriously so; prices claim an authority whose source is inscrutable. If modernity means anything, what it means, perhaps, is the struggle with this inscrutability. As I argue next, farmers undertake such a struggle when they feel price discipline every day. Prices create the sensibility of abstract labor without wages. Prices make farmers remember that they are working, even long after they have left employment behind—and long before any money from the market ever reaches their pockets.

COUNTING THE HOURS: LABORING FOR YOURSELF

Since farmers sporadically hire each other, a market for wage labor exists at Maracujá and Rio Branco, and even if embarrassed employers try to euphemize the relation, day labor throughout the villages nonetheless receives a standard wage. On any given day, everyone knows its value. Farmers pay that wage to their neighbors for installing fences or clearing fields, harvesting the crops or planting the manioc that eventually ends up in a central city marketplace.

Surprisingly, farmers sometimes act as if they are paying the wage to *themselves* (Morton 2019a). Even when no cash actually changes hands, they track their hours of toil on their own fields and measure their minutes in money. They count out the shadow price of their work. This shadow price is best illustrated through an example.

Relaxing inside his perpetually half-renovated house, the enterprising optimist Félix regaled me with a detailed accounting of the phantom wage. He was listing out the expenses associated with his coffee field that year. There was the R$300 he had paid to the laborers who harvested his coffee. There was R$295 in miscellaneous costs. And then there was R$150 of his own labor. This last figure represented the value of three days that *Félix himself* had devoted to clearing his coffee field with a machine. Félix told me that he would rate each of the three days at R$50.[4] He was not actually going to pay himself the R$150. Instead, he was using money as a tool for thinking about his labor. Félix's total coffee expenses—his own labor included—added up to R$745 that year. He had sold his coffee for R$710. Félix said that this equaled a loss of R$35.

At this point, I felt a bit confused. If we just took Félix's own work out of the account, I reasoned, then he had earned R$115 on coffee that year. After all, the R$115 was the actual cash left over in Félix's hands. But that was not how Félix

THE CARGO   125

	My accounting	Félix's accounting	
		Félix the farm owner	Félix the laborer *(on his own farm)*
Expenses	$R 300 for laborers to harvest	$R 300 for laborers to harvest	$R 0
	$R 295 miscellaneous costs	$R 295 miscellaneous costs	
		$R 150 for 3 days of labor with a machine *(worked by Félix himself)*	
Earnings	$R 710 earned from the sale of the coffee	$R 710 earned from the sale of the coffee	$R 150 earned for 3 days of labor with a machine *(worked by Félix himself)*
Profit/ Loss	Profit of $R 115	Loss of $R 35	Profit of $R 150

Félix's coffee harvest: Different accountings

saw things. In his accounting, it was as if there were two Félixes.[5] Félix the laborer had earned R$150 from three days of coffee work. But Félix the farm owner had lost R$35 on the coffee harvest. Félix was reckoning simultaneously as the worker and the boss of himself. He concluded dejectedly, "You see? I paid to work."

This was an accounting style that I heard from farmers over and over again.[6] Salomão once told me that, in the coming month, he would spend R$150 *of his own labor* clearing his field. On another occasion, Bruno explained that he had spent R$250 on his farm in 2011, all of it from "just my work." Neither Bruno's R$150 nor Salomão's R$250 was money that actually changed hands. Rather, the numbers represented the value of the time that Bruno and Salomão themselves devoted to sinking fence posts, preparing fields, and burning brush on their own plots of land.

These stories might lead us to conclude that the logic of the market runs deep. As farmers grow the food that they will sell in the marketplace, they turn themselves into their own time and labor disciplinarians. They summon the spirit of homogeneity and padronize their very minutes. They become the bosses of themselves.

But this explanation only tells half the story. For example, Bruno was a famously dedicated farmer who toiled in his fields day in and day out. So why had he told me that, during the whole year of 2011, the value of his own labor only amounted to R$250? The prevailing day wage rate in 2011 was R$25 per day. This meant that Bruno was only assigning value to *ten* days of his own labor for the entire year. What was he talking about?

As it turned out, farmers at Maracujá and Rio Branco used the wage rate to reckon some of their actions—but not others. What Bruno, Salomão, and Félix were valuing in cash terms was the time that they spent on major new projects that might produce commodities to sell in the marketplace. They used the wage to account for a field cleared, a fence built, or a crop planted. Each of these projects was a discrete, short-term task, the kind of task for which a farmer might hire a day laborer. Even if no day laborer was hired and the farmer ended up doing the work alone, the farmer still had the day wage as a mental tool for making comparisons. In other words, farmers were using the day wage to measure their own project work at a generic rate, acting as if they were their own day laborers. With this technique, farmers like Félix had a measuring stick for deciding if it had been worthwhile to plant the coffee, redo the fence, or clear the land for a field.

Not every moment of a farmer's day, however, was spent on major projects. Farmers also had to milk cows, feed chickens, give water to animals, and weed crops. I never once heard a farmer use the day wage to account for the time spent on these mundane, mandatory tasks. Why not? Perhaps because farmers tended not to hire day laborers to do that kind of work. Such tasks were too closely woven into the other rhythms of a day (Millar 2015), the cows watered as soon as one got out of bed or the pig fed the scraps after dinner. With no day laborers involved, farmers may not have thought about these tasks in terms of money.

But there seemed to be another reason for farmers, sometimes, not to count. Certain duties just *had* to be undertaken every day—like feeding the animals and monitoring the crops—in order for the farm to survive. A new field was optional: it could be opened up if the farmer possessed either time to toil or cash to hire a helper. The cows had to be milked no matter what. Perhaps it would have felt nonsensical—even disheartening—to tally the value of the chores that needed to be done regardless of results.

Instead of measuring these unavoidable duties, farmers aestheticized them. They talked about the duties as tasks they loved. "If you figure out what you spent on the farm," Dona Lola told me, "the farm doesn't cover what you spent. It doesn't. But because we were raised that way, we like the farm."

From Dona Mara, age seventy-seven, I heard the same analysis—a valueless farm and a beloved duty. When I tried to go over agricultural expenses with Dona Mara, she assessed her farm quickly. "It's not worth it," she proclaimed. "No way. We really just do it because—because of influence [*influença*]."

"Influence?" I asked. "What do you mean?"

"This is what influence means," Dona Mara explained patiently. "A person likes to bring back some little thing from the fields. A bit of beans. Corn. A pumpkin. Look at the happiness that I feel," she continued. "I end up with so much happiness that I seem renewed."

"Really!" I laughed.

"I make my little coffee, I drink it, I go to the fields, and then I feel better. When I come back, I feel fine. I spend two or three days in great shape, no pain in my body."[7]

Dona Mara and Dona Lola knew how to count their profits. But they also knew how not to count these profits. It was important for farmers to maintain a distinction between their farm as a business and their farm as a way of living. Indeed, perhaps *all* self-employed people end up creating this kind of distinction. Some part of one's daily activity needs to remain uncounted—it needs to evade being abstracted as labor.

For urban workers, the wage governed the predictable and boring parts of their lives. Village farmers flipped the arrangement: they used the wage to measure only their most unusual projects. The wage still existed in the distant villages, but it existed as an exception. And so maybe I spied the ultimate measure of distance when I looked more closely at the numbers in Félix's careful accounts. Serious, hopeful, hard-working Félix considered his coffee field for a whole year and tallied up all of his own days that fit into wage labor logic. He could only find three.

Part 2. The Back of the Truck: Seeing the Total

> The specialisation of skills leads to the destruction of every image of the whole. [. . .] Despite this, the need to grasp the whole—at least cognitively—cannot die out.
> LUKACS (1999: 103–4)

REMUNERATION THAT SHOWS THE TOTAL

When a cloud of dust blossomed at the blue edge between sky and road, villagers knew that the wheels churning dirt might not be from a bus. The cloud might contain a middleman's truck.

The middleman's truck, all metal and noise, provided another point of connection between the villages and the world market. Truck middlemen from the towns and cities would wander unpredictably into Maracujá and Rio Branco, searching for harvests they could purchase on the spot. By the time a truck left Maracujá or Rio Branco, its bed might be brimming with pineapples, pebbly coffee beans, or sacks of thick, white manioc flour.

The word for "middleman" is *atravessador*, which comes from the verb *atravessar*, "to cross a distance." Truck middlemen were crossers of distance; they made a living between village and market. Usually, when the price of a product rose high enough, middlemen weren't hard to find. A farmer might run into a middleman at one of the big central tubs where villagers dried out their manioc flour, with everyone chatting beside the fire that heated the tub from below. Or a middleman's phone number might get scribbled on a scrap of paper and passed from one family member to the next. Mostly, though, middlemen just appeared. Once I made the mistake of insisting to Analis that she should call a middleman about her slightly overripe crop. "They show up here!" she protested. "People aren't supposed to look for them! They go around looking." Someone would wander into the village sooner or later, searching for produce. Part of the point, it seemed, was that the middleman came to you. You had the chance to negotiate on your turf and your terms.

Often enough, a middleman would buy a full harvest, making a deal for all of your coffee or an entire field of your manioc. The farmer thus gained a view onto the total, the whole result of an agricultural cycle. Seu Milton told me that this was the advantage of the middleman's truck: "You go out there and, in the field, you sell it all." On another occasion, Lara reminisced about how it felt to contemplate her harvest in the moment of sale. "You know that you made one more result," she mused. "Because you got that money all at once." The back of the truck offered the panorama from the mountaintop: it was one of the special places where you could see your work expressed as a sum total.

Seeing the total, as it turned out, was a benefit that villagers sought in many of their economic arrangements. For example, when one farmer worked for another, the worker tended to prefer pay by the job rather than pay by the day. "It's miserable work," Maria told me, possibly remembering her exhaustion in the coffee fields, "that work by the day."

In day labor, a worker simply showed up at the standard time and did whatever the employer said for one day. In *empreita* (pay by the job), the worker and the employer went out to the field together and surveyed the entire task. They might consider the distance to be covered by a new fence, perhaps, or glance at the tree stumps to be removed from a field. Then the worker and the employer reached an agreement about the pay for the task. Often, the employer disbursed part of this pay in advance, and the worker, with minimal supervision, undertook the task at their own pace, over days or even weeks. Empreita thus relied on a broader kind of vision than day labor. "With empreita," Maria concluded, "you look at—" she paused. "At the total."

Farmers could also see the total when they organized their work through *meia* (half) or *sociedade* (society) ventures. These were two types of partnership. Villagers commonly shared cattle through meia or sociedade: a cattle owner would lend her cattle to a worker, who would raise them for a period of months. Both partners carefully measured the bovines before and afterward, and the owner would receive back what she had originally put in, plus half of the new calves born (in meia ventures) or half of the increase in the overall weight of the herd (in sociedade ventures). The remainder went to the worker, who had put in the effort of caring for the cows. Farmers implemented sociedade and meia agreements for more than cattle. You could split the construction of a house with a partner, for example, or you and one other person could divide the work of planting a joint field full of crops. Whatever the object of the partnership, sociedade and meia were grounded in the calculation of totals. Farmers used both arrangements as alternatives to wage labor—as forms of cooperation in which every partner had the chance to see the whole.

BISTUNTA: HOLISM AND HILARITY

In general, then, villagers tended to replace wage labor with agreements that allowed them to organize their work by considering a total result. This tendency was expressed in farmers' preference for empreita over the day wage and in their proclivity for meia and sociedade. But the tendency reached full bloom when middlemen drove their steel trucks out to the fields and indulged in the style of bargaining known as bistunta.

A bistunta deal was a deal made "just in the eye" or "in the looking," as farmers put it. The middleman and the farmer would both examine the item to be sold, maybe a plot of tall sugarcane stalks or a herd of cows in the pasture. The two bargainers would decline to measure anything. Instead, they would settle on a price. Only afterward, with the transaction complete, would the produce be weighed and its market value discovered. Bistunta thus carried spectacular risks, since one side might turn out to have lost a significant sum of money. Bistunta could also be uproariously funny.

One time, I heard Seu Milton leave his family in stitches while he described a bistunta deal. The middleman pretended not to see the full size of a cow, claimed that it was 30 kilos smaller than it seemed, and then finally compromised with the farmer. That middleman was "a big crybaby," Seu

Milton pronounced, and everyone cracked up. And it wasn't just the compromises that were funny. Sometimes, farmers recounted stories about bistunta in which they or their friends had ended up badly shortchanged. While they told the tale, they still burst out laughing.

What made bistunta hilarious? This was the question on my mind as I lounged on Lara and Rodrigo's battered couch, hoping they would offer me a scorching dark cup of coffee while I listened to them dissect a deal made by their neighbor Maurício.

It turned out that a middleman had recently rolled into Maracujá. His eye was caught by a field of manioc belonging to Maurício, and the two men bargained for the crop *na bistunta*. Maurício and the middleman settled on a price of R$1,050. The manioc was sold, ripped out of the earth by the middleman's own worker, and hauled to a processing plant.

"Even so," Lara concluded cannily, "the guy who bought it for a thousand fifty, I think he went on to make almost two thousand reais, you know?"

"He made more than two thousand," interjected Rodrigo.

"More than two thousand reais," Lara agreed. "When they weighed it."

This meant that the bistunta had been a hugely bad deal for Maurício. "He lost—more than a thousand reais," Rodrigo declared.

I felt instantly sympathetic and amazed by the extent of Maurício's shortfall. A thousand Brazilian reais, at that time, was well over a month's wages. But Lara and Rodrigo, seemingly puzzled by my amazement, were laughing.

My thoughts kept returning to Maurício. "And did he get irritated when he realized it?"

"No!" Rodrigo exclaimed. "He didn't get irritated. Here—" Rodrigo paused. "We're accustomed to doing exactly that. Losing."

Rodrigo laughed, possibly with a hint of bitterness. Lara began telling an unflattering story about him. One time, she said, Rodrigo himself had lost quite a bit of money selling the products from their family field *na bistunta*. "He didn't understand that kilogram stuff very well," she recounted. At first, she had a chuckle in her voice, and then she let it spill out into a guffaw. "That stuff about kilograms of manioc."

Unable to get the evening's gossip out of my mind, I guided the conversation back to Maurício again. "What a thing, to lose a thousand reais."

"Now he's taken some damage," Rodrigo offered optimistically. "Now he knows what it's about." There was more laughter.

"Yeah," Rodrigo suggested, as if Maurício were in the room. "Plant another field. And with this one, get wise!"

What made bistunta so funny? Why was it uproarious, even when you lost? By contrast, why was the city marketplace, with its single price, so deeply angering? Lara and Rodrigo laughed off their own shortfall at bistunta. When Félix carried twenty bags of passion fruit to the urban market, the cartel pricing didn't make him chuckle; it made him disgusted. What was the difference?

Bistunta was funny, I think, because bistunta was reckless, wacky, and given to surprising outcomes. And the surprise could happen to either party— to the farmer or to the middleman. This made bistunta, unlike sales in the marketplace, into a duel, a test of skill. In this sense, bistunta generated an equivalence between seller and buyer.

This equivalence came to the fore in the words that Lara used when she told me the story about Maurício's bargain. With verve, she imitated the negotiation between Maurício and the middleman, shifting her tone of voice to indicate the shifts back and forth between the two speakers. Here is a transcript of what Lara said to me:

> [Maurício] said, "Hey, you give me how much in bistunta, here?"
> [*imitating middleman's response:*]
> "I give it to you for such-and-such amount."
> [*imitating Maurício's response:*]
> So, he says, "No. I only give for such-and-such amount." [D: Mm-hm.]
> [*imitating middleman's response:*]
> The person goes and says, "Then I give it to you for such-and-such amount."

Somewhat strangely, Lara describes the *middleman* saying, "I give it to you for such-and-such amount [*eu te dou por tanto*]." The middleman's words, here, sound like the sort of thing that the *farmer* should be saying. And indeed, in the next line, Maurício the farmer utters a parallel phrase: "I only give for such-and-such amount [*eu só dou por tanto*]."

The middleman and the farmer, as voiced by Lara, use exactly the same verb over four turns at speech: the verb *to give*. This is not a situation where the seller is giving and the buyer is taking. They are both giving. Before the actual transfer of the manioc and the cash, they are exchanging prices. Each one is *giving* a price. In this sense, as they both propose prices, as they both do the same kind of act, they become equivalent.

Lara was not the only person to speak this way. Demétrio was a young farmer from Maracujá, and he used similar expressions in describing bistunta. The middleman, Demétrio told me, "is going to give you a price." Then "you offer a higher price." In Demétrio's description, both the middleman and the farmer *give*, and what they give is prices. "That's bistunta," Demétrio concluded.

This equivalence between buyer and seller is more than hollow etiquette. Both sides get a real chance to affect the amount of money that changes hands. This is what makes bistunta different from the city marketplace, and cleverly so.

The city marketplace only knows one price, the price per unit that the middleman offers, and one possible outcome—take the deal or leave it. In bistunta, the farmers do not challenge the middleman's authority to set the price per unit. Middlemen are experts on market pricing, and who would presume to disagree with an expert? But in bistunta, farmers do challenge the outcome. They make this challenge by haggling over how much their product *weighs*. Farmers, after all, should be expected to know a thing or two about the number of manioc roots likely to be lurking under the soil or the density of the sugarcane stalks swaying in the breeze. Thus, farmers can negotiate payment without ever disagreeing with the middleman's authority on per-unit prices. Farmers simply assert their own agricultural authority on weights.

Perhaps part of what is funny here, then, is the sense of reversal. Something is being craftily turned upside-down. Bistunta undoes the inevitability of the market; it creates distance from the market. This is *distance* from the market, not the *overcoming* of market—a point that Seu Milton and his son made to me after they recovered from their laughter about the "crybaby" middleman. When the weight of the cow shows up on the scale, Demétrio said, once the deal is over, then you discover "what she is really worth," "the market value."

I asked, "How do you know, um, the market value?"

"It's shown on television," Demétrio explained. "We see where the price is at." He was referring to the Globo Rural morning program, which showed the latest market prices.

Bistunta remains ultimately parasitic on the number reported on television. The final truth of the deal is discovered when someone weighs the produce. You win at bistunta by getting a bit more than you would have gotten in the city, by making yourself distant from the market, not separate.

Yet maybe bistunta holds more truth than is contained in the money itself. Bistunta allows a farmer to "sell it all," as Seu Milton said, and, in Lara's words, to "know that you made a result." In this way, bistunta makes it possible for you to do something difficult to achieve in the market. You can see the total—see it and, moreover, argue over what it means. You can tell a middleman that your cow weighs 30 kilograms more than he thinks it weighs.

When migrants watch their labor become abstract, at a nanny job or a construction site, part of what they are watching is the loss of their power to feel the total. The boss commands; the worker obeys; and, not by coincidence, the command is oriented toward *here* and *now*, as defined by the boss's location. Working in the city, migrants complained about the time-labor discipline of the hour, just as, on the plantation, they complained about the day: hours and days, the shortsighted regime of small units on which their jobs forced them to focus. Staring at *what I must do here and now*, you may find it hard to look at your own labor and *see the future* or *see everything that I have done*. The total is left in the hands of others. In other words, the total is expropriated.

Maracujá and Rio Branco are places where migrants avidly reclaim the total.[8] There, workers try to be paid by the job, not paid by the day. They create partnerships and divide the proceeds at the end of the year.

In these situations, farmers stretch out the time of reckoning, turning their gaze away from the hour and toward slower cycles, considering the outcomes over longer periods of time. They build distance. Distance makes for wider vision. The middleman's truck ultimately goes to market, but in the dusty moment when the truck drives away from your village, the sight you can see on its back is the total, the whole field of crops, the big view of what your work has brought into this world.

Conclusion: Leaving the Platoon

"I am quite sure," wrote Edmund Burke in 1795, "any given five men will, in their total, afford a proportion of labour equal to any other five" (2017: 73). Burke was thinking of farm labor. If you chose a single laborer at random, Burke argued, you would not be able to foresee the amount of farm work that the laborer would do each day. Some workers worked slowly, and others worked quickly. But if you chose a group of laborers at random, then the group, together, would toil at a predictable rate. This predictability could be found, Burke concluded, "in so small a platoon as that of even five."[9] Why did Burke feel so certain?

As Burke noted, something special happens to groups of people who work together. Newer workers learn from their more experienced colleagues; faster workers slow down and slower workers speed up so that they can stay in rhythm with each other. While they perform tasks together, workers develop altogether novel techniques and divide their labor more powerfully. What emerges is *average labor*: a new consciousness of what the human person can complete as a participant in a group.

It is hardly coincidental that Burke was writing in Britain at the very dawn of the Industrial Revolution. Industrial-era growth—and maybe *most* economic growth—depends on Burke's dynamic. Such growth is driven by the efficiencies and the learning that emerge when groups of people begin to work together.

If growth is (among other things) a new intensity about cooperating with each other, then one way to generate that intensity is to subject workers to a single point of command. Burke describes the employer, who stands at the point of command, as the person who can see the work of laborers "in their total." What sort of authority is this? Meditating on the peculiar form of command that flowered in the nineteenth century, Weber theorized it as rationalization, Durkheim as organic solidarity, Williams and Mintz as enslavement, Mies as patriarchy, and Marx as the creation of abstract labor.[10] So many elaborations on Burke's theme of the platoon.

When a migrant climbs into the bus and rides away from Maracujá or Rio Branco in the morning roar, that migrant is joining the platoon. Migrants sell their pigs for bus tickets, thus drawing a line between labor and capital, and entering a workforce where they will coordinate their toil with many co-workers. They will care for babies on the same schedule that every other nanny cares for babies; they will sew soccer jerseys at the same rate that every other factory worker sews soccer jerseys. They will cooperate by command. For migrants, this kind of command is hardly unfamiliar: it sounds very similar to the orders that they or their parents once heard in the fields of the plantation, where, too, they worked in tandem with their colleagues. Average labor comes into being as abstract labor.

But migrants can also desert the platoon. They can catch the bus back to Maracujá or Rio Branco. Back in the villages, migrants sometimes pursue their hope for autonomy by creating labor arrangements, such as empreita and sociedade partnerships, that minimize the supervision imposed on the worker. Other times, farmers work strictly by themselves. None of this, however, allows them to make a full escape.

The escape remains incomplete because you can also join the platoon by means of the marketplace. When farmers go to market, the single price sounds like a command, and it abstracts a farmer's labor as a boss does. To sell your harvest in the city is to collaborate, at a distance, with a vast number of other people. The pattern is your boss. You work on your own small field, but your labor is held up against the labor of countless other farmers, as if you worked alongside them on an assembly line: you must adopt their techniques, their rhythms, and their efficiencies. Otherwise, you will not manage to sell at the market's price and on the market's schedule. For some farmers, like Félix, the best response is to convert one part of yourself into the boss of the other part, measuring your days like a wage laborer's days, so that at least some side of your selfhood can see with the broad vision that is the privilege of the supervisor. For other farmers, perhaps, it seems better to adopt the phrase that I heard spoken by the man on the bus: "I'm not going to work for anyone anymore, not even for myself." Living without external bosses is not enough; you also have to learn to live without command.

As we pay attention to farmers' efforts to live without command, we learn some lessons about the quality of abstract labor in a farmer's life. First, abstract labor makes homogeneous objects. Félix's twenty bags of passion fruit turn into a source of indignation for Félix when they reach the marketplace and start to look the same as countless other bags, worth a single and unquestionable price. In place of this indignation, a farmer like Félix can enjoy a certain wry laugh through bistunta, which allows the farmer to affirm a unique and (momentarily) unmeasured knowledge of the merchandise. Thus, bistunta runs abstraction in reverse. This reversal helps give deeper meaning to an assertion from the beginning of chapter 3: abstract labor is the use of homogeneous time to produce homogeneous objects, so the unmaking of abstract labor involves the undoing of homogeneity.

Second, abstract labor emerges from command. A migrant encounters abstraction not in an ethereal system of categories, but, more specifically, in the moment when someone speaks a certain way. Commands have a recognizable style. They focus on a spatial position centered somewhere other than the listener; they orient to a sense of the present moment rather than the future; they are devoid of reasons. Commands do not only flow from the mouths of bosses: I have argued that a commodity price is the ultimate reduced form of a command. This is what makes commodity prices so different from the prices that propel a garrulous personal negotiation. Commands, by their nature, only succeed if they silence their addressee, and this silence opens a space for the thoroughgoing loss of specificity that signals abstraction.

Third, abstract labor deprives the worker of the view of the total. The laborer is made to gaze at the hour or the day, so as not to see the year or the life cycle. At Maracujá and Rio Branco, farmers go to great lengths to turn their eyes in the opposite direction and make the total visible again—through empreita, meia, sociedade, and bistunta. Similarly, while migrants are toiling in the urban labor market, those migrants can begin to detect a vision of the total as they imagine the closure of their personal round of migrations and the moment when they will step onto a bus heading away from the boss. The view of the whole, however fleeting or compensatory, already loosens the strictures of homogeneity. When you claim the total, labor becomes less abstract.

What makes abstract labor, then, is not a boss, not money, and not a wage. What makes abstract labor is a particular way of using time and objects. Hence the necessary limits on any political program that aims exclusively at confronting the boss. How do you fight the boss when the boss is yourself? Being your own boss does not cancel the constraints or undo the habits that make labor abstract. The hope of that undoing is what might animate the wish to live in a world without bosses—a world where you don't work for anyone, not even yourself.

There's no money, Seu Miguel told me, *that can pay for our freedom.* His words and his neighbors' can help us understand, in a deeper sense now, what may get lost in a moment of economic growth. This loss is not simply a process of painfully accepting the passing of beautiful but outmoded traditions. Nor is it only a matter of adapting to the rigors of cooperative supervised effort. Growth can rob the particularity of your time and things. It can expropriate your sense of the total. By virtue of its charismatic imperative, it can run counter to freedom.

Freedom, in my own analysis, sometimes appears in an unfortunately negative guise. I tend to figure freedom as the absence of a restraint, the lack of a boss, or the deferral of a market reckoning. One major achievement of the villagers at Maracujá and Rio Branco is their creation of more deeply positive, substantive understandings of freedom. As Seu Miguel explained it (see chapter 3), freedom is being able to go to the river tomorrow with a guest. Or, to listen to others around him, freedom means that you work when it seems meaningful for you to work. Freedom happens when you negotiate your price rather than having it pronounced to you, and there is freedom in seeing the total expanse of a job. Bistunta, empreita, and sociedade are all ways to live together as free people. To call someone not with a voice of command but with chamar—persuasively, hopefully—is to call on a person in freedom. And freedom is the chance to spend time with the people who hear your call.

*

When farmers confront the market's price, they find themselves negotiating over value—or evading it. Through their deferrals and distance, farmers also do something else. They envision the total sum of their efforts and, in so doing, they link their actions over time and consider the results. They watch themselves slowly build up a store of objects that matter. To ponder this process, we need more than an analysis of value; we need an analysis of accumulation. Value is realized in a single moment, the marketplace moment when one item becomes commensurate to another. Accumulation connects many moments and gives them meaning inside history. That sort of history, at once systemic and personal, is the subject of the remaining chapters.

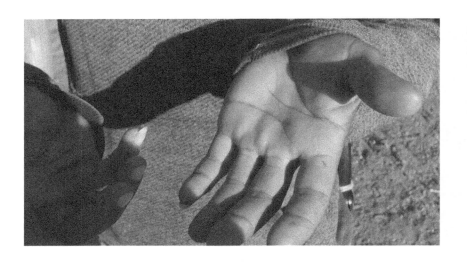

5

The Money

Asset Chains, Class Consciousness, and the Transfer of Value Out of the City

Stepping over a barbed-wire fence and heading toward Maria's kitchen, I could already hear the strange song. It was just one chord repeated over and over again, harsh and solitary. And when I stepped inside the mud-brick walls, sure enough, I found Josepe, who lived around the corner, slung out on a worn couch near the big plastic sink, strumming a guitar alone and singing tonelessly. He didn't know how to play. Maybe Josepe was making some kind of joke, I thought, but then I saw that the tears in his eyes were real. Dust from the dirt floor mingled with his song in the air. Maria floated back into the room—she felt no compunction about leaving guests by themselves in her kitchen—and she stared at him hard. She glanced up at me. Perhaps she remembered the romantic troubles that I myself had recounted on that same couch. *In this place*, she sighed, with irony and kindness, *it's nothing but lovelorn men.*

For many miles around, everyone lovelorn knew to come spend time in Maria's kitchen confessional. Josepe was no exception. A few months earlier he had been a construction worker in the city, nineteen years old, earning his money and living away from home. He returned flush. Back at Maracujá, Josepe fell tumultuously in love with Andreia, and the two of them began living close by my house. Sometimes I saw them lounging with Andreia's baby daughter on one of the village's empty cement porches. Other times they would shout and gesture, keeping a charged distance from each other. They lived these pieces of their joint life along the dirt street in front of the home they were trying to build together.

Josepe worked hard, and he loved music. Not long after the night when he sang, I found him back in Maria's kitchen, this time smiling his characteristic toothy smile, a smile that mixed swagger with friendliness. He was in the middle of an enthusiastic negotiation to purchase Suso's tiny, battery-powered mp3 player. Josepe would use it when he did day labor in the fields, he told me, so he had some music to listen to while he hoed or planted on land that he didn't own, earning wages far below his former urban pay rate.

Once Josepe left, having sworn to pay for the mp3 player, Suso and Maria started talking about him. "That man gave up a lot of money," Suso noted sagely. "How?" I asked. Maria explained. Josepe had come back from Conquista after a layoff from his job as a construction worker. He had the right to several months' worth of wages in the form of unemployment insurance, a right guaranteed by a letter that he brought with him when he returned to Maracujá. He kept the letter in the pocket of a pair of blue jeans. Someone washed the blue jeans. The letter was destroyed.

"Couldn't he solve that somehow? I asked. I could only imagine him smiling the smile while he looked at the spoiled letter.

"Sure," Maria answered, "he could try to get another copy of the letter from the company."

"Well, why hasn't he?"

Maria chuckled at my naïve question. "He's just not going after it! Lack of interest."

Josepe cared about the price of the mp3 player that would bring him music while he worked. He cared—to the point of tears—about Andreia and the life that he and she were struggling to create together. What he did not much care about, it seemed, was money.

No one in the villages remained unaware of value as measured by money, but people could demean its importance. Talking to me about women's Bolsa Família payments, Aristeu pronounced, "Money is what you work with. [. . .] But respect, no. Money doesn't bring respect."

Simão, discussing the same issue on another occasion, made a similar claim: "Money doesn't take anyone forward, you know?"

Rodrigo summed up: "We don't pay attention, dude. To money stuff."

This chapter will pay attention to the ways that Rodrigo and his neighbors do not pay attention. For there is a strange tension afoot here. How could people migrate to earn money—and then dismiss the importance of that very money? Why did people travel so far, work so hard, to earn something that they would later disdain? And why did Josepe allow his unemployment benefit to disintegrate in his pocket?

In this chapter, I argue that the puzzle arises because migration disrupts the careful arrangements that convert money into something meaningful. Cash becomes awkwardly prominent during migratory moments; it is strangely bundled into large quantities, uncomfortably disconnected from the regular rituals that tame its power. The awkwardness itself offers us a clue about the stable systems of meaning that have been disturbed. Once migrants settle into a specific labor relation, they develop a specific sensibility about *what matters more than money*. I refer to these various sensibilities as different asset chains. When someone engages in a particular kind of labor, the labor process itself ends up transforming the laborer's approach to time and objects. The laborer comes to embrace a particular vision about which objects, beyond money itself, have importance in their economic world. The laborer also sees a timeline for accumulating these objects. The vision changes as the laborer moves between class positions along the migratory circuit, from wage laborer to peasant farmer, or from small proprietor to liberal professional. To belong to a particular social class is to know a particular answer to the following question: What economic resource is more powerful than money?

This chapter looks at money in the context of the *asset chain*—the sequence of objects that a person is expected to acquire, bit by bit. Josepe had just moved to a village of peasant farmers. He found himself surrounded by neighbors who started out by planting their first asset, a field full of sixty-day beans. A young villager could parlay those beans into chickens, then pigs, then eventually a herd of mature cattle. This was the peasant asset chain, a distinctive timeline of objects, and each object needed to be acquired in order, after the object before it, and before the object after it. Money might give you a very useful boost from one object to the next, but money did not allow you to jump too far ahead. It would have been foolishness for Josepe to buy a herd of cattle before a pig, because raising the pig would teach him skills and build the good neighborly relations that he would need in order to manage cows.

In the city, Josepe would have known an entirely different asset chain. There he had been a wage laborer. He toiled among people who mixed piles of cement and turned that mixing into a month's pay, then into new clothes, then a cellphone, then a motorcycle. The wage laborer's asset chain, too, had an orderly sequence. It would have made no sense for Josepe to make a down payment on a motorcycle before he purchased a cellphone. On what grounds would he seem creditworthy? How could the dealership reach him to collect the monthly payments? Having money could only get you so far: you needed to find a way to convert your money into a place on the asset chain, and that conversion required time.[1]

Josepe, as he moved from city to village, perhaps found himself placed awkwardly between class positions. In the city, he may have felt it was difficult to deal with the bureaucracy required to pursue a worker's rights. At the same time, in the countryside, he was having trouble grasping even the first link on the asset chain of the peasant world. He purchased the mp3 player to satisfy his musical tastes while he toiled on other people's land; he did not have his own plot. Eventually, he might be able to buy land or obtain it through the landless movement, but at present, even though he came from the city with money in hand, there was not always someone willing to sell to a young man. He simply didn't seem like a trustworthy neighbor. So, for now, Josepe had no place to keep a herd of cattle or plant a manioc root. He needed to wait. Once he obtained his plot, he would still have to move slowly, starting with the simpler crops, putting in fences and improving the land bit by bit. Josepe required the kind of experience that could only be gained through trial and error in agriculture. He also had to create solid, thick relationships with his neighbors. Moreover, he would be obligated to follow the painstaking rhythm of his crops and livestock, which matured on their own schedule, and even the gradual enriching of the soil itself, before he could move upward. Even with a sizable sum of cash, he could not skip the steps in the sequence that led to becoming a peasant farmer.

Money can only get you so far. Josepe was facing a force much deeper than rural quaintness; indeed, the problem stands as a general characteristic of asset chains. In *every* asset chain, there are some things that people care about more than money, and I heard about these things when I talked not just to farmers, but to migrants in all sorts of positions.[2] During the first part of this chapter, I consider the social class positions available to migrants from Maracujá and Rio Branco, and I think about how migrants settle into one or another asset chain. This question is turned on its head in the chapter's second part. Here, I ask about disruptions in the chain: the cash remittances, cattle gifts, and other mechanisms that migrants use to take value out of one asset chain and put it into another. As migrants move between asset chains, they change their class position. They live out Millar's fundamental insight about "plastic economy" (2018: 127). Their economic action, like all economic action, is not an effort to achieve a single substance, such as "money" or "utility." It is an exercise in plasticity: an ongoing, historical process of giving and receiving form. When migrants shift value from one asset chain to the next, they do not pursue an unchanging goal; they change the shape of both their objects and their aspirations. They give a new form to their economic lives, all while receiving form from the asset chain that supplies them a new system of objectives toward which they can strive.

Josepe, at age nineteen, lacked access to the channels that would allow him to begin building a world outside of wage labor; he did not yet have the knowledge, agricultural resources, or support from neighbors that he would need to buy a cow or build a house—or even to get a piece of land. He had no way, at this point, to change his money into something lasting. I did not talk to him about this, but I suspect that the lack of access may help to explain his lack of interest in pursuing the unemployment benefits. At Maracujá and Rio Branco, cash counted when it could be turned into permanence. Otherwise, it was nothing worth paying attention to.

Part I: Settling into an Asset Chain

WHAT IS SOCIAL CLASS?

Famously, it is difficult to think about social class and economic growth at the same time. Standard growth theories tend to treat class as a distinction to be ignored or overcome through a growth process that, like a rising tide, will lift all boats (Friedman 2005). Some critical theorists have embraced the opposite view: they see "economic growth" as a euphemism for a darker mode of social change that takes from one class to give to another (Nash 1993) or that increases the inequality gap between a society's poorest and richest (Li 2014).

None of these accounts, however, can explain Brazil in the early 2000s. Economic growth was undeniably occurring, and it was *decreasing* the inequality between Brazilians. But social class, far from disappearing, became an extraordinarily salient feature of daily discourse (Klein, Mitchell, and Junge 2018; Kopper 2020; see the fascinating intersection with music in Enriquez 2022a). To understand such a moment, and to think about why people like Josepe would come back to the countryside in the middle of it, we need a concept of class that goes beyond money. We need to consider class as a relationship.

Social theorists have often argued that social class is not an attribute *of* people—not like red hair or Roman Catholicism—but, instead, a kind of relationship *between* people. These theorists sniff out class in relations between dominant and subordinate parties: between workers and bosses, teachers and students, wardens and prisoners, hipsters and squares. The theorists, undoubtedly, have a point. Yet in the perspective that I adopt here, class is a relationship between people only at a second degree. At the first degree, I suggest, we can think of class as a relationship to labor.[3]

The suggestion is a gentle one, aiming not to announce an axiom but rather to supply one more lens through which we might sometimes spy domination with a fresh eye. If we envision class as a relationship to labor, then we notice what makes class exploitation specific—how it is not just the same thing as other forms of oppression. Class analysis, in this light, is analysis that reveals how people relate to each other, at a remove, through the mediation of labor.

By focusing on labor, we see much more than employment, since abstract labor can be imagined as the making of homogeneous objects in homogeneous time. If class emerges from a person's relationship to labor, then we can also say that class emerges from that person's relationship to objects and time or, more specifically, from that person's relationship to the way that objects and time become homogeneous. Deep inside our collective representations about the things and rhythms of the world, class takes root.[4] Class endures longer than a job; a person belongs to a class before she ever works a day[5] and she continues to belong to a class after she ceases her employment.

My approach to class has important drawbacks. It emphasizes a person's relationship to the act of labor itself, not their relationship to the boss. It highlights a person's consciousness and concepts, not the unequal distribution of the money and other resources that the person receives. For this reason, it may be difficult to see, here, an account of the exploitation that workers face or of the related antagonisms. Other class theories may be more apt for that purpose. (Migrants themselves offer detailed theories of exploitation; see pages 109–13). Ultimately, I think, my approach does lead back to a reckoning with exploitation and the world market—and to some reasons why this exploitation can persist even in villages that have no boss. But first, let's consider the details.

With an eye to time and objects, I trace a provisional sketch of four different class positions: peasant farmer, wage laborer, liberal professional, and small proprietor. I focus particularly on that strange set of commodities called *assets*. An "asset," as I use the term, is a commodity seen with a view toward its value over time.[6] Assets thus direct our attention to the analysis of accumulation. Although assets exist inside the churn of the market, they are designed to stay in the hands of their owner for a relatively long period, and therefore they come to mark the owner as a particular kind of person.

An asset can help make you into a peasant farmer or a wage laborer, a liberal professional or a small proprietor. For each of the four class positions, I ask: What counts as an asset? Who gets to *define* what counts as an asset? Who can create authoritative knowledge about assets? How are assets lined up, one after another, to form an asset chain? And as you move through the asset chain, how do you represent the passing of time?

PEASANT FARMER

If they stayed stable in the village, toiling to maintain a herd of fattened cattle and a field of fruiting trees, then a migrant might eventually hear their neighbors refer to them with the honorific and slightly formal term *camponês*, "peasant." To be a peasant farmer was to stockpile subsistence assets, the kind that could be eaten if they were not sold. Each peasant farmer claimed their own expertise to evaluate these assets independently, through autonomous personal knowledge. And when farmers carefully built up their assets, bit by bit, in a long chain reaching over years, the farmers acted as *cycle stretchers*. In other words, they managed time by converting their quick-cycling crops into enduring wealth.

It took time to become a peasant farmer. A young person could start by finding a place to grow some sixty-day beans.[7] The proceeds from the quick beans could support them in the weeks and months they would spend digging holes and planting manioc stalks deep in the sun-dried soil, where a generous rain would make the stalks sprout and thicken over eighteen months or two years. The farmer would acquire livestock in a similar way, by progressing from short-term to long-term circulations. Chickens laid eggs every few days and thus enabled the purchase of pigs that required a year to reach full adulthood. With the proceeds from the pigs, the farmer might buy turkeys or even cattle, which grew for five years or more. A youthful farmer usually spent many days earning money through day labor for others, but as their livestock matured and their field grew deeper roots, they would be able to devote more of their effort to their own land.[8]

Then the farmer could dream of a house fit for a family, a dream that they would make real bit by bit, first raising a single room out of wood and adobe or wattle and daub, then separating out a bedroom, then covering the dirt floor with a concrete slab. They would slowly fill the house with furniture and durable appliances: a woodstove and then a gas stove, a mattress, chairs, a couch. The farmer might eventually construct a high-roofed kitchen spacious enough to host guests. With care, over decades, they would ascend the peasant asset chain, learning to "hold on" (*segurar*) to the slower rhythms and the goods that promise permanence. "You've got to have a manioc field," Rodrigo told me, "and hold on to it."

Rodrigo's manioc might end up in the marketplace or in his stomach. Like that manioc, the assets owned by a peasant farmer were usually objects that defied any distinction between production and consumption. Crops and livestock could be eaten as well as sold, and a house was indiscriminately a haven for rest and a workshop for all sorts of toil, carried out by women and men alike. Money materialized fairly infrequently in the form of cash. When it did, farmers favored spending the cash immediately on livestock or durable household goods. Peasant households thus enjoyed a high level of self-sufficiency.

Being relatively autonomous from the market, the residents of Maracujá and Rio Branco tended to accumulate forms of expertise that they regarded as idiosyncratic and personal. Villagers argued with each other about which moon phase helped the bean plants grow best. They had discussions on the best angle at which to plant a manioc stalk in the soil. They disagreed about the ideal age for purchasing a calf. These disputes felt exciting because there were so many possible answers. The only authority was the debatable opinion of your neighbors.

Amid particularity and autonomy, farmers were nonetheless guided by a shared orientation to time. They were driven by the imperative to make cycles longer. People in the villages admired the more enduring forms of agricultural produce. Two-year manioc made for a more respectable crop than sixty-day beans, just as the five-year cattle outshone the one-year pigs; rhythms elongated until they stretched to the limit of forever. Through this slowdown, a farmer made their world less and less homogeneous: its knowledge less standardized, its objects less frequently taken to market, its time less dominated by the small-bore rule of the minute and the hour, its distant future more steadily in view. Farmers were *cycle-stretchers*. A field of coffee trees or a solid house would last over time and become not a transitory commodity but a stable sign of its owner's personality. To improve, inside the peasant's class position, meant to move from the smaller cycles to the greater ones.

URBAN WAGE LABORER

Brazil's labor laws granted each worker in the formal sector the right to a *carteira de trabalho*: a booklet printed on starchy paper, bound like a passport, that a boss would sign to indicate that the worker was officially employed.[9] Migrants from the villages often hoped for a job like this, even if they had to start out by doing under-the-table work in the city. A carteira portrayed something quite personal: a wage worker's economic selfhood, understood as a bundle of skills certified by a supervisor.

In an important sense, the wage worker's first property was herself. She was defined by her ability to supply labor-power.[10] She did not own the tools that she needed in order to work every day. Wage-laborers drew an indelible distinction between productive tools, which largely belonged to the boss, and household goods, which the laborers themselves could dream of possessing. In the city, a laborer might not be able to aspire to own a factory machine or a restaurant kitchen—but, in compensation, the laborer acquired the power to purchase a scooter, a heating showerhead, or a tablet computer. A line separated the means of production from the means of consumption.

Wage laborers could use this same line to split their *own* assets into two types. On the one hand, laborers owned consumption goods. On the other hand, laborers owned themselves and, in particular, the productive skills they brought to the labor market. Laborers strove to improve their skills bit by bit, and hence laborers were *self-improvers*: they marked the passing of time by charting the change in their productive selves.

I learned about the distinction between consumptive and productive assets when Genaro introduced me to his car. It was bought with the wages from his city job and carefully parked in the garage that he had built in front of his tiny city condominium. Genaro was raised as a farmer in the village next to Maracujá, but after long study sessions, he passed a civil service exam and became a municipal street sweeper, then a municipal driver, in the metropolis. On a daily basis, Genaro took his partner to her job, drove to the other side of the city, left his personal car in a garage, switched over to a city-owned work car, and drove half of the distance back again toward his house until he reached City Hall, where he would pick up tax inspectors and shuttle them around all day. Genaro was careful about who rode in which vehicle. He drew a bright line between his work car and his personal car, between a productive tool and a consumption item. This was the very opposite of the rural merger of production and consumption.

Like Genaro's car, consumer products adorned a city laborer precisely because those products did *not* have any use on the job. Young migrants might acquire goods bit by bit, starting with fresh clothes and a cellphone, eventually advancing to a motorcycle, a car, and a condominium or a small house.

On the job, however, these workers had another kind of progress to pursue. They could improve their one productive tool, themselves. They could rise along the scale of skills. That was how Alexandra recalled for me the days that she spent restocking the fruit-and-nut section of an upscale grocery store in Belo Horizonte. "I always did it with love," she remembered. "I had the wish to do it. Because I had the wish to learn. More."

Wage laborers told me at length about their commitment to self-education on the worksite. Sometimes, they took jobs for the *purpose* of learning. "I went to work at that factory," Ana said, "thinking that from that place, I would gain greater knowledge."

Wage laborers like Ana described their labor not as mere drudgery, but as self-development. Migrants, energetic and penniless, came to the city and often began toiling at jobs considered unskilled, such as domestic service. Of course, these jobs, like all jobs, could in fact be carried out with tremendous talent and sophistication. What distinguished them was Brazil's famous system of labor regulation, inherited from the 1930s, which regulated some jobs as "professions" and granted benefits to employees in the formal sector, benefits that included the carteira. When a new migrant from the countryside found their first formal-sector job, they would get the first signature on the first page of their carteira. Each new signature was, very concretely, an asset that a migrant gained: one more work skill certified and useful for obtaining future employment.

Which dispositions counted as "skills?" And who decided? The answer in the city was not like the answer in the countryside. Farmers assessed their own talents by weighing the gossip, chiding, and advice of their many neighbors. For urban wage laborers, by contrast, skill was measured by a supervisor. A supervisor's job was to homogenize the worker's work effort and inscribe it through an assessment. One characteristic quality of wage labor, then, was that workers lost the authority to define competence and excellence at work.

Migrants often had elaborate memories of the methods their urban bosses had used to evaluate their capabilities. Ana, at the clothing factory, knew that her boss was surveilling the number of outfits she could pack per hour, so she herself began tallying that number every day before he did. Alexandra, at the supermarket, told me about her promotion from level 1 to level 3 on the market's employee measurement system. But it was Seu Ícaro who waxed most poetic with me, remembering the day when an electrician spotted him, a lowly laborer, on a construction site and chose him for advancement. The electrician set up a series of tests. First, Seu Ícaro had to connect electric boxes. Next he had to decipher an electrical blueprint. Finally, after many months of wiring a single building, Seu Ícaro was summoned by the electrician to flip the light switch. The lights came on. "From that day forward," Seu Ícaro recalled, "he classified me as qualified."

He classified me. Alexandra, Ana, and Seu Ícaro were monitoring their bosses as their bosses monitored them. Indeed, Ana was monitoring herself *before* her boss could monitor her. Often I heard migrants describe the improvement in their skills as "growing" (*crescer*). "I wanted a job that could help me to grow," Ana told me. Used in this sense, "growing" referred to the use of time to transform *oneself*.

A worker who gained enough knowledge could be said to have acquired a "profession," a portable identity registered in their carteira booklet. Wage workers were deeply concerned to determine exactly how a given job would advance this project of self-transformation. What skills would be learned? A struggle sometimes erupted between workers and bosses over this issue. Ana, for example, expressed anger that her supervisor had put her in the "finishing and boxing" department of the clothing factory rather than the "sewing" department, where she would have learned to sew. "Then, in any factory, in any tailor's shop that needed a tailor, if I put in my résumé, I could have been hired to sew," Ana explained. "Finishing and boxing isn't a profession. And tailor is."

In some sense, the wage laborer's progress in the city was an ongoing struggle to cobble together the skills that made "a profession." Once certified, the profession would allow the worker to go work for another firm.

But not every worker pursued this vision. Some wage laborers found stability, even meaning, by following upward the pathway created by a single good employer. "I sweated a lot to do well in that supermarket," Alexandra reminisced. "Because when you pass by, there's a really big sign: Green Sea. Green Sea Supermarket. So my dream was to wear the Green Sea uniform. And I achieved that."

What did you feel, I asked, when you saw someone in the street with a Green Sea shopping bag? Alexandra answered without a second of hesitation. "Pride to work at Green Sea."

Alexandra had started in the city as a housecleaner, then a desk clerk. Her pride pointed to the cycles she had been through, the wage laborer's slow spiral through job changes and promotions, résumé lines and managerial reviews, all leading toward the packet of recognized skills that a worker could hold as an asset. The skills themselves turned into objects and fell into an orderly asset chain. Precisely because a wage worker, unlike a peasant farmer, could not hope to own the means of production, wage workers talked with eloquence about changing *themselves* as a sort of process of bildung. They were *self-improvers*. They represented time as a flow of transformations in the self.

Hence it was no accident that migrants tended to describe their progression through the skills ladder as their *growth* (*crescimento*), as if the nation's economic progress had been miniaturized in their persons. My sense is that this ladder, more than the consumption spiral, defined the wage laborer's class position. The skills ladder held out the promise of acquiring an object that lasted longer than a motorcycle, longer than a cellphone, and longer than cash. "What counts," Alexandra told me, "is your reference." Even after she returned to the countryside, she retained the reference of her former supervisors, certifying both her bona fides inside the firm and the talents that she might carry to some other employer. "That's what circulates, more than any money."

LIBERAL PROFESSIONAL

In the villages, liberal professionals were easy to spot. They were the people trying to get you involved in one or another project: a new class at the high school, maybe, or an upcoming revival at the church. Professionals functioned as *project timers*. They split up the flow of everyday life into a series of discrete, time-limited projects and then recruited their neighbors into these projects. In order to carry out their work, professionals needed to accumulate certifications, such as diplomas and degrees, which the professionals treated as assets in their asset chain. These certifications were granted not by one's supervisor, but by the peers from one's own profession. In other words, professionals were villagers who launched projects that were endorsed and evaluated by an outside community of professional peers. The meaningfulness of this pursuit became clearer for me when I considered two professionals whom I knew well: Nelson at Rio Branco and Mariele at Maracujá.

Nelson kicked up miles of dust each week as he snaked his tiny motorcycle from farmhouse to farmhouse, meticulously writing down the vaccinations and doctor appointments of each family that fell under his responsibility, smiling with his neighbors, and taking coffee in their homes, since he was the area's dedicated community health agent.

Mariele boomed her voice through the classroom walls, loud enough to be heard far down the unpaved street, when she taught her passionately liberatory history classes next to the purple-flowered trees at Maracujá's high school.

Both Nelson and Mariele had spent nearly their entire lives as peasant farmers in the region. They still lived in the villages. They still cultivated their plots and still called themselves peasants. But they had also become professionals.

Thanks to social mobilization and left-wing governments in the 1990s and 2000s, Brazil's dawning welfare state had scattered a few liberal professional jobs throughout the villages. The countryside needed teachers to fill its new schools, health workers to staff its new medical programs, and organizers to swell its new unions and movements. While these positions tended to go to commuting urbanites, villagers sometimes got hired. The landless movement, in particular, managed to create job opportunities by channeling farmers into career-focused educational programs, ranging from literacy night school to advanced accounting class (Tarlau 2019; Meek 2020).

There also existed something of an alternative professional ladder inside the landless movement itself. The MST's Regional Leadership Collective (*coletivo de direção regional*) designated certain villagers as *militantes* (organizers), thus granting them the authority to run a protest march or a land occupation, and occasionally the MST compensated militantes with a meager stipend. For the most politically devoted, *militância* turned into a career that lasted for decades and reached far beyond the borders of Maracujá and Rio Branco.

Another alternative professional ladder came from the evangelical churches. Visiting pastors avidly sought to train villagers as preachers and missionaries. In church, the devout could serve as youth ministers or choir directors, worshiping through the microphone late into the night, traveling in tightly packed cars to revivals around the region. Leading a church, in fact, looked strikingly similar to leading a landless movement, and more than a few people made the move from one to the other.

Pastors, union radicals, health agents, teachers: what did these very different professionals have in common? They shared a sense of the kind of work they did. Their core work object was *the mission*. Liberal professionals represented their toil as a series of missions, undertakings, or ventures: a community of children to be made healthy, a plantation to occupy, a new congregation to found, a nonprofit to organize.

Among liberal professionals, the mission was constantly objectified—that is, it was discussed and treated as a self-evident *object* of desire, the sort of thing that everyone obviously wanted, just as skill was objectified for wage laborers and manioc fields were objectified for peasant farmers. But who objectified the mission? Who assessed it and defined it? Herein lay the first privilege of the liberal professional: one's mission was supposed to be evaluated by other people who belonged to the same group as oneself. Other teachers, for example, evaluated a class, while other activists evaluated a land occupation. One's peers judged one's work.[11]

In order to carry out their missions, liberal professionals accumulated a key type of asset: certifications. Teachers needed degrees. Health agents needed diplomas from trainings. Even religious leaders needed to formalize their calling: one friend told me bitterly that his denomination would not name him a pastor until he finished high school.

When I visited professionals at their homes, sometimes they would show me a folder of certificates that they kept in a special place. The folders all looked similar to each other, thick covers on the outside and the inside filled by the gossamer plastic of transparent sheet protectors surrounding each credential. As I flipped through, I would see the marks of major accomplishments intermingled with papers that seemed trivial to me: proof of completion of a one-day training session on agricultural cooperation, maybe, or a printout from a weekend convention. People lectured me on the importance of holding on to every such document. A professional could read his career as the sequence of certificates in his folder, each one a link added to his asset chain. If you decided to start keeping a folder, it was a sign that you had begun dreaming professional dreams.

A certificate folder represented an overarching pedagogical trajectory that was split into discrete, often disparate trainings. In the same way, liberal professionals tended to depict their work time by dividing the broader mission into a succession of major projects. Each project had a beginning and an end. A professional might undertake a revival at church, a vaccination campaign with a deadline, an activist march to the capital city, or a new class for the high school students. Projects were driven by urgency and by their own internal schedules; they lacked the repetitive regularity of the farmer's calendar or the wage laborer's workday. Indeed, professionals themselves were *project timers*. They earned their livings by making project time seem real and urgent to their constituencies: their students, their church members, or their patients. In turn, this same urgency disciplined the professionals, defining the characteristically episodic rhythm of their work process.

A liberal profession was always both a job and more than a job, recognized by the market but beyond the market. The professional's ideal trajectory led away from marketability and toward a kind of freedom. Eventually, it was hoped, you might be able to create a full split between the money you earned and the certificates you gathered. You could gain credentials that had nothing to do with the labor market. One day, I learned that Mariele had recruited other teachers to cover her history classes at the rural high school so she could make periodic thousand-kilometer trips to a university. She was pursuing a second postgraduate specialization degree, this one in Marxist theory. The degree seemed likely to have no impact on her earnings, since she was well established as a high school teacher. The second specialization degree was an asset that Mariele was accumulating because the professional's asset chain mattered beyond any considerations about cash. The new credential, the rumbling journeys to the university, the late-night class papers written near the darkened fields of the village, all of it with little regard for employment or money: Mariele had traveled far on the path of the professional.

SMALL PROPRIETOR

Maracujá and Rio Branco hummed every day with the energy created by local bar owners and van drivers, moneylenders and Avon saleswomen. In other words, the villages depended every day on a class of people who used their own capital to mount ventures serving the general public. These people were small proprietors. Proprietors made money by cobbling together bits of cash over time, and in this sense the proprietors were *time aggregators*, specialists in working with the time value of money.

For deals to take place, proprietors had to create a zone where people could deal with each other. The bar owner, quintessentially, needed a bustling bar. Thus, the key asset accumulated by proprietors, even more important than their particular merchandise, was public space itself. What counted as a desirable public space? This was a matter decided by the ultimate authority of the customers, through their decisions about where and how to spend their time. And one afternoon, I saw such evaluation in action at Maracujá.

Cinderblock walls were sheltering me from the noise and dust of Maracujá as I lounged in Felipe's bar and general store. Felipe had clear liquor in storage, meat from a local cow in the freezer, and enough time to show me the dirty, lined notebook where he scribbled down the money owed to him by every family in town. But his leisure ended abruptly, in the same way that it often did for Felipe: a customer walked in the door.

"How brave of you!" the customer shouted at Felipe's dog, who would not stop barking.

"He can't put up with anyone coming in this place," Felipe apologized gruffly. "What's up?" I realized that the customer was, in fact, Mauro, the owner of the new, rival bar located just around the corner on the dirt path.

"Floor wax," Mauro specified. "How much is it?"

"Floor wax," Felipe answered. "Three-fifty."

Mauro threw out his coins so they spun on the counter, deemed them insufficient, and handed them over regardless. "I owe you twenty-five." The wax changed hands.

Mauro was in no hurry to leave, so he and Felipe began gossiping about the wholesale price for beer. "Recently, it was at seventeen-something!" Felipe enthused.

"Give me one of those bitter liquors there," Mauro ordered gently. Over his drink, the two bar owners discussed the cost of running a freezer, the way to negotiate with a middleman, and the latest news about a worker who had quit his job at a construction company that was passing through the area. Felipe wondered, *How much severance pay did the worker get?* Mauro wouldn't venture a guess. Perhaps he knew more than he was saying: Mauro himself had once quit a job at that same construction company. In fact, that was how Mauro came to Maracujá. Sent to the region to toil on a gigantic pipeline project, Mauro liked the village enough to move in, leave behind his wage work, and open up the bar.

The conversation halted. Sérgio had appeared in the doorway, enthusiastic as ever and probably drunk. "Hey, Fel!" he called out.

"What's up?" Felipe answered quietly.

Sérgio noticed me. "Everything's fine. Better now that I'm with you!"

Sérgio began an amiable lecture on Cuban sports teams, his Portuguese ex-boss, and a nearby shoe factory that, he believed, produced Nikes that were actually cheap fakes. While I paid attention to Sérgio, Felipe and Mauro became engrossed in a discussion about the quality of different cognacs. The chatting was broken by Karola, Felipe's wife, who came in and mentioned lunch.

"My grub," Felipe explained to everyone, possibly with a hint of regret, as people began heading out the door. I lingered longer than the rest, and Felipe told me that Mauro's visit was nothing unusual. The bar owners from the village always dropped by each other's establishments.

If I decided to drink, Felipe mused, *I would go to someone else's bar.*

Drinking another person's alcohol in public: Lévi-Strauss once used this motif as the image of human sociability (1969: 58–59). For small proprietors at Maracujá or Rio Branco, public space was the key asset that one needed to accumulate—and sociability the primary tool. In the time it took Mauro to finish off a glass of bitter liquor, Felipe displayed the social talents that it took to thrive as a small proprietor. He was friendly and quiet. He made others talk. He demonstrated a tolerance for people and an ability to ignore them when necessary, as he ignored Sérgio, but without offending anyone. He built relationships that became automatic, just as Mauro automatically assumed that Felipe would give him twenty-five cents of credit. Through those talents, in a place that had no newspapers, Felipe managed to gather together the village's key information. During the few minutes that I spent watching him in his bar that morning, Felipe learned another proprietor's strategy for managing the expense of a freezer, and in turn he dispensed data about wholesale prices. He also kept track of the employment status and likely solvency of an itinerant construction worker—this news being significant to Felipe, since transient workers with well-paying jobs had a tendency to spend lavishly at the local bars, on credit, and a subsequent bad habit of leaving without paying their debts. All in all, Felipe channeled the flow of local information so that it swirled around *him*, thus carrying out one of the major functions of the small proprietor.

Small proprietors had an overwhelming tendency to live in the village they served, and from that base they ran a wide variety of business ventures that served the general public. By far the most common type of small proprietor was the owner of a bar and store (*venda*). But vendas were not the only possibility. A few small proprietors bought, resold, and slaughtered livestock for local consumption. Some small proprietors—all men—owned battered minivans and drove rural students to school each day, receiving compensation through a government contract. Other small proprietors—all women—retailed Avon clothing and cosmetic products from a catalogue. At least one small proprietor lent money at interest. It was especially common for a small proprietor with one such business to branch out into another field: for example, many of the van drivers also opened their own bars.

In all their varied pursuits, small proprietors made a living by managing differences in time cycles. The small proprietor detected a divergence between one circulation speed and another, then figured out how to bring the two together. Felipe knew his customers' habits, how much liquor they drank each night and how many cups of beans they cooked each morning, and he turned these daily rhythms into his monthly trips to the wholesale warehouse. Thus, Felipe took in money by the day and spent money by the month, earning profit by putting a price on the discrepancy. Diógenes, a school van driver, gained his profit in the opposite direction. He received a contract payment from the state government only a few times each year, but on a quite regular basis, he had to buy gasoline, oil, and new tires for the rocky country roads. Diógenes took in money by the year and spent money by the day, and through this translation he, too, made a living.

Small proprietors became adept at shuttling between cycles. Avon vendors monitored their neighbors' worn-out pants or empty perfume bottles, cobbling together orders from various families into a single shipment through the Avon catalogue. Livestock traders took advantage of the gap between the moment when one farmer wanted to sell a pig and the moment when another farmer wanted to buy one. Russo, the local moneylender, made loans during the coffee harvest so that farmers could pay day wages to the harvesters, and after the coffee beans were shipped and paid for, he received his money back (plus at least 6 percent interest per month).

In short, small proprietors were *time aggregators*. They were not time stretchers like the peasant farmers, who pulled time into longer and longer cycles. Instead, small proprietors arbitraged the difference between disparate time situations. They turned the short term into the long term, and then they broke the long term down into the short term again. Thus, uniquely in the villages, small proprietors stayed close to money, constantly tracking the conversion between hourly cash and monthly debts. They were experts at "working with money," as Russo put it to me. They knew the day's prices.

But working with money did not mean maximizing profit. Russo repeated a sentiment I had heard elsewhere in the village:[12] when he considered his cash, profit appeared as a minor detail. "As long as you've got a little profit," he postulated, "any profit is good." What mattered about money was not its power to make profit. What mattered about money was its power to circulate. "Every opportunity I get, I buy and I sell," Russo enthused. His voice hit an energetic high note: "Yeah, *any*thing that I have a good opportunity to buy to resell, I buy it."

"Mm-hm," I encouraged.

"Even a chicken, if I see that, that it's a good deal, I buy it." Russo and I both laughed. "And I go forward and I sell it."

Here, cash was a tool for circulating, not a vehicle for profit. Volume and turnover, not high margins, were the key virtues. Small proprietors devised vivid metaphors to describe money's circulator vocation. It was said to be bad to keep your "money blocked up" (*dinheiro empatado*) in an illiquid asset, like a house. A good proprietor would aim not to "stay with money sitting there" (*ficar com o dinheiro parado.*) "I'm always moving money around," Russo told me. "That way, it doesn't run out."

In the parched climate of Maracujá and Rio Branco, proprietors spoke about this abundant circulation by using liquid language (Sanabria 2009; Mayblin 2013). Felipe, during the middle of the recession, moaned to me that "the money isn't flowing." Just a few minutes later, he shifted the idiom. Felipe was warning me that he had to be quick in paying back the farmer who had given him a cow to slaughter on credit. If Felipe waited more than thirty days, no one else would want to sell him a cow again. "The news flows, and you're done."

Reputation flows just as money does: perhaps it was not a coincidence that Felipe reused his metaphor here. If village store owners like Felipe represented money preeminently as a medium of circulation, this was because, for small proprietors, money itself was not the key asset to be accumulated. The key asset was public space—public space understood as relational space. Small proprietors managed flows of publicly relevant information, whether that information came embodied as money or reputation, prices or gossip, and a talented small proprietor could channel the information in order to bring a public into existence inside the villages.

The villages' small proprietors built public space in the most literal sense. Each night, the bars assembled a mostly male crowd that debated and guffawed around a few plastic tables and chairs set out in the dirt adjoining the bar owner's house.[13] The same locales had a more integrated feeling by day, when virtually anyone in the community might stroll up to buy or simply to chat.

The school vans, too, served as public spaces. Their vinyl bench seats became daily sites of encounter between young people from throughout the region, who might otherwise have few chances to see each other. Indeed, this was one of the goals behind the government's major push, in the 1990s and 2000s, to make school transportation (and hence schooling) universally available in the countryside: by going to school, students broadened their social worlds. Van owners toiled, in a very direct sense, to make the broadening happen. They took that element of the job quite seriously, tolerating and even encouraging noisy conviviality during the long, tooth-chattering rides along the dirt roads that led from farmhouse to farmhouse to school. Indeed, nonstudents—myself included—frequently imposed on the drivers by asking them to carry extra passengers, packages, produce, or messages to be passed along to the remote parts of the countryside. A public had been built.

To be a small proprietor, then, was to use your command of information to create a public space under your aegis. A talented small proprietor accumulated these public spaces as their own assets: everyone knew, after all, that the bar belonged to Russo, the in-home candy shop to Dona Maciele, and the van to Diógenes. The authority to define and rank these assets, however, rested elsewhere. For the most part, an asset was judged by the whole mass of people who engaged with it each day. Villagers collectively decided whether a particular bar felt friendly or boring, which Avon vendor or cattle seller to use, and how much to trust the moneylender. Villagers ranked each public space and created its reputation.

A small proprietor built up their assets progressively, over time, in the sequence of a distinctive asset chain. To move up this asset chain meant to lay claim to a more lasting relational space in the public sphere. A small proprietor could make the asset longer lasting simply by strengthening its infrastructure. A venda, for example, might begin as nothing more than the window of a house whose owner would sell topped-off glasses of clear liquor over the windowsill. Felipe opened his bar and general store with just the investment of a month's wages and a promise to his wife that they would try it together. They specialized in soft drinks and food, running the entire operation in their living room, and this setup allowed them stay close to their baby. Once the baby grew into a toddler, Felipe cleared space on one side of their house and laid down three walls of adobe mixed with cow dung. The new venda turned into a meeting-point for the village. Eventually, Felipe tore down the initial walls and replaced them with cinderblock. The venda now had a freezer for meat, a bar stocked with various drinks, and a storage room for rice and beans. Villagers flocked there every day and stayed until Felipe, exhausted, would close down shortly after dark. He had, very literally, built an enduring public space at Maracujá.

Small proprietors also moved up the asset chain by building their public spaces in a different sense: by strengthening the relationships that held those spaces together. When starting off, a small proprietor needed to establish a coterie of clients; consequently, new proprietors might extend very generous terms of credit. This generosity could draw in a whole network of villagers. Their purchases became the foundation for the new public space.

Famously, however, such foundations proved fragile, as customers made demands for credit that pushed the proprietor to the brink of insolvency. A well-established proprietor, then, was one who could say no judiciously. Solid proprietors developed loyalties and acquired knowledge of each customer's creditworthiness. Generosity mattered as much as rectitude, and store owners in particular operated as social safety nets, allowing destitute customers to take out "credit," perpetually unrepaid, that amounted to food donations. Many villagers established somewhat more ambiguous arrangements with a store owner, never quite clearing the debt completely, but usually managing to scrape together enough of a payment to persuade the proprietor to allow them to buy one more sack of rice or box of floor wax on credit. These habits demonstrated how the public space became enduring: not simply as a cluster of chairs but also as a hardy web of relations.

Small proprietors were thus the villages' conduits of information, and they summoned their expertise to knit together the disparate time cycles that made daily action practical in the countryside. Small proprietors might seem to accumulate money, but in a deeper sense they put money to work in order to produce public space, building this space as an asset that they themselves could hold.[14] They climbed their asset chain by rendering their space more and more lasting, less vulnerable to the shock of conflict, more permanent.

The great lessons of the small proprietor were perhaps best exemplified by Russo, who was said to have grown wealthier than anyone else at Maracujá. He had done it by turning himself into the impresario of public space: owner of the loudest bar, only source of big loans, and the person you should see if you wanted to buy or sell a cow. Interestingly, though, Russo never showed his money. He dressed, ate, and drank as he always had; he lived in the same kind of house as his neighbors. One day I asked Russo what his dream was, and he paused. His dream, he told me, was to open up a supermarket so that all four of his daughters could work there together, never having to be employed by someone else. Russo did not dream of getting rich or of making strangers toil for him. He dreamed of converting his money into the ultimate stable enterprise. Here was a vision—the public space so deep that it absorbed the family, the network so stable that no one ever had to leave their kin behind—and here was that vision expressed as a business plan. To me, it sounded like the most beautiful aspiration of the small proprietor.

CLASS IS A LINK BETWEEN TIME AND OBJECTS

Josepe did not simply want money. The shreds of a letter in his blue jeans bore witness to that. At Maracujá and Rio Branco, money gained its meaning when it could fit inside an asset chain, a series of objects arranged into an order in time. A migrant began to climb the asset chain as soon as they started to work in a particular way. The labor process itself—the very act of laboring—ended up shaping a person's sense of time and things, sharpening their attention to sequences and objects that suddenly came to feel important. Through this sharpening, social class came into being. Your class position gave you an answer to the question, *What economic resource matters more than money?*

Different classes came up with different answers. The key asset might be a certificate or a patch of public space, a herd of cattle or a passel of work skills.

THE MONEY

These assets would be judged by one or another authority, depending on your class position: by your supervisor, if you were a wage laborer; by your peers, if you were a liberal professional; by your customers, if you were a small proprietor; and by arguments with your neighbors, if you were a peasant farmer. As you strung your assets together, you would develop a distinctive approach to time. You would become a cycle stretcher, a self-improver, a project timer, or a time aggregator.

In every case, you would be building a sense of your relationship to the things and rhythms of the world. An asset chain emerges as a story about what you are gaining bit by bit in the course of time, what your labor is starting to mean, and not in a fully personal sense but rather as part of a standard progression shared by many other people. Each such story becomes, ultimately, a recipe for producing and consuming commodities.

Thus, as migrants moved along an asset chain, they were devising a specific response to the market. They were dealing with the unavoidable fact that, in the marketplace, their time and their objects became homogeneous, indistinguishable, and colorless, vanishing into a standard: one more hour on the construction site or 10 more kilos of fruit at the wholesale warehouse. Already I have noted migrants' negative responses to this homogeneity, their acts of rejection. In chapter 3, we saw how workers disparaged the measurement of the "hour" and the "day" through which the boss had made their time homogeneous; in chapter 4, we heard how Félix angrily portrayed the marketplace as a "cartel" that homogenized his objects.

But migrants did not simply defy this homogeneity. They also invented their own names for it and their own ways of comprehending it. They invented, in particular, a sequence that could help them understand how one object might lead to another, over time—an asset chain. The asset chain held out the hope of allowing you to define yourself as something more than raw labor power. By following an asset chain, workers became workers of a particular kind, members of a particular class, strivers in pursuit of a recognizable goal, people who would labor one way and not another. Class consciousness arose both from acts of rejection and from the positive imaginations that workers developed in order to understand their action inside the commodity order.

What, then, is social class? As we focus on the asset chain, we attempt to articulate a theory of class that is grounded in time and objects, not in the domination of a supervisor. Such a theory is well worth trying. It may speak to the situation of people who have no boss, such as the small farmers at Maracujá and Rio Branco. In a theory like this one, it is not necessarily your boss who exploits you. Exploitation comes already included in the sort of abstraction that removes your sense of power in your work, in the homogeneity conveyed by a command. Here, we understand class as a person's relationship to abstract labor and hence as a person's response to homogeneity. Your class is the condition under which you generate homogeneous objects in homogeneous time, thus becoming homogeneous yourself.

An asset chain loops you into this homogeneity. The asset chain brings you into sustained interaction with the market that buys your skills or sells you a motorcycle. At the same time, in a hegemonic gesture,[15] the asset chain tames that market, integrating it into a comprehensible life plan and giving you a goal. Thus, an asset chain both facilitates exploitation and places a limit on its extent.

An asset chain is a hermetic system of meaning, a wholesale account of the times and objects that make up the world, a map of the authority that regiments labor. But the asset chain is not unbreakable. People do in fact change their class positions in the villages, which means moving from one asset chain to the next. How they carry out this translation—how they transport wealth from one form to another—is the subject of the chapter's next section.

*

Josepe's fights with Andreia grew worse. From Maria, I heard that Andreia and Josepe, at the point of desperation, had gone to a service at Maracujá's evangelical church. They stood inside the thick white walls of the sanctuary, and both sobbed. On the spot, they answered a call and accepted Jesus. The two of them resolved to stay with each other. They left Maracujá shortly afterward, moving in with Andreia's parents in a nearby village.

A few days later, I visited their new home. Josepe seemed freshly committed to beginning a rural life. He and Andreia were living packed in with her siblings, amid the dust of a dirt road. Andreia's parents offered to give them a corner of the yard. Andreia and Josepe had begun forming adobe bricks out of mud so that, a little at a time, they could raise their own house. Brick by brick, Josepe, the former urban construction worker, was literally building the foundation that a peasant farmer would need in order to start out in the world.

Part II: Changing Classes

GETTING MONEY OUT OF THE CITY: TRANSITIONS BETWEEN ASSET CHAINS

When Stefania and her husband decided to leave São Paulo, after seven years of toiling with begonias at a flower nursery, they took their preschool-aged daughter to a store and told her to pick out a doll. She chose one from the top shelf—so high that a clerk had to fetch it. Once the doll reached their daughter's hands, it turned out to be nearly as tall as she was. And (as Stefania told me later, with undisguised disappointment) it wasn't a nice Barbie. It was a rock star. Their daughter loved the colossal rocker, so, mastering her own feelings, Stefania bought it.

Beyond the doll, Stefania and her husband took a careful look at the other items they had acquired during their years in the city. They owned a refrigerator, two televisions, and a stereo. They debated if it made sense to bring all this back to Bahia. Stefania chased down a truck driver in the northern suburbs of the megalopolis and wheedled him to his best price: R$3,500, or one-third of the family's total savings.[16]

Stefania added up the market value of her appliances, which came to R$5,000. She decided that she could not leave that much value behind, so they paid the trucker and rode back to Bahia.

Tellingly, Stefania tallied the family assets in money terms. Money tended to become painfully, awkwardly salient, despite every disavowal, during moments of migration. Money mattered when a villager needed to buy a bus ticket to go join the wage labor market, like Diego riding on the cash from his father's pig (see chapter 3). And money mattered when a migrant moved into the village, trying to find some way to bring the earnings from distant wage labor and convert them into respectable agricultural wealth. In other words, money rose to awareness when people tried to shift from one asset chain to another.

How do you move wealth between different systems of meaning? Like Stefania with her bulky furniture, migrants were confronted, in the first place, with a formidable logistical challenge. One solution was simply to send cash remittances—but this turned out not to be so simple after all.

The nearest ATMs were more than 100 kilometers from Maracujá and Rio Branco, in the city of Conquista. So when a relative sent money through an account, someone would have to spend an entire day going to the ATM to fetch the remittance cash. During the evening bus trip from Conquista to Maracujá and Rio Branco, the bus was often filled with these little stores of money, carried inside pockets and purses. Thieves knew this. On one memorable occasion during the period of my fieldwork (thankfully, not on a day when I myself was traveling) a pair of unknown men stood up while the bus was traveling down a deserted stretch of highway, drew guns, and ordered the driver to keep driving. They began methodically collecting each person's money and any cellphones. *I wasn't born to be robbed!* an older man protested angrily. The robbers answered him by shooting a hole in the floor of the bus, and he gave up his cash, too. At an especially desolate location, the robbers ordered the bus driver to pull over, and, after helping themselves to the beautiful black leather jacket that one of the village teachers was wearing, they disappeared into the brush.

Thieves weren't the only enemy. Migrants had a constant battle to fight inside themselves over how much money to send back and how much to spend in the city. Often, they paid for urban computer classes or business courses for themselves, as in the case of Alexandra (see the introduction). And, as Marcos put it to me wryly, "There are a lot of things that you can do here at night, in Brazil." Young people, in particular, talked about how quickly they got used to spending at nightclubs, tiny bars, and snack shops. "I spent my money very carelessly," Tamara laughed one day, "at that McDonald's."

Melchior reminisced about "seeing that abundance" when he arrived in São Paulo. "I'd party from Thursday to Sunday," he told me. "Then, on Monday, I'd go and ask my boss for a voucher to buy food. Because I wouldn't even leave anything for food." But even Melchior in his wild days remembered to send money to his mother. On top of the cash for her food and her cooking gas, he bought her a bus ticket to come visit him each year.

Indeed, the "little sacred money" (*dinheirinho sagrado*), as Alexandra called remittance cash, had a solid hold on those migrants who cultivated ties to the village. Among the cluster of young men who toiled as firefighters at the mines, Marcos reckoned that everyone sent at least something—and not a trivial amount. Marcos considered it almost negligibly minimal for a worker in his group to send only 12 percent of their salary in remittance form; Marcos himself sent half, every month, supporting his aging parents and his three sisters and brother at Maracujá. He could do this because, like many other migrants, he "worked free" (*trabalhava livre*; see Gudeman and Rivera [1990: 106]), meaning that he lived in a dormitory provided by the company and paid no rent. Older men might remit especially sizable amounts. Ivan calculated that he was currently sending 40 percent of his city salary, and Joaquim remembered that he used to remit 75 percent to his wife and children in the village.

Money was not the only way to get value out of the city. Value could be conveyed in the form of impressive merchandise, like Stefania's appliances on the back of the truck. An especially common dream was to come home with a motorcycle. Sérgio roared into Maracujá with a large white bike. Marcos, quieter and more meticulous, had saved his earnings from the urban yogurt factory and made the down payment on a dark red Honda motorcycle that the village's children loved to borrow for zips around the four dirt streets.

Sérgio's and Marcos's bikes were bought legally, brand new, from a dealership. But once the bikes left the city and arrived in the villages, they, like so many other objects, began to change their nature. They slowly drifted toward the demimonde of "Pokémon" vehicles.

The term *Pokémon* played on the similarity between the name of the popular Japanese cartoon character and the participle *pocado*, itself derived from a Tupí word meaning "to explode" (Navarro 2005). An "exploded" motorcycle was one that had no legal title because of debt problems: its owner had not paid to renew its registration or, more seriously, had simply stopped paying the installments due to the dealership. Rural people avidly bought and sold these illicit vehicles, albeit at a steep discount. If Marcos or Sérgio stopped making payments, he could still ride all around the countryside, since the police in rural areas rarely checked vehicle documents. But he would not be able to drive the motorcycle back to the city, under peril of having it impounded.

For a vehicle to become "exploded" was for it to begin belonging to the rural zone. Quite literally, an exploded vehicle could no longer circulate in the city; more figuratively, it dropped out of the cycle of urban commerce, since, being unusable and unsalable in the metropolis, it no longer had value.

This sort of transformation was a symptom. Something was happening to objects on their trip into the countryside. Not just motorcycles, but also gas stoves and roof tiles, radios and refrigerators became more immobile as they passed from city to village: more difficult to sell, in this place with so few customers; less capable of circulating; more likely to stay put. They were cycling more slowly. Cash, too, underwent such a change. People in the villages (as we will see) speedily converted cash into forms that fixed it into place. Here was the mark of a successful transition to the new asset chain: money lost its salience. An object became less marketable, less comparable to every other object in the marketplace, more attached to a person, and hence less of a commodity.

Even the enormous doll seemed to feel the alchemy that accompanied the transition to rural life. Stefania's daughter introduced me to the doll while her grandmother cooked lunch in back of the house, near the fruit trees and the manioc plants. I noticed that there were no more rock star clothes to be seen. Someone had replaced them, by hand, with a plain and modest cloth dress.

KEEPING WEALTH IN THE COUNTRYSIDE: EARMARKED FIELDS, CHILDREN'S CATTLE, AND APPLIANCES ON CREDIT

Once migrants managed to bring money back to the countryside, they needed to find a way to integrate that cash into the peasant farmer's asset chain. The money had to become something meaningful, something stable and unlikely to slip out of one's hands. It had to turn into an asset. Migrants responded to this challenge by pouring their money into fields, herds, and houses. These three devices were so effective that villagers often used them to take value from various different asset chains and convert that value into the peasant regime.

Consider Carlos, Jamaira, and Nelson. All three of them ended up crossing class lines, and, while crossing those lines, they invested in a field, a herd, or a house. Carlos, an urban wage laborer, returned to the village and devoted his resources and sweat to planting manioc fields. Jamaira, who was married to a small proprietor, turned cash into household goods through the intermediation of the mascate truck traders. Nelson, a professional health agent, exchanged his earnings for livestock that he gave to his children. In other words, the peasant's asset chain successfully digested the value brought in by a wage laborer, a small proprietor, and a professional.

But the digestion was hardly autonomic. In order to assimilate value and render it stable, villagers engaged in specific practices for managing fields and furniture, cows and chickens. These practices made each asset less fungible and tied it more closely to the personhood of its owner. The examples thus reveal something of the ambivalence of the asset. An asset is a commodity, but because the owner envisions holding onto the asset over time, it loses something of its commodity quality and edges toward inalienability.

CHILD OWNERS: NELSON'S GIFTS OF CATTLE

Nelson, the region's community health agent, had graduated from professional training and received a (very modest) professional salary each month. But Nelson also described himself as a peasant farmer. On his daughter Tara's third birthday, he gave her a cow. Through this gift he converted his professional income into the kind of wealth that fit onto the farmer's asset chain.

Tara and her sister owned more than just one cow, in fact. And they were not the only child owners of livestock. Maracujá and Rio Branco both had a swarm of barnyard animals, from ducks to donkeys, and many of these animals belonged to children. Typically, a child became an animal owner when an adult relative or a family friend gave the animal as a gift.

One might wonder what it meant for Nelson's daughters to *own* cattle. At age three, Tara could not take care of her cow. She could not decide by herself to sell it or eat it. Perhaps, I thought, Tara's ownership meant that no one else could sell her cow, either, that it had to stay in her hands until adulthood. Nelson was lecturing me soberly on the importance of this privilege when his wife Martina put on a sly look and muttered under her breath, "You yourself have already sold animals like that."

"Me?" Nelson exclaimed. "No way!"

But the truth was out, and a few minutes later, Nelson admitted it.

To sell a child's animal, however, did not necessarily mean to do away with the child's property. What made child ownership so powerful was that, in some circumstances, it persisted even *after* the animal in question had died. If an adult farmer peddled or consumed an animal belonging to a child, that farmer was obligated to "put another one in its place," to buy a replacement animal for the child.

Thus, child ownership of livestock was not simply about possession of one particular animal. Rather, it meant that a child had title to a share of livestock, in an enduring sense. The family needed to set aside not just this one cow for the child, but rather a whole chain of *future* cows, each replacing the last. Child ownership was the warrant that a certain stock of wealth would stay in the child's hands, hence in the family's hands, over the long run.

EARMARKING: CARLOS'S MANIOC FIELD

Many of the fields at Maracujá and Rio Branco had ephemeral lives. They were planted in a fortunate rain and lasted only until the sun squeezed the last water out of the topsoil a few months later.

Other fields, though, were built to last.[17] Carlos had recently returned from construction work in São Paulo, and he was trying hard to gather money so that he could bring his son back from the megalopolis. Carlos could already point to his green ocean of sharp-leaved manioc, planted several months earlier. The manioc would take a year or more to mature. He planned to make the wealth of that field last far longer than that, by means of an accounting practice known as *earmarking*: separate money set aside for special objects (Zelizer 1994).

It was Carlos's neighbor Rodrigo, standing in his own field, who explained to me how earmarking worked. Rodrigo and his family could eat the product of their field without thinking twice. But when they earned *cash* from that field, they took care to earmark every dollar and return it to the field itself. Money from the field could only be reinvested in the field, not spent on clothes, school notebooks, or furniture. The family purchased those other items with their earnings from day labor.

Through earmarking, Rodrigo broke the fundamental assumption that money is fungible—that any one dollar is the same as any other dollar. To Rodrigo, a dollar from the field simply was *not* the same as a dollar earned at wage labor. A dollar from wage labor was for clothes, shoes, or any other purpose. A dollar from the field was for the field.

Rodrigo was hardly the only villager to think this way. One day I asked Carlos if all money was the same. He offered a beautifully ambivalent answer.

"For me, it's all equal," he proclaimed. "Except—" Carlos paused. "I say it's all equal, but it's not."

"I drink beer," Carlos continued. "On weekends I'll have a beer."

"Mm-hm," I mumbled confusedly.

"But the—I, I drink out of the money from my day wages. If I work somewhere, then I'll go over, I'll have a beer, and I'll pay and everything."

Carlos drew the conclusion with emphasis. "I, I don't, don't, don't, don't put money from my own field into bar stuff. No way."

Carlos's will was tested on a Sunday, when he returned from selling his homemade manioc flour at the fair. "It's like, 'Ah! Hey, Mr. Carlos is coming! Come on, let's have some beer!' I said, 'Hey.' I said, 'Money from my field isn't going into a bar. No way, my son.' [. . .] Money from my field doesn't go into a bar. No way. Money from my field is for my business."

Carlos felt so strongly about this issue that he sometimes went into debt at the bar even when he had plenty of money in his pocket. If the money came from his own field, then he preferred to borrow from the bar owner rather than paying cash for his beer.

Earmarking was, in this sense, a mechanism for making sure that the field became a self-sustaining entity. It was a method for integrating wealth into the peasant asset chain. To put things another way, earmarking was a tool that helped Rodrigo and Carlos to turn the value that they earned from their wages into something more permanent and lasting.

MASCATES: JAMAIRA'S HOUSEHOLD ASSETS

On certain days, while the roosters sang, word would spread through the villages that one of the roving truck traders, or mascates, had arrived for a visit. One such day I sat relaxing in Seu Jacques and Dona Lúcia's living room, a dry blue sky visible through the windows behind us, with their neighbor Jamaira on the worn couch beside me. Then Jamaira's fourteen-year old daughter Karina burst through the door.

"The money for the mascate is *where*?" Karina demanded breathlessly. A mascate was at Jamaira's house, and he was pressing for the credit payment that the family owed on some household item they had purchased from him.

"Under the bed!" Jamaira shouted back. Karina and her mother had a brief yelling match. Karina worried that she would not find the money. Jamaira explained that it was next to her government ID card. Karina added that this guy was that uptight little mascate (*nervosinho*), the kind who might hit you. Jamaira did not budge from her seat, and I got the impression that she might be visiting her neighbors' living room that day precisely for the purpose of avoiding debt collection. Finally, Karina, resigned to the fact that her mother was not coming along with her to talk to the mascate, went back to negotiate with him on her own. "He wants three hundred," Jamaira told us. He would get less than that.

Mascates crisscrossed the Brazilian drylands in impossibly battered and dusty trucks filled with pots and tables, jewelry and ceramic water filters. These traders sold on credit, delivering the item when they received the first payment, but this was not the kind of credit available in the city. Mascates almost never checked a person's legal credit history or, for that matter, asked for any documents at all. Instead, they relied on reputation and personal networks, building up links of trust in a small cluster of villages, counting on the likelihood that, in the rural context, people would not disappear without leaving behind at least some kind of family connection. A mascate came to one's door every month. People knew that mascates did not charge interest and that one could renegotiate a credit payment over and over again, giving something less than the agreed amount, asking for forbearance in times of illness or unemployment. People also knew that, for this reason, mascates vastly inflated their prices, charging, as one mascate estimated for me, about double the urban value of an item.

Jamaira's husband worked as a small proprietor, a merchant who wandered to Paraguay to convey goods across the border. When Jamaira made a credit arrangement with a mascate, she was separating a part of the household income from these itinerant pursuits and securing it in the village. As soon as she made the first payment, the mascate brought the new sofa or chair or water filter directly to her door. The persisting presence of the item reminded everyone, each month, that a stream of disposable cash would need to be redirected to paying for that lasting asset. As she solidified her rural household, Jamaira was taking her husband's flow of small proprietor money and converting it into a place on the peasant's asset chain.

Installment payments existed as a woman's realm. By setting aside a careful bit of cash each month, a woman could transform unstable money into a more durable form of wealth—a mattress, maybe, for the new child in the family, or a stove with four gas burners to supplement the firewood hearth in the yard. People dreamed of these acquisitions and planned them out in advance, in sequences that stretched years into the future. Martina recounted for me her purchases over a decade. In that time she managed to buy a television, a blender, a gas stove, and a sofa.

No less than agricultural assets, these objects conveyed autonomy from the labor market. They allowed the members of the household to stay in the countryside and enjoy a respectable life. They served as guarantees against the alternative that many villagers have known: wandering from plantation to plantation in search of a plantation owner who had houses where his employees could live. Tables, beds, and stoves were resources that promised a margin of freedom from the need to work for a wage. They were a tool for making money into permanence.

Conclusion

Josepe, back from his construction job at age nineteen, was having trouble converting his city cash into a lasting rural asset. It turned out that money could not simply purchase a place on the asset chain. Hence—I believe—the washed blue jeans, the destroyed letter, and the tranquil smile.

Why did Josepe let the letter slip through his fingers? How can we account for the *unimportance* of money? Class, as a theoretical concept in the social sciences, is designed precisely to answer this sort of question. The class concept shines a light on the stickiness of social hierarchy; class explains (some of) those situations where more money does not necessarily translate into higher rank.

In the moment when a migrant shifts from one class position to another, the migrant's wealth becomes unmoored, desocialized. It takes on the form of an awkward bulge of cash, a bulky cargo of appliances to be carried home from São Paulo. Migrants then resocialize this wealth. They mold its plasticity into a particular form. They reconnect with an asset chain—that is, with a sensibility about what matters more than money.

This sensibility derives from the labor process. Class, I have argued, is a relation to labor. If Rodrigo, Jamaira, and Nelson turn their wealth into slow-cycle assets, this is because they have come to live as peasant farmers, devoted to stretching time into longer and longer units. Assets look different to professionals, who are project timers, and different again to the self-improving wage laborers and to small proprietors, the time aggregators. An asset chain, I have argued, is a disposition involving time and objects. Out of these relations to abstract labor—these particular habits of using homogeneous time to produce homogeneous objects—social class emerges. It does so, as Adam Sargent has brilliantly noted, in the form of an *ideology* of labor, that is, a conception of what "labor" means and how it changes the laborer (2020, 2021). Indeed, each asset chain is the repository of its own ideology of labor.

Class is a relation to labor that includes the grounds of opposition to labor. As a classed person, Josepe or Carlos or Tamara exists as something more specific than a simple unit of timed work: each one exists as a person with a definite set of aspirations and plans, morals and habitus, willingnesses and unwillingnesses to toil. In the asset chain, these dispositions acquire shape. Class is the mode of belonging that people build so that they are not simply laborers, but rather laborers of a certain kind. Class exists as a negotiation with the category of labor rather than a capitulation to it. A classed person works with a specific kind of time, not abstract time in general. A classed person generates assets of a given sort, not any marketable asset. And so a classed person's time is never fully fungible with money; it trades only under certain terms, in exchange for certain rewards. In this sense, class is a bargain with exploitation. Your class provides you with the conditions under which you accept the command of a boss—or, beyond any boss, the command of the world market—and the conditions under which you refuse. At Maracujá and Rio Branco, two communities built by people who have left labor behind repeatedly over the past two centuries, those conditions are very limited, very particular, very exacting.

Class membership means laboring only under specific circumstances and holding on to characteristic forms of insulation against the vagaries of labor. Here we can find a reason why people say that money is not worth paying attention to, and why Josepe has trouble turning his cash into countryside wealth. People create a class precisely as a stormwall against the abstractions of the labor market; thus, class membership is not available for purchase through the abstraction of the universal equivalent, money. Maracujá and Rio Branco are places where the stormwall has been built especially high. If a migrant has trouble acquiring a respected herd of cattle, the reverse becomes true as well: once that migrant gains cows, the market will have trouble taking them away.

Economic growth is often described, and politically justified, as a singular tide lifting all boats. It looks like a rising number. But growth only looks that way if you are a consummate migrant, infinitely malleable and able to move to any labor opportunity, counting your wealth as a sum of awkward cash. Seen from the perspective of any person who has settled into a class position, economic growth is perceived not in money terms, but as a step forward along one's own asset chain. More than that: growth is a delicate compromise in which my advancement, along the asset chain I know, has become linked to the progress of other people, from other class positions, along other asset chains. My new certificates in my plastic folder have come to mean that someone else can hold on to more enduring wealth in the form of new cows, which means that someone else can put out more chairs in front of their bar. Growth thus is a matter of connections and inclusions, always a translation between different people's meaningful systems, always susceptible to the suspicion that someone has been left out. Growth arrives as a bond between my asset chain and another person's dissimilar principle for reckoning their own position. In these terms—never as a matter of money alone—growth persuades.

*

The last time I heard about Josepe was when Martinho became enraged by the thought of him. Thin and wiry, Martinho always greeted me with bright eyes and a smile, but others had told me that he had a rough temper, and now he was unleashing it. Josepe, he accused, had stolen his chickens.

His anger made no sense, at first blush. Chicken theft happened commonly, and Maracujá's residents seemed to regard it as an unfortunate but humorous tendency of young men. Zé, for example, was reputed to be in the habit of stealing a chicken and then telling its owner, the next day, that the meat had tasted delicious.

But Martinho explained a difference. His stolen chickens were *galos de raça*, purebred poultry, an especially gorgeous variety that might be sent to cockfights or sold for a good price. On the peasant asset chain, they mattered.

Martinho's accusation was a jolt that I never knew how to interpret. Did Josepe, a farming novice, simply not understand the distinction between a regular and a purebred chicken? Had he stolen Martinho's livestock as a joke, failing to spot the crucially different nature of those particular birds?

Or did Josepe know that difference all too well? Perhaps he had grown tired of his setbacks as he tried to climb the slow and painstaking asset chain that led toward enduring rural wealth. In an environment where his cash and his work experience counted for little, maybe he saw an opportunity to get something that mattered to farmers, something beautiful and important, and maybe he took it.

Or maybe Josepe did none of that. The accusation could have been false. Young and socially isolated, Josepe lacked the support, relationships, and resources that might have shielded him. He was easy to blame.

Josepe struggled to find a place for himself in the system that made for meaningful rural wealth. Did he want to fit into this system? What was his next step? These were questions I did not get to ask him. Right after the accusation, I was told, Josepe moved out of the region. He returned to city living.

6

The Things You Hold

Against Saving

In the city, Suso stayed up much later than he ever had in the village. It was around midnight, the sky as thick as the black coffee he loved, and Suso seemed not to notice the time as he chatted and chatted in the darkened doorway. Around him stretched hundreds of other doorways, all thin metal on scratchy new plaster, in this neighborhood that the federal government had barely finished building on top of the brown scrub brush at the edge of the city of Vitória da Conquista.

Suso had just moved in. In fact, everyone there had just moved in. It was 2013, the crest of Brazil's economic wave. Recently, much had changed in Suso's life: he had turned eighteen, he had moved back to the city after his brush with the law,[1] he had found work cleaning and repairing buses. And he had found God, in a new way. Suso's neighborhood was dotted with tiny evangelical churches, which had just moved in as well, and Suso's church friends were helping him to build up a little wardrobe of formal clothing (*roupa social*), the kind that evangelicals should wear. In the darkened doorway, Suso was talking with the neighbor's son and showing off a recent acquisition: a beautiful suit jacket. Suso's kid brother observed while the neighbor's son clownishly tried on the coat. It was too big for him. Suso plunged his finger into the depths of the fabric and pointed out the pockets sewn into the inside lining. *See?* he proclaimed with a joking smile. *If you want to rob a rich person, that's where he keeps his money.*

That's where he keeps his money. Suso's words took me back to Maracujá, the village he had recently left, with its rows of bitter manioc and jagged pineapples. I was reminded of my fumbling attempt to conduct a household survey there.

As soon as I started the survey in the village, I ran into a practical problem. I wanted to ask people how much money they were saving and what they were saving it for. How should I translate the English word "save"?

At first, I tried a dictionary option, "poupar dinheiro," but my interviewees responded with blank stares. So I shifted to "economizar dinheiro." My interviewees usually recognized this term, but they seemed to use it to refer to finding a less expensive option—as in *saving* money by shopping at a discount grocery store or *saving* gas by riding a motorcycle instead of a car.

Finally, I was introduced to the phrase "guardar dinheiro"—literally, "to store money." That seemed to fit my purpose. But now a new problem appeared. Almost all of my interviewees told me that they were not saving anything at all. Many of them had savings accounts in the city, or at least they had relatives who had savings accounts. But the interviewees spoke emphatically: they were not saving.[2]

This chapter is concerned with saving and, especially, with not saving. I will try to revive some of the strangeness of "saving." And I will argue that what many of us call "saving" is really a very specific, very monetized, very limited manifestation of a much more common human gesture, the gesture of withholding an object from circulation. When people save, what are they doing? Perhaps saving is not, in the first instance, about retaining value or transferring consumption to the future. Perhaps the act of saving, in the first instance, is the act of refusing to exchange.

So why did people in the villages tell me that they did not save? That question became a little stranger when I considered the results of that household survey I conducted. One of the striking conclusions from the data was how many durable assets were owned by households, compared to their incomes. On average, I calculated, a household at Maracujá was holding more than two years' worth of its income in reserve, in the form of livestock and domestic goods: couches and stoves, cows and chickens. A household at Rio Branco, on average, was holding a little more than one and a half years' worth of its income in reserve. Why were people telling me that they saved nothing?

Saving, it turns out, is hardly the only way to hold on to an object. In this chapter, I will highlight certain objects that migrants do strive to retain. These are objects that promise to allow a person to live without performing the type of labor they have previously known—objects like rural houses, cattle herds, and special tools—and I refer to these objects as *premios*. A rural house, for example, gives a domestic worker the freedom to quit their live-in job in the city. A herd of cattle transforms a day laborer into an independent rancher. A special tool, such as a passenger van, gives a wage worker the power to hold the means of production and become a small propri-

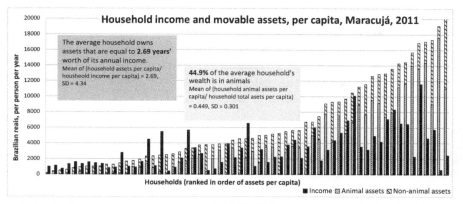

Each pair of columns corresponds to one household. The black column represents that household's per capita income for 2011. The adjoining column represents that household's assets, with the dotted portion of the column representing animal assets and the hatch-marked portion of the column representing other assets (all per capita). Graphs reprinted from Morton (2019b). Data from survey conducted by author; see Morton (2015a: appendix) for method.

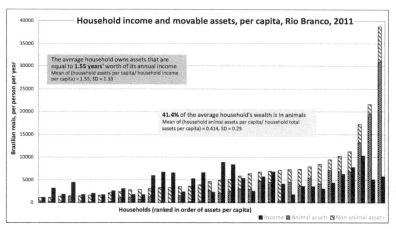

Each pair of columns corresponds to one household. The black column represents that household's per capita income for 2011. The adjoining column represents that household's assets, with the dotted portion of the column representing animal assets and the hatch-marked portion of the column representing other assets (all per capita). Graphs reprinted from Morton (2019b). Data from survey conducted by author; see Morton (2015a: appendix) for method.

etor. Premios serve as the end point of an asset chain, the anchor holding it in place.

Premios stand at the end of an asset chain because premios should, by their nature, endure. The widespread dream is that a premio, when well maintained, will stay in one's hands forever. The herd of cattle will become self-reproducing. The passenger van will make enough money to pay for its replacement. In other words, a premio is made out of value that a migrant has extracted from the market and rendered inalienable.[3] Each premio, as it turns out, encodes a recipe for undoing the abstraction of labor. This act of undoing is not an act of saving. Indeed, at the right moments, it becomes a critique of saving.

Reasons Not to Save: The Limits of the English Word "Save"

As I spent time talking and listening to small farmers, I realized that *not saving* is not a casual matter. People give each other advice about not saving. According to this advice, saving money is an unwise strategy, a risky strategy. One day on the bus, I overheard Marília tell her friend, "Money isn't good for saving. [. . .] If you save it, the thief takes it." On a different occasion, Patrício offered a similar maxim. He said, "Money in the hole won't yield anything." O'Dougherty, in her study of São Paulo's inflationary days, heard such a message from one of her interlocutors: "In Brazil, to save money is not an advantage" (2002: 36). Millar, in her ethnography of Rio, asked a bar owner how she and her husband had managed to save enough money to build the bar, and the response was a laugh. "Ha! We never saved a single cent" (2018: 108).

Saving was not only unwise. People frequently described saving as something far worse. It was a rude gesture, even an antisocial one. Declining to save was a virtue. Stefania, for example, told me about her husband. His relatives constantly asked him for loans, and because of this he had difficulty putting money in the bank. Stefania explained, "He was always, like, a good person, like that." Then she concluded with a tone of deep respect in her voice: "Since I've known him, he doesn't, he hasn't had anything, you know, anything in his hands."

I found it difficult to understand how saving could be considered a vice and how Stefania could fall in love with her husband's tendency to leave no money left over, *nothing in his hands*. But it all became a bit clearer to me when I talked to Suso, with his good job in the city, his new suit jacket, and his urban co-workers. He spoke to me about saving, and I could hear his anguish and passion as he spoke.

"My co-workers give me a bunch of horrible advice," Suso began. "Saying, ah, that I can't get married, that I can't stay with my mom, that I have to have my own things, that I'm working, that I'm a single guy, that I have to save money.

"I was about to let my mind get affected by that stuff. But the reality that I live in—and that I *have* lived in—is different. You know what I mean? I can't let my family perish. I can't let my family lack anything, if I have financial resources. What good would it be for me—for me to have my drawer right here, for example, full of money—and know that at home they're in need of something?"

"Mm-hm," I murmured, very struck by his words. "Mm-hm."

"What kind of pride would I have? What good would that be?" Suso was sounding more agitated.

"Mm-hm."

"What goo—What kind of man would I be like that? That's not something that a human being does, a man *[literally, "that's not the work of a human being, a man"]*. You understand?" Suso drew a conclusion. "There's no point in me saving money and spending money."

As I mulled over Suso's image of a drawer full of money, I recalled a seminal argument by Gudeman and Rivera. They point out that it was two eighteenth-century European economists, Adam Smith and Baron Turgot, who created the contemporary economic notion of "saving." To make the "saving" notion, Smith and Turgot mixed two quite distinct concepts: on the one hand, the parsimonious use of household resources and, on the other hand, the stockpiling of money (1990: 176–78).

I came to realize that something was at stake in my difficulty in translating the survey question. The English term "to save," in my own social world, was combining a number of disparate meanings. As I naïvely spoke the word "save," I was pointing, first of all, to the habit of storing money in a bank account. But "save" in English also has other meanings. It can refer to the practice of holding on to objects, as when a farmer at Maracujá or Rio Branco *saved* part of their corn harvest by keeping it sealed up in plastic soda bottles. "To save" can also mean to find a cheaper way to do something—for example, *saving* time by inventing a better technique for sewing. And the word's extension reaches even further. One can "save" a person by rescuing them from drowning, and God might "save" our souls.

In the English that I speak, these meanings easily become tangled up with each other. The act of storing money, in the English language that I speak, seems naturally to overlap with the act of reducing costs. It is as if putting away money naturally made things cheaper and more efficient.

Thus, the imagery of keeping strawberries in jars in the basement comes to sit in a cozy parallel with the imagery of depositing cash into an ATM; even more strangely, all of this joins up with the imagery of discovering a more efficient technique for sewing a pair of pants. Above all, each of these meanings gets bathed in the warm moral light of *lifesaving* and divine soteriology. This tangle of meanings even helps to explain the irresistible native appeal of the doctrine of austerity, a doctrine that insists, however illogically, that government belt-tightening will lead to efficiency and even national salvation.

My survey ran into trouble because, in the villages where I worked, these things did not overlap. Keeping money in the bank was not understood to be at all the same as retaining a soft drink bottle full of seeds. Neither one was similar to discovering a faster way to sew pants. Nor was any one of these acts necessarily virtuous. I was struggling to find the right word for *save* in my survey because I was struggling to appreciate the limit of my own concept. Thus, it was hard for me to hear the conclusion that, to Suso, seemed like a truism: "There's no point in me saving money."

But while there was no point in saving money, there certainly was a point in holding on to certain important objects. In the village, as we have already seen, Suso's neighbors avidly sought to plant fields full of long-term crops, such as fruit trees and coffee bushes. They bought cattle, and often they gave those cattle as gifts to their infant relatives. And they did all of this precisely because it was hard to uproot a fruit tree, and it was hard to sell a bull that belonged to an infant. As Zelizer (1994) or the Bohannans (1968) might point out, here, trees and cows are objects with limited fungibility. They are the sort of objects that can turn into premios. During my fieldwork, Aldo, a young man at the village, gave a cow as a gift to his baby son, just as Nelson had done with his daughter (see chapter 5). Aldo told me about the reason behind the gift. "Really," he mused, "we give it to him for—for that very reason, so that we won't sell it. So that it doesn't end, you know?"

Suso's neighbors had a word for this kind of act. To maintain a long-term asset was *segurar*—literally, "to hold on."[4] As we saw in chapter 5, farmers could hold on to earmarked fields, to cows and pigs, to houses and mattresses. But people insisted that *to hold on* to something was not the same as *to save*. One evening, I naïvely congratulated Lara for having saved her money by buying cattle. She interrupted me to correct my mistake:

L: Yes, and you know a lot of times we don't get to save, you know? [. . .] Sometimes we find a little thing, something like that, to buy. [. . .] We put the money toward that, you know?
D: Mm-hm.
L: Then—but, like, there's no way for us to be putting it in the bank, sometimes, you know?

For Lara, buying "a little thing" like a cow was not saving. Cows and money in the bank were simply not the same species of object.[5]

Here I might end this chapter and conclude that saving is a culturally limited concept, indeed a strange concept, one that mixes the notions of retention, efficiency, and salvation. Perhaps this concept, in rural Brazil, simply does not make sense. Perhaps we are at the interface of incompatible worlds, untranslatable signs. Saving does not belong, as Suso says, to "the reality that I live in." Or perhaps it does.

Buried Money and Its Danger

If rural Brazilians deny that they save money, perhaps this is not because they are unfamiliar with saving. Perhaps they are all too familiar. After all, many farmers in the villages, in their lifetimes, have seen Brazil's government implement eight successive currencies, each one replacing the last in an inflationary race. For people who live far from the nearest bank, these transitions can prove devastating. Nearly everyone knows someone whose saved money became worthless because of a currency change.

In northeastern Brazil, the practice of *not* saving has a long-term connection to the history of inequality. Even long before the inflations and the devaluations of the 1980s, some of the oldest stories in the villages are stories that contain what might be called a critique of saving. Here, I am referring to stories about buried money.

These stories build from a very common theme in the Catholic world, but in the villages, they have a special meaning and use. Some people in the villages tell of the time of the great landowners, a time that the tellers themselves still remember. In that time, many villagers toiled as sharecroppers or house servants or cowboys out on the vast, dry fields of the plantation or in the warmth of its wooden manor. They raised the manioc, the cattle, and the coffee that fed the world market.

Dona Zaida told me about that time, in her girlhood, she who was now a great-grandmother living on top of her own hill. She described the local plantation and the many plantations that stretched beyond it. "There were some guys who were rich for real. That's what is said. When they had a big sum of money, safe, if they'd sold some cattle, sold something like that, they would go along putting the money together. So as not to give it to the poor, they would take the money, fill up jars, and bury it."

The jars, made of heavy baked clay, held the money fast under the earth.

But Dona Zaida's neighbor Carlos explained that jars could not prevent the problem that a rich man feared.

"He would get to the point where he would die, and then that was it. Then because—the, the story is that—"

Carlos was a boisterous person, but at this moment, he grew hesitant and serious.

C: —because—the soul doesn't, doesn't, doesn't, doesn't have salvation.
D: Ah...
C: As long—as long as that money is not dug up.
D: Ah!
C: But I don't know how a thing like that could be. The only one who knows is God.

Carlos did know, however, what a suffering soul might be able to do.

C: A lot of them manage to come back and speak with someone.
D: Ah, I understand!
C: A lot of them manage—I don't know, the soul there manages to come back and offer it to someone.

Dona Zaida, who was talking to me on a separate occasion, told me about the same hope. "When he would show the money, where it was, and someone would go there and dig it up, it would be then that he would gain salvation."

Dona Zaida gave me details:[6]

DZ: The spirit would return to talk to—talk to any person who was around there so that the person would go dig up where he or she had buried the money.
D: Really!!?
DZ: They would ask, "Where is it buried?" And then the spirit would say. The spirit would say. The spirit would talk to whoever had courage. "I buried it in such and such a place, like this, like that. You go there so that I can show you where it is. Go at such-and-such time of the night." See! They would set a time. They didn't have watches, but they would say something like that. Maybe "Go—around—early morning." Or "Go at midnight." "At the hour when the rooster sings. You go out there, and I'll take you to where the money is."

Now the person who had courage would go. When the person would get there, they say that the person would go up to that—thing. [. . .] Like it was a person there, accompanying them. They would get there, "Well it's there, in such and such a place. Go there." *[inaudible]*[7] as the person dug in with the shovel, the person would land on top of the pot of money.

D: Hm!

DZ: Then the person would dig up the pot of money. That person would get rich.

Here, in the buried money stories, is saving. Here is saving with some of the same meanings that seem familiar from my English-language verb "to save." Here is the act of depositing money—money as a relationship between people that is frozen in time. But here, too, is holding on to an object, the pot buried in the ground like a parody of a seed planted. And here we can also find saving as salvation, as God's saving work.

But in the buried money stories, these three meanings are connected backward, it seems. The seed of savings does not sprout. Holding on to money offers you the *opposite* of salvation. It is as if the stories worked to undo the tangle of meanings around my own native verb "to save," to separate those meanings, and then to invert them.

I take the buried money stories as evidence that people in the villages, in fact, were not at all unfamiliar with the notion of saving that I carried inside my own native language. No neophyte proletarians, they came from five hundred years of experience with capital, with the fluctuations that had brought cycle after commodity cycle and that would, within a year, destroy the same prosperity that had built Suso's new neighborhood at the edge of the city. Their narratives, in Michael Taussig's sense (1980), made Marx's metaphor literal: capital really is dead labor. I read the buried money stories as an indication that my interlocutors were not misunderstanding my concept of saving. Instead, they were critiquing it, disagreeing with it, undermining its very bases. They were questioning whether saving meant salvation.

The Premio: Holding without Saving

Dona Zaida and Carlos remained alert to the dangers of hoarding cash. Beyond cash, they seemed to have other some methods for holding on to things of importance. Dona Zaida, the child of a sharecropping family, spent part of her old-age pension building a house for herself on top of a steep hillside. Carlos returned from his construction jobs in São Paulo and sweated to plant the roots of manioc, a slow-growing crop that might eventually become the centerpiece of his lasting green field.

What made the difference between a money hoard, on the one hand, and a house or a farmer's durable field, on the other? These other stores of wealth were what I dub "premios": they congealed value into a form that promised to allow a worker to exit the type of labor they had known.

A premio is an object that enables a realistic fantasy about how you might leave behind the conditions under which you work. For some moradores and farm laborers, that fantasy involves a piece of land with a house solidly fixed on it. For freeholding peasant farmers, the key wish might be herd of cattle, a herd so large that it secures the household's sustenance. Urban wage workers, for their part, may imagine themselves owning the means to open a hair salon, a grocery store, or a bar.[8] In all these cases, a premio amounts to something more than one more step along the asset chain that structures the worker's everyday aspirations. A premio is something more than a better pig or an electric showerhead, an extra résumé line or a new motorcycle, or even an earmarked field. A premio serves as a final point to that asset chain, providing a vision of how you might finish the chain and move on to an altogether different set of plans.

A premio is the dream of leaving labor, and it is that dream made concrete. Premios do not necessarily offer you the chance to avoid abstract labor altogether (much less to give up on human exertion in general). With a premio in hand, you may still work, but you will cease the kind of labor you know best. Each premio thus serves as a detailed, targeted rejoinder to the unfairness of a specific labor relation. We can understand premios to be critiques of labor as that labor takes on a definite form. In this way, a premio differs from a money hoard: the hoard gains its power because it could be used to buy anything, and thus it remains abstract, representing value in general, while the premio has power because it incarnates one stratagem for rejecting the particular labor that surrounds you, and thus the premio undoes abstraction.

Premios tend toward inalienability. When you gain a premio, you remove that object from the circulation of value and aim to preserve it for good. In this chapter, I address two types of premio, *the rural house* and *the tool*.

First, the rural house appears as an especially compelling premio for sharecroppers and other landless workers. This sort of house becomes inalienable because, sturdily built to last through the years, it has the feeling of permanence.

Second, the tool serves as a premio in those cases where migrants acquire equipment that allows them to live out their dream of becoming a store owner, a cook, a musician, or another specialist small proprietor. When incarnated as a tool, the premio becomes inalienable because of its connection to the personhood of the worker. This tool manifests some internal, lasting quality of the worker as a person; it helps the worker demonstrate that they are, on the inside, an excellent chef, a talented musician, or the bearer of some other talent that turns into an enduring feature of their personality.

Permanence and *personhood* serve as two rebuttals to the abstraction of labor. The house, as a repository of permanence, rebuts the first sort of alienation that the young Marx described: alienation from the product of labor, alienation as a tidal force washing all commodities away from the person who made them (Marx 1994: 66). The house undoes alienation because the house endures.

The tool, when understood as a marker of the worker's personhood, rebuts Marx's second sort of alienation: alienation from the process of production, which leaves the worker feeling distant from the activity of their own laboring. The tool undoes alienation because the tool reflects and transforms its wielder (Sargent 2020). The hammer, as Jackson Browne sang, shapes the hand.[9]

In these two premios, the house and the tool, the worker renders the object inalienable, at least in a small sense. But how?

The Rural House as a Premio: Inalienable Permanence

I heard a tale, Seu Catulo told me, brightening his words with the genial humor that befitted his role as head of Rio Branco's Protestant church. He gave me a title for the tale: "The Boss and the House Servant."

"The servant took care of every last bit of the work around the house, and when she finished every last bit of it, she went to serve God," Seu Catulo said. Meanwhile, the servant's boss had a vision of the world beyond this life. "The boss saw some very beautiful houses [*casas bem boas*] and some lesser ones [*inferiores*]."

The boss asked, "This house right here is whose?" She heard a response: "That is so-and-so's." Then, as she gazed upon an especially wonderful dwelling, she heard more. "This house right here is your house servant's. And that lousy one right there is yours [*é de você*]."

"Why?" the boss asked. "I have money."

"Your servant sent plenty of good material to build a good house. And the material that you sent was only enough to build this house."

Seu Catulo concluded by asking me to tell people that this story is about preparing for eternal life, sending material by acting rightly on earth. As I listened, I heard, too, about the house servant who finally got a house.

Just a few steps from Seu Catulo's cool white living room, where he regaled me with the tale, stood the home that Tamara had purchased at Rio Branco while she toiled as a nanny a thousand miles away in Higienópolis, São Paulo, when she was a teenager running away from a marriage proposal (see pp. 3–5). Why did you buy the house? I asked her. "To employ the money in something!" she exclaimed, using the same verb, *empregar*, that described her boss's relationship to her.[10] Her boss employed her, and she employed her money. And then she quit her job, left São Paulo, and moved back to Rio Branco, where she raised her own four children in her own new home.

For migrants like Tamara, a house is a premio, an asset that allows you to leave behind the kind of labor you have known. When migrants worked as domestic laborers, as Tamara did, the job had an inextricable link to their living situation: domestic workers often resided in the house where they worked, especially if they had just arrived in the city. Construction workers followed a similar pattern. Sérgio remembered sleeping in an elevator shaft on the work site when he came to São Paulo, and Diego, in the metropolis in search of his synthesizer keyboard, resided along with the rest of the construction firm's crew in a wooden hut with an inadequate kitchen, eating rice so gelatinous that it took on the shape of the pot. These workers had to accept specific jobs in order to have a place to lay their heads at night. The more they could create their own houses for themselves, the more freedom they had to leave behind the labor they performed.

This problem reached its peak among moradores. *Morador* means "inhabitant," and moradores were sharecroppers who resided in houses lent to them by the owner of the plantation where they toiled (see chapter 1, note 8). If you were a morador, gaining your own permanent house could quite literally allow you to leave labor.

Moradores might hope to obtain such a house through a practice known as "paying the times" (*pagar os tempos*). Dona Dorotea lived as a morador on a plantation near the villages, and she explained the practice to me bluntly: "It's a right of ours." Then she specified, "The right to a house." Dona Dorotea, her husband, and her children had spent sixteen years on the land of the plantation owner, and when her husband retired, the owner would have to buy the family a house in a local town or city of their choosing.

On a different occasion, Mathias explained the practice to me in more detail. "Sometimes, a guy had worked ten years on a plantation, fifteen years. So when he would leave, the boss would go and buy a house to give him to live in. So the guy didn't end up in the street."

Such a house was understood as a payment for the morador's total time on the plantation—and, specifically, as an alternative to cash. If the plantation owner didn't buy a house, Dona Dorotea specified, "he has to give the times that [the worker] stayed." Dona Dorotea added, "In money." "When someone is leaving a plantation," Seu Jacinto noted to me, "other people go up right away and ask, 'Have you gotten your times yet?'"

"This is now a matter of law," Seu Jacinto stipulated. "That thing comes from—from a president." But what did "the times" mean? As a number of villagers were ready to explain to me, "the times" served as a cover term that referred to the labor rights that the Brazilian state, over the course of the twentieth century, had bit by bit extended to rural workers. These rights included holiday pay, unemployment insurance, and the "thirteenth salary," an extra month's wages to be received at Christmas. Plantation owners tended not to provide these benefits when they were actually due. This omission meant that a departing morador could take the plantation owner to court [*botar na justiça*]. To avoid the court process, a plantation owner might instead make an informal arrangement to purchase a house for a morador, with both sides agreeing to let the house stand in for the many benefits ("the times") left unpaid over the years.

The times were more than a legal obligation. In Seu Jacinto's view, the times were a reward for "the responsibility that the person had for that time." He elaborated: "When the end arrives—of all of that firmness that I stayed [*essa firmeza que eu fiquei*], ah, on your plantation—well, then you pay me something else that's different. Some other money different from that which I already earned." Seu Jacinto, here, echoed Mauss's famous argument for social democracy: laborers give a gift of themselves when they work, and this gift is never fully repayable in regular cash (1967: 65). It requires "something else that's different," a money different from normal money.

Domestic workers like Tamara and moradores like Dona Dorotea had an especially strong reason for building a house, since they actually lived at their jobs. But migrants in general felt the same imperative. Seu Catulo's tale had portrayed the servant realistically: urban workers really did send construction material to the countryside to stockpile bit by bit. The villages were full of piles of bricks and stacks of roofing tile.

During the recession that began in 2014, while economic activity slowed down in the cities, migrants accelerated their homebuilding projects. Urban workers were returning to the countryside, where they could live cheaply. Even the existing villagers, perhaps newly skeptical about the urban alternative, seemed to be entrenching themselves. By 2016, the main dirt road into Rio Branco was crowded with Luca's new tidy bungalow and the unfinished sprawl of brick walls where Gerardo, a São Paulo truck driver, was now living with his family; all these people had recently moved back to the village. Even Félix, one of Maracujá's earliest residents, had gotten in on the expansion. In 2016, I found his living room covered in dust. He explained that it was simply impossible to keep things clean until he managed to pour concrete onto the dirt floor in the sizable room that he had just added to the back of his house.

When migrants like Tamara or Gerardo decided to build a house, they had a major decision to make: should they build in the city or the countryside? Many migrants selected the urban option. Patrício and Valentina, having fallen in love through the cellphone sent in the package (see pp. 46–50), ultimately constructed a house along the rural-urban edge (Harms 2011), mobilizing for this purpose a complex mix of store credit, bank loans, and remittance cash. Other migrants took the same route as Suso, the young convert with the new suit coat. They moved into government-built city housing from the Minha Casa, Minha Vida program and improved their dwellings slowly over time.

What was the difference between a city house and a country house? When I asked migrants this question, I heard a single word over and over: *value*. In the countryside, "a house doesn't gain value," Nelson explained to me. "In the city, it evolves." On another occasion, Melchior told me that urban housing can "pick up value [*pegar valor*]." Patrício spoke even more assertively than Nelson and Melchior. A house in the countryside, Patrício said, had no value at all.

What did it mean to say that a countryside house had no value? Rural homes existed at a distance from the market's valuation. This distance already appeared in the building process itself. Certain construction materials might be brought from the city, but you could make your own mud bricks instead of buying them, and someone might let you cut down free wood for the roof beams. And once the construction was complete, houses in the villages did not circulate like their urban counterparts. It was rare to buy a rural house; usually, a person in need of a dwelling would simply build a new one. On the occasions when people did sell a countryside house, they had difficulty settling on a price, since there existed no robust market. Nelson told me that villagers sometimes set the price by counting up the cost of the construction materials that had been used to build the house, as if the house were nothing more than a pile of cement and roof tiles.

People did not build homes in the village with an eye toward selling them ever again. The reason to build, as Patrício put it, was if "you want to get comfortable, calm down." In this sense, a rural house was very precisely a premio. Such a house came at the end of a cycle of abstract labor, as it did for Tamara, who left behind her nanny job, and as Dona Dorotea hoped that it would for her family, once they had finished their years on the plantation. Like the servant in Seu Catulo's parable, the house's occupant had arrived at a final place. A rural house did not promise you that you would never labor again. But it did serve as a demonstration that you had reached the end point of an asset chain, a chain of objects leading you through (and ultimately out of) a specific labor relation. You had achieved the kind of stability that would prevent you from needing to submit to a construction boss or a plantation owner simply in order to have a spot to sleep for the night. The house's own solid shape served as a riposte to the perpetual transience of migratory work, a transience built into that work as one feature of a worker's subjection to the supervisor. Thus, a rural house gave you the space to reject certain kinds of laboring—and to imagine new ways to labor.

Tania Li, writing from Indonesia (2014: 121), and Julie Chu, in China (2010: chap. 6), both describe seeing a striking sight in villages that are undergoing migration-led economic growth. The villages are crowded with elegant, brand-new houses that are sitting vacant. Maracujá and Rio Branco, of course, are not different, except that, especially in the wake of Brazil's 2014–16 recession, those homes were increasingly filling up. What do vacant houses have to teach us about growth? Often, growth is envisioned as a perpetual process of expansion, an arrow always pointing forward. Yet the very people at the heart of the growth process—people like Tamara and Carlos—may, themselves, be toiling precisely for the purpose of leaving growth behind. They may be building something back in the village. Growth itself can be driven by an aspiration for something very different: permanence. An understanding of growth that misses the wish for permanence is, in the end, as hollow as an empty house.

"I bought construction material," Dona Cássia told me, remembering the origin of her house. "And I made a future."[11] A future, not *the* future. A house was a way to make the future specific. In the villages, a house contained value taken out of circulation, yet houses were not a form of saving. Unlike buried cash, that house could not be imagined as an object to spend again. It could not transform into anything else in the world. Firmly planted, a village house removed human effort from the realm of homogeneity. It represented that effort in the shape of a particular aspiration, a space made vivid and nonnegotiable, certain walls to enclose one's daily steps, windows facing a given direction, a specific vision about how a person should live.

The Tool as Premio: Inalienable Personhood

On one of his last days in São Paulo, Diego went into the restroom of an electronics store. Out of his underwear he pulled the first reddish bill, R$50, a spotted jaguar's steely gaze printed on the back. Then more and more. "I counted," Diego remembered, "eighty jaguars!"

Diego had spent hours negotiating with a clerk over the price of a synthesizer keyboard. This synthesizer was the meaning of his months spent toiling on a city construction site; it was the object he had dreamed of since childhood, when his parents heard him singing to himself while he worked in the village fields. Now, inside the bathroom, he was R$800 (US$400) short of the asking price for the instrument.

When he summed up for me his time in São Paulo, Diego highlighted that synthesizer, "the tool that I went in search of." Diego's synthesizer provides an example of a particular type of premio: *the tool*. A tool, when it is a premio, holds out the hope of transforming the worker's relationship to labor altogether. The tool promises not an incremental improvement, but a wholesale leap that enables the worker to leave behind wage labor and become, in one sense or another, a small proprietor.

At Maracujá and Rio Branco, tools appeared in various guises. Rodrigo returned from the plantation coffee harvest with a chainsaw that could make him into the region's woodcutter. Carlinhos gathered up cash and made a partnership with his father to purchase a battered Volkswagen van so he could get contracts to shuttle students to the rural schools. Aninha and Orestes left the villages to work in São Paulo; they aimed to raise enough money to buy food service equipment for the lunch counter they had opened in an abandoned house in Maracujá.

Here, I focus specifically on the synthesizer as it appears in the stories told by Diego and Melchior. A close look at these stories can demonstrate how the tool-as-premio is imagined as the end point of an asset chain. The migrant acquires the tool through the careful accumulation of value, planned over time. The tool safeguards the migrant's position outside wage labor. Thus, the tool resembles a buried coin stash. But unlike the buried coins, the tool is not an instrument of saving. The tool reflects something internal to the individual who wields it, something deeply personal, something not subject to the judgment of others. The tool becomes inalienable thanks to its connection with the personhood of its user.

Diego and Melchior are musicians. And in a very practical sense, the synthesizers function as their work tools. To understand this type of work, a brief detour into musicology is apt.

Forty or fifty years ago, when the older villagers were young people, a joyful party involved "dragging your sandals" [*arrasta chinela*] and "raising dust" [*levantar poeira*] by dancing all night long to the music of a band composed of three people: an accordionist, a triangle player, and a drummer or tambourine player [*pandeirista*]. Over the past two decades, the synthesizer, as a musical instrument, has allowed for a reconfiguration of the same structural logic. The new bands comprised one synthesizer player and one singer. As in the old days, these new music groups were small, transportable, and oriented toward rhythm—a rhythm now incarnated in the synthesizer's preset backbeats. Both the new and the old instruments allowed for the development of a high level of virtuosity and flair, and yet a person could teach themself to play at a basic level relatively quickly. Moreover, the new instruments and the old instruments both could be played while seated, meaning that musicians could endure grueling sets that lasted from midnight until dawn. Thus, the synthesizer, like the accordion before it, served as the fuel for parties where the main attraction was dancing.

A young person with a synthesizer could form a band and slowly start to build a reputation, playing with friends or at the start of parties that featured better known musicians. After a little exposure, the band might make a deal with a person who had a reputation as a good impresario in one of the nearby villages or towns. A date would be chosen, and the band would scramble to pay for small, glossy posters that would soon appear at two-table bars and dusty general stores throughout the region. On the day, young people from miles around would wind their way through dirt paths on foot, horseback, and motorcycle, all coming together at the venue—often a town square or a field near someone's house. Sometimes, attendees would pay for admission. Other times, a local political figure or fraternal organization would foot the bill; on special occasions, the inhabitants of the village might pitch in by purchasing expensive tee shirts that commemorated the moment. At the end, the impresario and the band split the proceeds, saving some money in order to prepare for the next event in a town down some other country road.

This was the kind of future that Diego and Melchior could have envisioned when they imagined bringing a synthesizer back to the countryside. But how did the two of them tell the story?

For Melchior, the synthesizer arrived as an object that expressed something in himself he never knew. At age thirty, he had never played music. He had spent years wandering back and forth between Bahia and São Paulo, toiling at construction and factory jobs. His skin grew white from overexertion.

Then one day, entirely without planning, Melchior ran into something in the city's refuse. "I was walking around," Melchior reminisced for me, "around São Paulo and there was a little synthesizer, like a little piano, really tiny. Battery-operated. In the trash, you know? And I didn't even know if it worked.

"Anyway, I thought it was—interesting, cute, you know? I took it just because it was pretty."

Melchior felt intrigued. "I went to the market. I bought—four batteries, because it took four of those little batteries, the thin ones. And I put them in it, you know. So it started working. And I turned it on, and it was working. Then I started to learn to play—'Happy Birthday.'"

Along with the tiny piano, Melchior discovered something about himself. "I think that I *had* the capability of learning to play, but I didn't believe it. [. . .] I discovered it by accident because I found that instrument in the garbage [. . .]."

"A gift—inside of me—but there was, there was no way for me to bring it out, to the outside, you know? Because I didn't know what it was—Because I didn't have the financial resources to buy an instrument."

Rapidly, Melchior taught himself the secrets of the keyboard. He returned to Bahia and became a touring musician with a band, riding from concert to concert on a bus. Melchior eventually grew tired of the wandering life and settled opposite his mother's house on a plot of land, where he planted neat rows of coffee.

In the village, Melchior met a tractor driver, Alex, who was a singer—and who owned a synthesizer. Melchior and Alex began playing at parties in the nearby villages and towns of the coffee zone. Their schedule started to fill up with what Melchior referred to as "our work [*nosso trabalho*]." Melchior knew that the duo could get gigs if they kept up good relations with the local politicians, and he cultivated a bond with the region's city councilperson. I interviewed Melchior shortly before the municipal elections; he was already preparing to play at an old folks' dance sponsored by the incumbent administration.

Melchior had a goal beyond dances. He wanted to set up a music course to teach his talent to children in the village. Maybe he might even receive a stipend from the municipal government for this purpose. One of the candidates, in fact, had given Melchior his word that the stipend would come through—if the candidate won the election.

For the time being, Melchior relied on Alex, the tractor driver, because Melchior himself did not own a synthesizer. "There is talent, but there are no instruments to work with," he noted. "Just the talent itself." Melchior had not achieved autonomy, but between music and the coffee field, he hoped to get there eventually. "What I want is to work for myself," he stipulated. "I don't want to stay working for other people anymore." Melchior did not intend to go to São Paulo, where he might be invited to play in bands. "I want to continue with this dream. But here."

Melchior spoke of his music as a *gift*, "the gift of God [*o dom de Deus mesmo*]." It had a deeply personal quality. But the word "gift" (*dom*) captured the duality that lived inside this personalism. His musical talent was both a unique quality of his selfhood—he was *gifted*—and a singular obligation to other people, a *gift* he had received from God and that he now needed to pass on to children.

Melchior hoped that the synthesizer could help him enter the realm of generous gift exchange, the realm of full-time music, and leave wage labor and the city for good. A hoard of cash, too, offered removal from the urgency of wage labor, *not to work for other people anymore*. Both the synthesizer and the hoard of cash were promises of autonomy. If they differed, the difference arose because money, the universal equivalent, promised autonomy to anyone who held on to it. The synthesizer's autonomy had its roots inside Melchior himself.

Melchior was not yet at the point of autonomy: he described himself as a person waiting and planning. In the week when I interviewed him, he needed to postpone a gig. The tractor driver, his partner, had gone to the metropolis of Belo Horizonte to do a short spell of city work. "For the purpose," Melchior explained, "of us buying a better little synthesizer, you know?"

*

For Melchior, the tool revealed and enacted his gift. But the tool-as-premio was not only a gift, it was also a dream. The aspirational nature of the tool, its quality as an object of desire, shone brightly in the story that Diego told.

On the day when he ended up counting his cash in the electronics store restroom, Diego had spent seven months on a construction site. His father had slaughtered the pig and bought him the bus ticket he needed to get to the job in São Paulo. His mother had sold her best calf and sent him R$800 toward the instrument. Each payday, he himself had stored a chunk of money in his mother's bank account. But he was R$1,200 short of the synthesizer price.

Diego's family made extraordinary sacrifices for the synthesizer because they knew its extraordinary meaning to him. As a child, Diego "started to—to have a dream, like, of going into music. [. . .] And it's a thing you can reach," he told me. "As long as you have the gift." For Diego, as for Melchior, music was a gift, a deeply personal quality that demanded an exchange with others. But even before Diego knew his gift, he dreamed the dream.

In Diego's São Paulo life, the predominant object of exchange was not music, but labor, and that exchange, on the construction site, came with great frustration. Diego found himself marked with a regional-racial identity: he was one of "the big bunch of peons from Bahia [*a peãozada lá da Bahia*]." He slept in a row of bunk beds. His boss spoke to him disrespectfully. "I was humiliated like heck there," Diego remembered.

Diego found his relief by wandering on the weekends to Saint Ifigênia Street, São Paulo's center for electronics. Along that street, he would "research [*pesquisar*]" and "make love with the synthesizers [*namorar com os teclados*]." He eventually began talking to a sales clerk in one of the stores. When Diego narrated the story to me, he described the clerk's words in detail.

DIEGO: The sales clerk was like, "How can I help you, friend?" I said, "Nah, I'm just looking around a bit. *[pause]* Um—um—well, I just was wondering, how much is this synthesizer?" He said, "This synthesizer right here is priced at five thousand two hundred reais."

DUFF: Whooa.
DI: I said, "Yeah, dude." [He said,] "How about it? Will you be buying?"

At that point, Diego had only saved up a little over a thousand reais.

DI: I said, "No, there's really no way for me to buy it because—Because I, I just got here." All that. I explained the situation.

Diego, in his narration to me, depicted a stark difference between his own speech and the clerk's. Diego's speech was full of the pronoun "I," as he provided a stream of justifications for himself (*I was just wondering, I just got here*). By contrast, the clerk spoke not about himself, but about Diego (*How can I help you, friend? Will you be buying?*) This dynamic would repeat itself as Diego continued telling me the story.

After months more of labor, Diego managed to accumulate R$3,200 in the bank.

DI: Then I went down there again, to Saint Ifigênia Street, to make love to the synthesizers.
DU: Hmmm.
DI: I said, "I want this one. I want this synthesizer. Hey, dude! How much is this synthesizer?" The guy looked over, and he saw that it was me again. "What's up, dude? Will you be buying today? You came to get it today, right?" I said, "Nah, nah. *[pause]* I just came to take a look at it again. To do a little research." [He said,] "Man, this keyboard goes for—we can manage to give it to you for—we can lower the price from R$5,200 all the way to—R$4,800."
DU: Hm.
DI: [He said,] "If you pay all at once, no credit." I said, "Man, for real, dude?" "Yes." I said, "Next week, I'll drop by."
DU: Mm-hm.
DI: And I went back to the construction site.

This was when Diego called his mother on the village pay phone and she agreed to sell the best cow. Diego took that cash, combined it with the sum in the bank account, rolled all of it up inside a small bag, and stuffed it into his underpants. On a Sunday, he met up with a friend who liked music, and they went back to the store—Diego nervously stopping every few minutes to pat his own underwear.

Diego negotiated for hours, bouncing between the salesperson and a supervisor, winning a price reduction from R$5,200 to R$4,500, then to R$4,300.

THE THINGS YOU HOLD 193

But Diego only had R$3,800. "I went on imploring him," Diego remembered for me, and he recalled the words of supplication he uttered: "'I'm not from here. For the love of God.'"

Diego's friend took him aside and made an offer: he could lend Diego some money, and Diego would pay him back after returning to Bahia. With the promise of a R$200 loan from the friend, Diego now had R$4,000 to spend.

D1: I went—to the manager with that thought. [. . .] I said to him, "Hey, hey, buddy. It's like this. I'm going to be sincere with you [*você*]. I can get R$4,000 for the synthesizer."

Here, for the first time in his narration, *Diego* addressed the *sales staff* with the word "you." The story was changing.

The salesperson said the offer was impossible.

D1: Then he showed me other synthesizers. "There's this one here, man. Why don't you take this one?" Whatever. I said, "I want this one."
DU: Mm hm.
D1: The guy was like, "Yeah, dude. Do this. We're going to leave it at R$4,100 for you."

When the price came down to R$4,100, Diego saw an opening and he seized it. As he described his next move to me, his voice rose loud and harsh.

D1: I said, "I am going to give 4,000 for the synthesizer and that's that. This is finished. You can wrap up the synthesizer."

Hearing the tone in Diego's words, the clerk disappeared to ask the manager. The manager returned. "I'm going to let you have it," he conceded. "But—I don't even know why I'm doing this."

Inside Diego's narration, his decisive final words take on a particular form. They are commands (see chapter 1). Diego speaks in short sentences, built around an imperative (*you can wrap up*), oriented to the immediate present (*this is finished*). He uses deixis that requires the listener to adopt the spatial perspective of the speaker (*I want **this** one*). He refuses the other party's different deictic frame: Diego insists on describing the synthesizer he wants as "this" rather than "that," thus rejecting the clerk's attempt to provide another referent for the word "this" (*Why don't you take **this** one?*) In other words, Diego gives commands.

At the beginning of his story, Diego is a speaker who mostly justifies himself to others. By the end, he speaks in the voice of a supervisor. It is the store manager, ironically, who has to account for himself: *I don't even know why I'm doing this.*

Diego paid for the synthesizer, then called a friend to ask for a ride, and the friend pulled up in a Chevy Monza. Diego had entered the store at ten in the morning. By the time he walked through the door to the Monza, a brand-new synthesizer in his arms, it was three in the afternoon. As Diego strolled out, the sales clerk called out to him in wonderment, "Man, I don't know how the manager did that for you, dude."

I don't even know why I'm doing this: Diego has managed to flip the manager. In my understanding, Diego's story about the synthesizer is also a story about the humiliation that he himself knew as a laborer in São Paulo, a story about how to reverse that humiliation. He demystifies the authoritative speech of command. Just a few days after buying the synthesizer, Diego refused a command from his boss on the jobsite—a story told in chapter 1—was fired from his job, and caught the bus back to the village. It was, he told me, "a crazy happiness."

When Diego counted out eighty jaguar bills and paid them to the store, he was taking value and removing it from the cycle of exchange. But it would be wrong to say that he was saving. Like Melchior with his keyboard from the trash, Diego was finding a way to exit the wage labor he knew. He was gaining a premio.

Dream, gift, tool: the premio, here, has power because it roots itself in personhood. It matches up with your *dream*. It reflects your *giftedness*, and it then requires you to pass the *gift* on to others, transferring the meaning of your toil out of labor market calculus, recasting your effort as generous exchange. In these stories, you even receive the synthesizer itself as a kind of gift from others, borrowed from the neighboring tractor driver, paid for by the sacrifice of your parents, acquired with a loan from a friend. Such premios transform value into a more lasting form of obligation. And it is not just musical instruments that possess this power. Restaurant equipment has its oneiric qualities, too. In 2016 Aninha and Orestes were away in São Paulo earning the money to buy gear for the village eatery that they had opened with so much devotion. I stopped by the abandoned house where they ran their establishment, and I saw the logo they had painted there. It had a halo, a tiny geometrical hamburger, and, in curved red and blue words, the restaurant's name: *Lanchonete Sonho Meu*, "My Dream Lunch Counter."

From deep fryers to chainsaws, from synthesizers to school vans, some premios reverse the fundamental quality that makes a person a wage laborer.

A wage laborer does not own the means of production and relies on someone else to provide the tools they need for their work. The premio can solve this problem. But Diego and Melchior did not go into music as a business venture. If we see such tools only as enterprising investments—only as a form of saving—then we miss out on their power to turn the person who holds them into a certain kind of person.

We miss, too, the critique of abstract labor that migrants might be making as they stockpile money for a synthesizer. To be a wage laborer is to have your abilities constantly evaluated by the person who owns the tools. But Melchior and Diego invoke a dream and a giftedness that live inside them, beyond the judgment of any job supervisor. The synthesizer is a vehicle for expressing part of themselves, a way, as Melchior said, "for me to bring it out." "What," the young Marx once asked, "constitutes the alienation of labor? First, that the work is external to the worker, that it is not part of his nature [. . .] It is not the satisfaction of a need, but only a means for satisfying other needs" (Marx 1994: 66). In imagining a tool that corresponds to themselves, workers imagine work no longer external to their natures.

Self-expression does not happen in response to a supervisor's command. As Diego demonstrated when he defied the salesperson and his construction boss in the same week, self-expression can become a refusal of command. Sometimes even a parody of command. After Diego returned to the countryside, he founded a band with a friend of his. They named it *Xaveco de Patrão*, "The Boss's Talk."

Withdrawing from Circulation, Refusing to Exchange

When Diego unrolled the bills to buy his synthesizer, or when Tamara sent cash to pay for her new rural house, they were withdrawing value from circulation and fixing it in the countryside, as if they were burying a pot of money. The synthesizer and the house were objects that transferred value out of the wage labor market.

These same objects then opened up new, more restricted circuits of exchange. The synthesizer would animate the flow of people and resources inside a festive economy. The house would turn into the central place of hospitality: as Nelson told me, the reason you wanted to build a house was because "you have to welcome your family members." In these cases, villagers did not simply retain value at a remove from the world market, they generated new forms of exchange that cycled wealth outside that market.

Not so with the pot of money. Burying money meant withdrawing cash from circulation and then refusing to begin a new circuit. Dona Zaida said that the rich saved *so as not to give to the poor*. In this theory of saving, to save is to refuse to exchange. This quality—the refusal—may reveal something about what makes saving special.

In the buried money stories, the refusal took on a particularly dangerous meaning. Noncirculation kept the soul from salvation. The way a living person could solve the problem of saving, then, was to produce an exchange relation, by agreeing to dig up the treasure. And the new relation called for a key personal quality: the quality of boldness.

Carlos put it this way:

c: People are scared. Because they say that at the moment when you're digging it up, when you're taking off the seal, they say that the soul comes and stays there right by you.
d: Hm!
c: Now a lot of people aren't scared of dead people. They can see them there, even talk to them. But others don't have the courage.

They don't have the courage. It bears remembering that these wealthy souls, in life, had owned the great plantations where the villagers toiled. In some cases, a villager could not eat at the same table as a landowner. Sometimes a villager would not even dare to enter the owner's house. Landowners were to be addressed with deference and obeyed.

Now the same landowners beckoned, still fearsome, but fearsome now for a different reason: they were dead. To overcome inequality and to undo savings, a villager needed to break the barrier around the rich by engaging in the bold act of talking to them.

To establish an exchange relation, one needed to negotiate with the rich without deference. It bears noting that when the tellers told me these stories, they were often talking about people that I myself knew—their own relatives and neighbors. Carlos told me, for example, about what happened when a soul gave some money to a man named Walter. The conversation sounded almost like . . . a labor market negotiation.

c: That old soul gave—gave the money to Aunt Maria's son Walter.
d: Mm-hm.
c: But he said that he didn't have the courage to—to go dig it up by himself.
d: Mm-hm.
c: Then [the soul] said, "So you choose someone, so that you guys can go—so that he can go with you." So he went and chose Victor. *[Carlos laughs, and I laugh, too.]* But the thing is that Victor—he just went and got scared.

He said that he wouldn't dig it up. But then *[inaudible]* then he couldn't change it and ask another person to go with him, because that's not what was in the contract.

In this fair negotiation, a contract is a contract, even a contract with a soul, and both sides have to stand by it.

And so it is by undoing saving, by digging it up, that an exchange relationship is established and people are brought together again. Exchange, of course, can involve both boldness and trickery. Carlos told me about his bold neighbor Carolina.

C: They say that a little old lady gave some to her, too.
D: Hm!
C: But [Carolina] was like, "But I'm not going by myself, no way." Because—Little Carolina is gutsy.
D: Mm-hm.
C: "Can I choose a person?" "You can." So she chose—I don't know if he's her brother. I don't really know if he's her brother or not. He's a guy named Frankie, Marco's Frankie. [. . .] So she said, "Can, can I take Fr—Frankie with me?" "You can. You can take him, anyone you want." "Okay, then, I'll take Frankie." So then they got there and—*[inaudible]* There the earth is hard to dig. [. . .] Frankie—she—said that they were there like, "Hey! You can dig here to see." So Frankie went at it, he went at it, he hit the earth with a big pickaxe, and he was digging and digging and digging, and when he was just about to uncover the mouth of the jar—"Ah, wow, here it is. Hey! Look at the mouth of the jar here." Then they say that the little old lady sat down beside them.
D: Mm-hm.
C: Then *[inaudible]* Frankie, then [Carolina] was like, "It was this woman right here who gave the money to me." When Frankie saw blood, or maybe a stick stuck into the middle of her chest—
D: Hm!
C: Frankie ran off into the world *[slaps hands]*, into the underbrush, and she shouted, "*[inaudible]*, come on, this is no big deal," and Frankie went off with the blood turning around in his feet. She went chasing after Frankie. *[laugh]* She ran down chasing Frankie to see if she could catch him, to make him come back, to make him dig it up. Frankie ran off; she couldn't catch him. She went back. When she got back there, well—you know, it was just exactly the same way that it had been.
D: *[laughing]* I like that.

c: Just as if they had never dug anything at all. [*laugh*]
d: Very interesting.
c: Because he ran away. [*laugh*]

In stories like these, saving functions as the opposite of salvation. It is as if the storyteller were disagreeing with a saving logic that they know only too well. The tales reveal an unexpected richness hiding inside the concept of saving. They dig up the hidden assumptions and make saving available for debate once again.

Standing against Saving

Often, our first assumption is that saving is nothing but the negative of consumption—nothing but money that an agent decides not to spend for now (Browning and Lusardi 1996). But this view is limiting, and in any case anthropology has its own theories. The discipline points to "wealth in people" (Guyer 1993) and shows how the powerful can accumulate loyal dependents instead of accumulating cash. Or anthropologists can cite Bourdieu's notion of symbolic capital (1977), that is, the conversion of economic resources into acquired signs of power, like a taste for refined art, a beautiful vocabulary, or a college degree.

Yet something remains unresolved. Wealth in people and symbolic capital: these are concepts that aim to demonstrate how humans can save without ever using money. They are concepts that allow the analyst to look at the most varied acts—from a feast for one's friends to a trip to a museum—and see these acts *as if they were* acts of saving.

But people at Maracujá and Rio Branco insist on just the opposite. They insist that they are *not* saving, even when I might think that they are. When Stefania's husband lends money to his family and leaves nothing in his own hands, we *could* say that he is accumulating wealth in people. Or when Lara buys a cow, we *could* say that she is acquiring a locally relevant form of symbolic capital. We could say that, in some sense, they are saving, after all.

But this is the opposite of what *they* say. And if I interpret Stefania and Lara as symbolic capitalists, as covert savers, then I am not just contradicting their own stated views. Far worse: I am denying the critique that they pose against capital itself. I am failing to hear their argument that owning a cow differs from opening a bank account, that saving is not salvation. For there are so many, very different human acts that can lie hidden inside the English word *to save*. Keynes believed that the verb *to save* covered a multitude of actions—he himself named eight motives to save. We need to take seriously what Keynes referred to as "the independence motive." Sometimes, Keynes argued, people hold on to wealth in order "to enjoy a sense of independence and the power to do things, though without a clear idea or definite intention of specific action" (2016: book 3, chap. 9).

The power to do things without an intention of specific action. Here, it seems to me that Keynes opens the door to a much bigger project, the project of rescuing money's third function. Many textbooks tell us that money's third function is to serve as a store of value.[12] But often enough the textbooks cannot resist subordinating that third function to the first function: money's function as a medium of exchange. Often the textbooks seem to assume that people store money *only* in order to defer consumption, as if people stored money only in order to use it, later on, as a lubricant for trade.[13]

But saving is so much more than deferred consumption. Money enables us to do much more than buy something in the future. The third function is the power to hold on to value and store it, and that power has a subordinate and even a dangerous role in classical economics, a role kept alive by thinkers like Malthus and Marx (Harvey 2006: 77; also Hunt 2002). It was Marx who taught us that this third function can turn money into something else—it can make money into capital. It can make a hoard of coins seem less like a pile of symbols to be exchanged and more like a general power, as if the coins held the power of abstract labor itself. One might also refer to this as the power to do things without the intention of a specific action.

But in analyzing buried money, one would do well to look beyond capital to an even more general power, the power of *not giving*. Inside what we call "saving" there lies hidden, so often, a refusal of exchange. The drama of "not giving" lies at the heart of the anthropological arguments of Marcel Mauss (1967) and Annette Weiner (1992). For if there is some common thread that unites the synthesizer, the cow, and the rural house with the landlord's buried pot, that thread is the refusal of general exchange and the determination to render an object inalienable. It is the insistence on circulating that object only inside a special circle, just as Stefania's husband will lend money only to his family, just as the cow will be passed on only to one's infant heir, just as the pot remains encased in the ground and unknown to the world. To hold on to the object means to define the edges of an exclusive social group. You can save for the very purpose of *creating* such a group—not for the purpose of consuming, primarily, but for the purpose of demonstrating that you exchange with some people and not others. Here we find the "independence motive" indeed: the drive to make oneself and one's small circle independent from all other people.

Suso and his neighbors in the village know very well how to refuse general exchange; they know how to buy a cow for one's daughter in the same way that a rich landowner knows how to bury money in the ground. They know how to cut the boundaries of belonging to a social group. Suso and his neighbors also know the danger of this act. They are familiar with the peril of the myth of saving—the peril of believing that to withhold objects from exchange means to achieve efficiency and even to attain salvation. For Suso and his neighbors, as perhaps for all of us, I argue, withholding objects from exchange is not, in the first instance, about accumulating wealth in people or accumulating symbolic capital or indeed accumulating anything. Withholding objects from exchange is, in the first instance, about removing oneself from other people.

In my rural household survey, I asked about saving, but upon reflection, what I wanted to ask about is a human gesture much broader and vaster: the gesture of refusing to exchange. People refuse to exchange *without the intention of a specific action*, without any plan to consume in the future; they refuse because refusing to exchange is a key tool that one may use to produce a special social group. This gesture of refusal can become manifest in children's cattle, a royal jewel, or a sacred heirloom. The gesture can also become manifest in what I natively refer to as "saving," that is, in the bank accounts and buried monies of contemporary capitalism. And there, I believe, Suso and his neighbors make their critique of the folly in saving, the folly of mistaking money withheld for efficiency gained and mistaking efficiency gained for virtue. To refuse exchange is to exclude others. This refusal has power, the power to build a group, a power that Suso and his neighbors know well. They make use of this power every time they buy a cow that they will pass down inside the kinship line only. This is a power that comes with danger attached to it, the danger of closing down exchange with the other.

Suso's neighbors also know how to reopen exchange that has long ago been shut off. They can listen to the soul that tells them to dig up the pot, and they can speak back to that soul boldly. They can also create the premios that generate a new cycle of exchange at a distance from the market, like Diego's rural dance parties—or outside of it altogether, like Nelson inviting his family members to his new house.

In 2013, as Brazil's growth adventure reached high noon, Suso stood in his new neighborhood at midnight and explained to me where rich people keep their money. But it might be relevant to remember an incident that occurred years earlier, when Suso and his family first moved into their previous house, a whitewashed bungalow out on the dry plains at Maracujá. Suso's kid brother William went digging around the back yard for fun, and there, under the hard earth, he discovered a clear plastic bag. The bag lay round and fat with something that shone in the sun. It was full of coins that an unknown hand had buried. All brassy and weathered, the coins seemed exciting. But they turned out to be worthless. They were an old currency, one of the eight that Brazil's government ran through over the course of the twentieth century, and they would circulate no more.

Suso's mother, Maria, held on to the bag of devalued specie in her kitchen, and it was there that I spied it. I am not sure *why* she kept the coins. But I would like to think of it as something of a lesson that she was sending. In an economy marked by five hundred years of commodity booms and commodity busts, where sugarcane gave way to gold and gold gave way to coffee, where coffee gave way to rubber and today to iron ore and soy, the realm of value always disappoints. Objects come and objects pass. It is not by holding on to value that one can make one's place in the world. This, too, is the conclusion of one of the arguments for which Keynes is most famous: the paradox of thrift. Let us see if we can read Maria's memento, that bag full of worthlessness dug up by a playful child, as something like a critique of the concept of saving itself.

My Dream Lunch Counter.

Conclusion

Wait for the Coffee

"With coffee you conquer a person. With a small cup of coffee." I heard these words of advice from a smiling seventy-nine-year-old man seated next to me on a bus. He did not explain the enigma. But his phrase helped me see how Clarita, one of the quietest people at Maracujá, managed to defeat my survey.

Clarita and I met during an early trip that I made to the region. At the time, she was living with her adult son in a stark white house near the edge of the village, and I was attempting to carry out a community-wide mental health survey, which I ultimately abandoned. One day I came to her home to ask her if she would complete the survey with me. She creaked open the door, listened to my request, and then proclaimed, "Enter."

Once I stepped into the darkness of her house, a seat was suddenly available, and Clarita offered a new and warmer invitation: "Sit!"

"Wait for the coffee," she continued, and then she turned her back to me and wandered into the kitchen, where she juggled pots, water, and fire, emerging some minutes later with a steaming glass cup of coffee. We spent the next ten or fifteen minutes absorbed in gracious and friendly conversation about the things that might be discussed with a stranger. When I tried, awkwardly, to maneuver the discussion back toward the survey, Clarita suggested that I should return and visit her house again, at a better time.

So I did return, and in fact I returned repeatedly over the next few weeks, always hearing the same requests to sit and wait for the coffee, always politely reinvited for a future visit whenever I brought up the survey. Through our hospitality banter, I confessed my own reasons for being in the village, my wonderment and confusions, and she described her time in the city, her faith, and her worries about her son. I became a frequent visitor. Finally, on the last day of that fieldwork trip, I explained to Clarita that this was my final opportunity to have her take the survey. Would she like to complete it with me? "No," she answered simply, and she proceeded to describe in extraordinary detail a story of family secrets and anxieties that I will not repeat here. It included much more soul-baring than I would have requested in my yes-or-no mental health questionnaire. We bade each other farewell. When I returned to Maracujá several years later, she had moved away, and I have not seen her since.

Eventually, I learned that Clarita's three-part litany was a common hospitality script for welcoming people into one's house: *Enter! Sit! Wait for the coffee!* (*Entra! Senta! Espera o café!*) The final phrase had special resonance for me. It embodied a very common sensibility about coffee, a feeling that the beverage possessed a unique power to tame the outsider who stepped into one's home. Coffee was warmed over the cookfire or stove, far off in the kitchen, and then brought into the sociable space of the living room, where it served as a synecdoche for the house itself turned outward in relation to the world beyond. To lack coffee for the visitor was to fall into embarrassment. "Coffee just doesn't stay! [*não fica o café!*]," exclaimed Lara on one of the evenings when I perched on the family couch in front of the television, and her coffee's rapid liquidity was the sign of her household's generous habit of welcoming, up to and beyond the limit imposed by her means. *Isn't there any coffee prepared there?* she called out to her teenage son. *Put on some water to boil!* I would have to wait for the coffee.

Once the coffee was being heated for you, you could not leave, not until you had drunk down to the clear sugar crust layered on the bottom of the cup. Here, the act of waiting seemed to me to have a special importance. People tended to frame a hospitable visit as a moment removed from one's productive pursuits, a period in which the visitor and the host were doing nothing, just waiting. The language of hospitality, in general, was peppered with references to this kind of time. When a guest got up to leave, the host would formulaically object, "It's still early! [*está cedo!*]," no matter what the time of day or how lengthy the visit. A guest who finally left would be dismissed with the phrase "Thank you for the little hour [*obrigado pela horinha*]." This term—*little hour*—was the same word that Ademir used to contrast work in the village with work in the wage labor market (see page 102). For a boss, you had to work *the right hour*, but in your own field, you could work *a little hour*, starting and stopping to come back into the house and then starting again. Visiting, too, created a little hour. Visitors and hosts contrived to build a moment that pushed against the constraints of a greater external time. The little hour extended itself and deferred any other reckoning. A good host did not ignore the ticking of a grand singular time outside the house door—indeed,

CONCLUSION

the rhetoric of hospitality called time constantly to mind—but a good host rebelled against the clock's imperatives.

So it was, I believe, with Clarita, who masterfully counted down my fieldwork calendar to the very last day, deferring time till the end. Clarita had conquered me with coffee. Her gesture did not simply refuse my request. She repositioned me as a guest rather than a social scientist, and, being a guest, as a mark of her household's dignity.

Farmers at Rio Branco and Maracujá drank coffee, and they also grew it. Village fields were sometimes lined with the deep green of a few coffee bush rows, but the vast majority of the region's coffee blossomed and fruited on the great plantations. Long, harmonious rows of plantation coffee reached for the dry horizon, then ended abruptly once they came to the middling towns, packed with russet brick houses and the landless day laborers who inhabited them. Villagers at Maracujá and Rio Branco strove not to live like these day laborers, reliant on the pay of the estate masters. But when the coffee harvest season arrived and the day laborers rushed into the abundance of heavy-duty work, many villagers tended to get swept along as well (see the testimony by Analis on pp. 107–8 and 110). Toiling directly for the world market, they all, for a time, earned steady cash.

Here was another meaning of *wait*. The region's workers flocked for a few months to produce a major export crop. For the rest of the year, they chased other pursuits and anticipated the world market harvest again. They waited for the coffee. This book has been about that second moment, the time that workers spend waiting beyond the edge of the dominant economy—beyond the edge (Harms 2011) of the coffee field, the lunch counter, the nanny job, the factory line, or some other site of wage labor. Maracujá and Rio Branco are places located a good distance beyond that edge. In the villages, peasant farmers do not simply wait for the coffee. They have turned the waiting into an art and an alternative. They stretch this alternative time so far that it extends to cover most of their days; it defines their dispositions; it guides the rhythm of the bus ride home. It becomes the organizing principle for a way of life.

When I first arrived in Brazil, in 2005, landless activists expressed tremendous optimism about the prospects for nurturing and expanding this organizing principle. Perhaps, through land redistribution and social democracy, a capitalist growth model could become democratic enough to leave space for its alternatives. The landless movement was aflutter, seeking spaces in which to build these alternatives, "occupying," in the words of one activist, "every corner we could find."

By 2012, landless leaders had a darker outlook; they sensed that Brazil's current growth model had reached its limits. Vividly I remember a somber weekend retreat where dozens of rural organizers slept on the concrete floor of a sports center, ate from a common pot, and discussed the possibility of a new conservative backlash. They seemed worried.

Those worries proved accurate. Between 2014 and 2018, Brazil underwent a devastating recession, the impeachment (on a technicality) of left-wing president Dilma Rousseff (Sosa 2019), and the election of a far-right successor, who campaigned with a promise to confront the MST. Disasters multiplied for the landless. But well before disaster, already in 2012 and 2013, I talked quietly with activist after activist who wondered with anguish about the meaning of the movement. What, really, had the MST achieved during the years when the Workers Party held national power? The MST did not create socialism in one country and not even "islands of socialism" (Branford and Rocha 2002: 92). The MST did not always build highly productive farms. It did not always end poverty for the families that entered it. And yet, the movement made a certain way of living possible.

This book is a meditation on what the landless movement has accomplished in the first four decades of its history, although I have carried out that meditation through a displacement, since the MST lies nowhere near the center of the narrative. I have tried to show how the MST fits inside a much longer history built by the people who have lived at Rio Branco for over a century. Indeed, we might say that the MST itself is one instrument through which that history realizes itself in the present moment. This is a history, as Jonathan DeVore insightfully argues (2014, 2016, 2017, 2018, 2020), of emancipation.

To listen to such a history is to think differently about Brazilian progress. Since the end of the dictatorship in 1985, progressives have repeatedly focused on the notion of citizenship (*cidadania*). They have narrated the past thirty years as a story about how people become better citizens, more capable of asserting their rights.[1] Buried inside *citizenship* is the word *city*, in Portuguese as in English. This is no accident: Fernando Henrique Cardoso, later to become Brazil's president, made the argument explicit in his 1972 essay "The City and the Countryside" (Singer and Cardoso 1972). Brazil, Cardoso says, never had real cities; the nation sank its roots too deeply in a rural soil dominated by authoritarian plantations. On this view, democracy happens when Brazilians finally make a genuine move to the city. There they learn to demand basic services, to articulate their rights, and to speak through the legal system. The polity *is* a city writ large, as Athens and Rome were cities writ large, and rural-to-urban migration, with all of its travails, is ultimately a school of citizenship.

But how does our social theory change if we consider democracy outside the city? What if we center the people who spend their time waiting for the coffee? Instead of *citizenship*, we might then focus on a different concept, *autonomy*. Autonomy is no less a democratic virtue, and it has its own habits and heartlands. Autonomy is illuminated by the energy that drives urban-to-rural migration. In the context of that reverse flow, autonomy appears as a space that you can open up somewhere along the edge of the world market, at the far point of Mintz's permanently unbalanced oscillation.

In Brazil, theories of citizenship fit nicely with the imperative of economic growth, represented as a drive toward the city. Theories of autonomy, however, have a more mixed relationship to growth. Certain kinds of economic growth can generate and nurture autonomy. Pay phones, for example, render the villages more powerfully available as an aspiration for migrants in the city. Bolsa Família and government retirement pensions are funded by Brazil's growth model; these social benefit programs make it possible for farmers to acquire a critical distance from the wage labor market. And after all, it was the residents of Rio Branco, heirs of a century of autonomy, who set off fireworks in 2006 when the first electric line was connected to their houses. The moment was, as Hirsch says, a "scene where economic growth could be felt" (2022: 3), felt as part of a project of freedom.

But the autonomous tradition does not sit well with the act of command. Villagers, instead of commanding, hone their talents at giving advice and calling on each other; they defeat capital accumulation by insisting on growth through the gift. They aim for accumulations of other types. Through their patient conversions between motorcycles and pigs, between one asset chain and the next, villagers exemplify Millar's argument about plastic economy: economic action is not the pursuit of a singular substantive goal, but a movement *between* forms. Migrants travel the space from city street to village field and embrace the "interplay between different forms of living" (2018: 150).

The autonomous tradition encourages an aspiration to permanence. Often enough, migrants throw themselves into economic growth, taking a long bus ride into the world market, for the purpose of creating something that does not grow but rather lasts. Thus, I have argued that a truly democratic growth model is one that makes the alternatives to growth *more* possible. Growth, when cast as an undeniable path, becomes undeniably authoritarian. Economic growth is democratic only if it opens more widely the space for forms of nongrowth.

The lack of growth does not imply the lack of accumulation. This book has striven to show that migrants can accumulate both inside and outside the growth process. They can use their wages to buy urban consumer goods, or they can convert this value into bean fields and rural houses that help them stay beyond the edge of the world market. From the perspective of a migrant, the two sides of the coin may seem like incompatible opposites. Either you spend your money on a fresh urban motorcycle, or you try to shore up your family's countryside home. But, here, the anthropology of accumulation sees a deeper unity, an underlying similarity that connects all the gestures through which people multiply and proliferate the objects they cherish. Economic growth is only one kind of accumulative process, and once growth steps aside, the others rise to the fore.

We can begin to spot the speculative outlines of an anthropology of accumulation. Such a project would need to consider, comparatively and capaciously, such accumulative practices as the building of friendship networks, the amassing of spiritual merit, the recruitment of soldiers, the planting of forests, the emergence of religious revivals, the generation of fan bases in popular music, and the expansion of encyclopedic collections like those held by museums and zoos. The project would try to understand visions of amassment as progress, economic growth being one such vision.

Those who criticize the shortcomings of economic growth sometimes extend their criticism into a wholesale rejection of the notion of progress. Such a rejection may not fully capture the complexities involved in waiting for the coffee. The time of waiting is indeed one species of progressive time, since the person who waits is anticipating the future and orienting to it. When you wait, you are living toward the future, just not right now.

The artful host knows how to mediate this tension. Dona Rosalinda described that art to me when she recalled, at age ninety-six, the parties she had given in her youth. Back then, neighbors danced barefoot in the dust; snacks flowed in overabundance; anyone at all picked up the triangle to beat its thick metal in time with the drum and the accordion. The evening grew longer and longer. Midnight gave way to morning. "The day would dawn," Dona Rosalinda remembered. "I would go make food to give. And the people were there until it was nearly nighttime."

"Mm-hm," I urged.

"They had no hurry to leave. No way."

No hurry to leave. Good hospitality unfolded this way: it canceled any reason to rush. It undid the lessons of the labor market. A "true party, a big party," in Dona Rosalinda's words, exuded enthusiasm but not cooperation, since partyers produced togetherness for no goal.

The villages nourish these moments of undirected togetherness, like the day when the occupiers at Maracujá learned that the land was now theirs with no further obligation, and also like the instant when someone steps off the creaking bus and back onto familiar ground. More microscopically, the same sensibility comes built into the hospitality ritual itself. The guest waits, and the host delays; both of them see the future and they can accept it, but they generate the terms and the timeline on which it arrives. Pushed to its extreme, this logic of hospitality becomes a dream in which time, rather than pounding relentlessly or melting away, enters into the hands of the guest and the host. Time becomes the artifact that they produce with each other. That dream, anyway, is what I heard from Pedro, the pastor at Maracujá, one day when I stayed deep into the night chatting on his giant red couch. I apologized for taking too much of his time. "No," Pastor Pedro replied. "We have our time. Because we are the ones who make our own time, man."

"Mm-hm," I said uncertainly.

"We are the ones who make time."

Afterword

After she returned from Belo Horizonte, Alexandra stayed at Maracujá. She moved into a house hidden behind the laundry hanging in her parents' back yard, and she cared for her children with the help of family. She left the luxury supermarket and the business class far behind. But now, back from Belo Horizonte, Alexandra found a new way to study. She caught a rural bus, government-subsidized, that ferried her each evening to the night program in a nearby town. After many tired class sessions—and after repeatedly sneaking into the office of the village elementary school to type up her senior thesis—Alexandra earned her high school diploma. As of this writing, she is one of the leaders of the MST in the region.

*

Dona Eva, who rose early to roast her light and buttery pastries, who once watched her father and her uncle resolve a dispute by going to the plantation owner, who trekked to the Secretariat of Education to enforce the village children's right to a school van, was also my exuberant and endlessly generous host for a year at Rio Branco. She is one of the most adventurous and kindest people I have known. Several years after I left, she discovered a small skin spot that grew larger and larger. Doctors finally diagnosed it as malignant melanoma, and she traveled across Brazil in search of medical care. Patrício, who once received a cellphone in a package from his girlfriend Valentina, is Dona Eva's son. He poured all his resources into obtaining a car so he could drive her to a public hospital thousands of miles from her home. Valentina accompanied him, and the two of them cared for Dona Eva, all three sleeping in guesthouses and on the floors of people's homes while Dona Eva sought treatment.

Several international drug companies produce medicines that are effective in fighting Dona Eva's type of cancer. The companies even have programs to make these treatments affordable in the United States. In Brazil, however, she was eligible for no such assistance programs, and the treatment regimen would cost US$70,000. Her family searched everywhere for the money. I wrote a letter to Jimmy Carter, who also had melanoma and who was treated effectively with the same medicine that Dona Eva needed. I did not ask Carter for money, but requested that he publicize the problem of people overseas who were ineligible for drug company assistance. He sent me back a brief, handwritten note promising to do so. Dona Eva's family ultimately raised enough money for one dose of the medicine, which she received. She died a few weeks later.

*

Carlos, who used to share cheese breads during his overnight bus trips, struggled mightily to get his child Bruno to move from São Paulo to Rio Branco. Carlos had a plan. In this plan, he would no longer have to paint varnish on tall buildings or toil in the hated chemical factory just so he could see his son. His earmarked fields of manioc would pay off. Perhaps Bruno, just barely an adolescent, would never need to work for a city boss. At any rate, father and son would live together on their own land.

"When you come back to this place," Carlos had once told me, "God willing, he will be around here." On a return trip to Rio Branco several years later, one weekend morning, I meandered up the thin path, through the gray spindles of scrub brush, up to his little adobe house, and I peeked inside. Carlos stirred himself awake for me, possibly embarrassed to be still in bed at what by village standards counted as the middle of the day. Then he told me his big news, and any embarrassment vanished into joy. His son was living with him now.

But I couldn't meet Bruno just then. Carlos had no idea where his son had gone that morning. Carlos seemed to feel no concern at all about Bruno's wandering. This was Rio Branco: the child had surely found a spot in a kitchen or a field with a cousin, an aunt, or a friend. Wherever he was, he was close to his land.

*

Suso was the son of Maria, the brilliant woman who heard confessions on her kitchen couch at Caldeirão; he was the grandson of Arisosvaldo, who was shot at Mocambo while struggling for the land. Suso eventually made a place for himself in the metropolis of Conquista. His earlier effort had ended on the terrible day when a police officer called him "Black man," plucked him away from his umbu fruit cart on a city street, beat him, and detained him in the police station without evidence. That time, Suso went straight back to the village. But a year or so later, Suso, his mother Maria, and his brother William all moved together into the freshly built city neighborhood of government houses, and things started changing for Suso. He found a job maintaining the grittiest of the long-distance buses. He entered a church, a different church than his mother's, and when he had small opportunities to preach, he preached. He pored over a study Bible with extensive academic footnotes. After several years, Suso became an evangelical minister.

In 2020, because of the coronavirus pandemic, churches had difficulty meeting in Suso's neighborhood. Suso invented a solution. He announced an outdoor service, with himself officiating, right in front of his house, and his younger brother, a few feet behind him, picking out a song on the guitar. From their windows, from spots on the pavement, people in the neighborhood looked on.

Later, I reached out to Suso on WhatsApp to ask permission to write about his arrest.

"You can use it," he enthused, "as a story of overcoming!"

He explained, "That day when I was arrested, for me, was a day of shame. There were maybe twenty or thirty people looking.

"So why do I say it's a story of overcoming? Today the audience that I preach to is an audience of three hundred people."

Much had changed in the intervening years, but some of it had come full circle. Suso was back in the city. He was standing on a street corner again.

"So," Suso concluded, "it was a turnaround in my life."

*

During one of my return trips, Maracujá was vibrant with the news of an upcoming party. An MST village some twenty miles away would soon host the three-day Manioc Festival.

So I found myself crammed in with young people and old folks on the back of a truck heading to the party, and then, when the truck could not hold our weight going uphill, trudging through reddish mud. We arrived a day early. With enthusiasm but no skill, I tried to help the general effort to run temporary electric wires, hoist tents and tarps, and clear space for a contest where horseback riders stood in their stirrups to put a nail through a hanging hook while the horse charged forward.

At last the party started. There was a cavalcade and the singing of the landless anthem, and then dusk fell on a warm Saturday night. The stage filled with contestants for the Miss Manioc prize, each attired in a different homemade dress designed to imitate the shape of the plant's long leaves. An emcee awarded the prize, and the stage remained empty for some minutes. Suddenly, dance music poured forth and I glanced up, past the multitudes who had started to shake and sway. At the front of the stage, I could make out the shape of a synthesizer. Who was behind it? My eyes focused in, and I felt a happy recognition: it was Diego. The crowd recognized, too. As he strutted and shouted and crooned, they cheered for him, their neighbor, the boy who had grown up in the fields next to them. His days on the construction site at São Paulo had made a difference. He looked huskier. He handled a synthesizer. He sweated and sang for hundreds. Now, he was a rural rock star.

Acknowledgments

The task is an impossible one: nobody can sum up the influences that have led to a text. The fact that a task is impossible, though, does not mean that one should not try it.

The first thanks go to my Aunt Whitney McCauley, who cared for me when I was a baby and who welcomed me many times into her life. Repeatedly, I left her, to travel to Brazil, to go to graduate school. Still now I can remember returning to her one evening after time in Brazil. Then I left again, and I did not come back. Aunt Whitney left her poetry and art, and I hope that we can stay with her and she with us.

Second, I must thank the people who can't be named because their stories are in this text. If you are one of those people, you are still today teaching me more than I yet know how to say. Thank you for your extraordinary generosity. For Maria Silvani Vieira Ferraz, you are a hero of hospitality, a brilliant thinker, and a person open to the world; I admire you so deeply. To that other Maria, your genius is breathtaking—insights all of the time that fill up notebooks. Your generous friendship is one of the greatest gifts I've ever received.

Isaiah Christopher and Little One: you give the reasons for everything, and vividly I remember the first time I saw each of you move. Emily is my most honest and best reader; I feel constantly grateful for her genius and the chance to walk alongside her. My parents and my sister remain, to this day, the most creative and energetic people I know. My mother's sharp artistic analysis made me want to interpret the world—and her relational gift-giving, to people around the world, is unquestionably the reason that I wanted to become an anthropologist (with a corresponding raincoat and hat.) My father had a special generosity that he expressed most fully by speaking, his words big with the openness of curiosity, and the current text is, more than anything, a snippet of my conversation with him. My sister's stunning ideas have constantly motivated me, and so has her crystalline writing, but both of these pale in comparison to her unashamedly loving spirit.

Often, for me, the best conversations begin in wonder. That wonder always seems to hover over the head of Enrique Mayer. His class veered from the poetry of struggle to the ecology of potatoes, everything delivered with warm irony and a joke. There's not a way for me to describe the influence he had—and has. Eric Hirsch's model for thought and life moved me deeply (in Rhode Island—later, in Chicago, a scholar of the same name would also move me). Inspiration sparked again for me right before graduate school, when I met Summerson Carr, who taught me a new meaning for analysis, and Jean Comaroff, who mixed brilliance, commitment, and laughter. Later I would learn from the generous readings of Julie Chu, the human warmth of Harold Pollack, the limitless ideas of Dain Borges, the expansive vision and endless welcome of Susan Gzesh, the wisdom of Manuela Carneiro da Cunha, and the rigorous commitments of Bill Sites, with whom I still feel like I am talking constantly. The vibrancy I learned from Marshall Sahlins, Robert Lucas, and Moishe Postone kept me awake to the world. All of this I know through the genius of Anne Ch'ien, who saw more clearly than everyone else how the ideas connected to each other, who pointed me gently in the direction of right living, and whose endless generosity creates its own legends. On the day of my qualifying exams, I accidentally slept until two minutes before the exam was to begin. Anne thought of me, understood what I needed, and got me there.

James Green may not know it, but this project exists because of his arrival at several moments. In 2005, nearly a decade before I met him, he emailed with me (although I think he doesn't remember) when I needed to find my way to the MST, and he guided me successfully. Long afterward, he welcomed me to his academic world—and then into the constant, turbulent flow of activists all around him. To him, I am so grateful.

Just as I count on the foregoing wise guides, I count on the lessons learned from my peers. They taught me the most. Although I can hardly list them here, I should say that the work of this text is due in large part to them: Averill Leslie, Kathryn Mariner, Jay Sosa, William Feeney, Eli Rose Thorkelson (every day that is a good day for thinking, I think of an idea from you), Jordan Schoenig, Erin Moore, Carly Schuster (my first host in grad school), Toussaint Losier, Joe Grim Feinberg, Alex Goldenberg, Aaron Ansell, Sean Mitchell, Hannah Appel, Tara Peters, Richard del Rio (an inspiration from the first day of class together), Dominic Surya, Adam Sargent (an extraordinary and brilliant collaborator and co-thinker), Yvonne Smith, Matt Spitzmueller, Erik Levin, Eric Hirsch (the Chicago one!), Ben Merriman (I think of your ideas

ACKNOWLEDGEMENTS

all the time), Gabriel Tucinski, Matthew Rich, Joshua MacLeod, Jason Zhou, Angelica Velazquillo, João Gonçalves (so glad to know Belo Horizonte because of you!), Kerry Chance, Florian Sichling, Tamara Kamatovic, Youngjo Im (so faithful to our world), and Yazan Doughan. María de los Angeles Gutierrez Bascon walked together with me for many days, with her brilliance, clear vision, and care for others—so much the same as Ifrah Magan. Will Hartley generously kept me housed and safe. In Rhode Island, the world is made brighter by Janice Gallagher, Megan Smith, Catherine Lutz, Julia Chuang, Elizabeth Williams (whose ideas are equaled only by her generous welcome), Patricia Agupusi, Ali Kadivar, Cam Piero, Yusuf Josh Neggers (the most inspiring office-mate), and Michelle Jurkovic, who came to my door every day until I submitted my writing. In upstate New York, I felt guided by Laura Kunreuther, Yuka Suzuki, Sophia Stamatopoulou-Robbins, Jeff Jurgens, Peter Rosenblum, Phil Pardi (who has made me believe both in teaching and in teaching about teaching), Kwame Holmes, Michelle Hoffman, Mike Thicke, Stephanie Savelle, Peter Klein, Susan Elvin Cooper, Edwar Aviles-Mercedes (an extraordinary worker and a reason for me to have hope), and Alexa Murphy (such a good collaboration!) Recently, I have become grateful for the wonderful ideas and welcome of Lotti Silber, Ramona Hernandez, Norma Fuentes-Mayorga, Waldemar Morety, Terri Watson, Matt Reilly, Asale Angel-Ajani, and Sarah Muir. Miles Aiken offers a constant supply of new thoughts.

Mary al-Sayed provided conceptual, collaborative editing of such gracious intensity that many of the ideas are co-authored by her. The "anthropology of accumulation" framing comes entirely from conversations with her. Dylan Joseph Montanari generously and effectively took over for Mary. Fabiola Enríquez Flores and Beth Ina have thoughtfully advised every part of the process. Lys Weiss of Post Hoc Academic Publishing Services provided skilled copyediting.

Many others have shaped my opportunity to write. Jonathan DeVore, your genius and your friendly engagement have changed me. If I consider freedom, it is because of you. Your generosity matters even more: you gave me, among so many thoughts, the title of this text.

Over the last few years I have had the extraordinary chance to write alongside Narges Bajoghli and John Mathias, my closest scribblers, and with Meghan Morris, Lashandra Sullivan, Lee Cabatingan, and Tariq Rahman. Kevin O'Neill, your guidance changed the way I write. Frutuoso Santana speaks as if he is writing a masterwork, and my phone calls with him stay with me as precious stores of wisdom. Oscar Dupuy D'Agneac gives me an example that I cite constantly to students. Judith Miller makes me think nonstop. Every chat with George Borg is a whole world glimpsed.

This manuscript comes in the shadow—the luminescent shadow—of Father Ray Tetrault. So far, I have not met anyone else who combines contemplation and radical social change as he did, does. His brilliant thoughts were exceeded by his love for the beauty in the world. He saved me often and taught me how to be, although I have not done my best yet.

There are so many others whose names I can't manage to write before the filing deadline expires.

This research was supported by the Tinker travel grant, the Social Science Research Council International Dissertation Research Fund, the Inter-American Foundation Grassroots Development Fellowship Program, the Watson Institute postdoc, and the National Institute for the Humanities summer stipend, all of which I gratefully acknowledge. The generous assistance of the Center for Health Administration Studies (Harold Pollack) and the Dominican Studies Institute at CUNY (Ramona Hernandez) is also very much appreciated.

In Brazil, a few names can safely be named. Tatiane Lima welcomed me with her powerful ideas and the care in her spirit. Seu Jovelini allowed me to visit his house constantly, and I remember the songs that we learned to sing together. In the United States, Falina Enriquez's brilliance gave me the energy to continue working, with a smile. Ed Soares brings me hope and struggle every night. Helen Corino guided me, and her lessons stay with me. The welcome, love, and generosity of Ana Khoury is without measure, but her storytelling even more so, and I am so glad every time I see her. Evelyn Woodson taught me about joy, stories, the fight for faith and justice, and the possibility of taking action. Alan Thomas continues to share his genius with me, and he will, I hope, for a long time. Ignácio Martín-Baró, Fabio Santos, Marcos Matos, Augustine, and Thomas Aquinas all helped along the way, and I hope that they will for a long time, too.

Notes

Introduction

1. All names of people (except major public figures) are pseudonyms, and so are "Maracujá" and "Rio Branco."
2. Throughout the text, quoted words are direct quotations if they are in quotation marks, indented, or in transcript format. (In this case, the words are a quotation of a person quoting another person: Alexandra was telling me the story and quoting her mother.) Words in italics are paraphrases, usually based on notes that I jotted down that were not word for word.
3. This was not the first time. Years before, Alexandra had nearly obtained a high school diploma while studying in a boarding-school program for promising rural students. She made it to the last months of that program. Then her youngest daughter became painfully ill. Alexandra heard the news and she returned to the village, giving up her high school plans. It is worth noting the parallel between this situation and the Dakota student described in Ella Deloria's classic anthropological text *Speaking of Indians* (1998: 117).
4. Data from Instituto de Pesquisa Econômica Aplicada 2012: 6 and 19.
5. Seu Jairo actually arrived in Maracujá in the 1990s, somewhat before the economic boom. He came with the landless movement—a story told in the next section.
6. The notion of growth has a close alliance with a different social science concept, development. Daly, for example, distinguishes between "development," which he describes as a (helpful) improvement in the state of the art, and "growth," or the (dangerous) use of finite planetary resources (1996). More humorously, Lucas suggests that "growth theory [is] defined as those aspects of economic growth we have some understanding of, and development defined as those we don't" (2002: 31). What Lucas is alluding to, I think, is a meaningful difference. "Development" is often described as a problem for poor (underdeveloped) economies, while "growth" is what all economies are supposed to experience. If development discourse always requires a reckoning with the gap between rich and poor nations, the language of growth tends to presume that rich and poor nations share common dilemmas. In this discourse, "development" is described as an unquestionably salutary event. "Growth," in contrast, is more questionable, and since the earliest days of growth accounting, its major practitioners have raised serious questions about whether or not growth should take place (Kuznets 1934: 5–7, Keynes 2010). In this book, I have focused almost entirely on the notion of growth, not development. This is, first of all, out of sheer habit, because "growth" (crescimento) was the term used by my interlocutors to describe what was

happening in Brazil at the beginning of the twenty-first century. Second, I speak of growth because I think that when my interlocutors used that word, they were staking out an important position. Neither they nor the economists and policymakers in their nation imagined themselves to be primarily imitating the "developed" world in order to join it. Thus, they lived out what Mitchell has aptly dubbed "the decline of mimetic convergence" (2017: 28–33). They described themselves as people doing something genuinely new, trying to find a new way to live as a society.

7. Tamara arrived in São Paulo in the late 1990s, so the events of this anecdote took place just before the growth boom of the 2000s. Tamara and her family would make a number of trips to live in São Paulo during the boom years as well.

8. Thanks are due to Hannah Appel for this idea, which she explained with rigor. See Meek (2020: chap. 4), on repeasantization.

9. Brazil's extraordinary rates of violence—including violence against women and police violence against Black communities—have been powerfully described by a wide range of scholars. For anthropological analysis, see Caldeira (2000), Savell (2016), Smith (2016), Rocha (2012), Drybread (2016), and Larkins (2015). For a more quantitative approach, see Vargas and Alves (2010) and the Atlas da Violência series, published each year by IPEA (http://www.ipea.gov.br/atlasviolencia/).

10. Economic growth, of course, has been eloquently defended by a panoply of thinkers across generations and continents. (To glimpse the dizzying breadth, consider Yan Qinghua's insightful discussion of Mencius's advocacy—2,400 years ago—for the division of labor in China (2014).) Surveys of contemporary positions are ably supplied by Lucas (2004), Friedman (2005), Oulton (2012), and Mokyr (2017). The correlation between economic growth and life expectancy is represented by the Preston Curve. For data from the whole world over the past century, the Preston Curve demonstrates an undeniable relationship between national income per capita and life expectancy, although this correlation is strongest in lower income nations and is not necessarily due to economic growth per se. See Deaton (2004).

11. The arguments against economic growth are no less venerable and no easier to summarize. Long ago, Aristotle condemned overreaching, which he understood as a characteristic of retail trade; see Parts 9 and 10 from Book I of *Politics* (1996). Today, feminist theorists point to the destructive and warmongering bias of the growth imperative (Waring 1988; Mies 2014) and, in particular, to the fundamental incompatibility between growth logic and the act of caring, which requires one-on-one attention and thus cannot be made more efficient. You cannot accelerate the speed at which you care for another person (Donath 2000). Ecologists note the basic incompatibility between a growth-driven economic system and the environmental system in which the economy is contained (Daly 1996; Vettese 2018; but see Pollin 2018). One result of these criticisms has been a proposal to reject or revise Gross Domestic Product (GDP) as a measure of human flourishing (Ul Haq 1995; Stiglitz et al. 2010; see Coyle 2014 for an amiable defense of GDP). Another thoroughgoing approach has been developed by the degrowth school. These thinkers conclude that growth is not simply irrelevant to human flourishing, but actually harmful to it. Degrowth theorists thus call for a rejection of the growth aspiration. Arguments are presented in Kallis et al. (2012), Latouche (2009), and Norgard (2013)—and, in some senses, prefigured in Schumacher (1973). Kallis, Kerschner, and Martinez-Alier refer specifically to the idea of a degrowth alliance that includes landless peasants (2012: 178).

12. This question comes from a long anthropological tradition. Anthropologists have distinguished themselves by asking, *How does economic growth happen?* or, relatedly, *How does it come to appear that there is such a thing as economic growth?* By the mid-twentieth century, the growth problematic inspired considerable debate inside the discipline. On one side stood scholars who

believed that anthropology could have some useful role in humanizing and promoting growth, and, on the other side, scholars who took growth to be an ethnocentric cover argument for the destruction of noncapitalist lifeways. See contributions from Redfield (1947, 1955), Herskovits (1956), Kottak (2017), Salisbury (1962), Deloria (1998), and Geertz (1963a, 1963b).

By the 1980s, anthropologies of growth had taken a critical turn. Scholars increasingly asked epistemological questions: why it seemed that growth existed, how the discourse of growth became persuasive, and what knowledge/power constituted that discourse. This scholarship refused to take for granted the definition of growth. Sahlins (especially 1994) served as something of a bridge to the new approach. Major contributions came from Mitchell (1998, 2002), Ferguson (1994), and Gibson-Graham (2006), with an important analysis of the intersection with colonial process in Comaroff and Comaroff (1991, 1997). Escobar (1995) offered a summation of the critical position.

Since the turn of the millennium, anthropologists seem to have taken an increasingly postcritical approach to growth. They are more willing to accept that, whatever the conditions in other historical moments, something called "growth" is happening now, and they are curious about how people handle it—through a mix of resistance and resignation, appropriation and hopeful embrace. See Appel's virtually programmatic question: "What might an ethnographic account of economic growth [. . .] look like? More work on national economies could help us think through the intersection of growth imperatives with the imperatives of the Anthropocene" (2017: 315).

As the specter of global environmental crisis has come to occupy a more central place in left-wing imaginaries, growth has become both more tangible (no longer simply an ideological side-effect of capital) and more urgent. The growth/ecology pairing has given (some) progressives the vocabulary they need to articulate a totalizing analysis and envision the social whole, now framed as an enviro-planetary world system. More generally, anthropologists now seem dissatisfied with "unmasking," the scholarly gesture that reveals the fundamentally performative nature of economic life. They wish instead to attend to the details of the performance.

Hirsch, for example, provides a thoroughgoing theorization of economic growth as a collective affect: "Growth is not an objective description but an aspirational composition, a public feeling rendered palpable [. . .] actively orchestrated, deliberately staged, and constantly managed" (2022: 10–11). In tandem with Hirsch's intervention, the recent generational shift has produced exemplary and characteristically ambivalent ethnographies of growth and its travails, including Rogers (2005), Tsing (2005), Li (2014), Besky (2013), Harms (2011), Schuster (2015), Appel (2019), Mitchell (2017), and Ferguson (2015). Livingston (2019) provides a stronger condemnation of growth in Botswana, a condemnation carried out through close attention to the details of economic activity. All these scholars are united by their move away from the critical analysis of discourse and by their fascination with mundane action in a moment of growth.

13. Here I use the word "object" in a broad sense, covering all those entities that can serve as the object of a verb, or, perhaps better, as the object of a desire. A high school diploma, for example, is an object here. For an overview of value debates in anthropology, see Graeber (2001) and Sahlins (2013).

14. Classic texts for an anthropology of accumulation include Sahlins (1972), Munn (1992), Weiner (1976), and Barth (2004).

15. Grateful thanks are due to my teacher Jordano Quâglia, who first told me about the MST, the Movement of Landless Rural Workers (Movimento dos Trabalhadores Rurais Sem Terra).

16. Dawn Plumber, James Green, and an anonymous student helped me get the number, via a chain of emails and phone calls. Only many years later did I actually meet James Green, a major scholar of Brazil's social movements.

17. Expropriation is a legal process that Brazil's federal government can undertake when a sizeable plantation has been determined to be unused or when it has been the site of serious environmental, tax, or labor law violations. The government's land reform agency, INCRA (Instituto Nacional de Colonização e Reforma Agrária), often initiates expropriation proceedings in response to protests by local small farmers, and these protests are often organized by a movement like the MST. The government pays the owner for the land. Land rights are then transferred to the federal government, and the government uses the land to create a settlement for small farmers. For details on the MST and Brazil's land reform, see Morissawa (2001), Branford and Rocha (2002), Wolford (2010), Ondetti (2008), Loera (2010), Meek (2020), Pahnke (2018), and Tarlau (2019). On related rural movements, see Klein (2022).

18. See the very persuasive account in Jonathan DeVore's important series (2014, 2015, 2016, 2017a, 2017b, 2018, 2019a, 2019b, 2020) and DeVore and Paulson (2006). DeVore has consistently argued for increased attention to the emancipatory claims that people enact when they insist on taking up small farming in the context of Brazil's plantation zone.

19. Much of the research was specifically concerned with Bolsa Família, the largest conditional cash transfer program in the world. In this book, Bolsa Família is barely discussed, but results have been published in Morton (2013, 2014, 2015b, 2018b, 2019b, and 2019c).

20. See Morton (2015a: appendix) for detailed information on the surveys.

21. I am grateful to Jonathan DeVore, who pointed out this usage of "world" to me and who generously donated the title for this book.

22. "The banguê sugar estate inaugurates industrial production in Brazil, as early as the sixteenth century" (Menezes, Muniz, and Silva 2013: 10, translation mine). For classic descriptions, see Gorender (2005), Stein (1985), Palmeira (1976), Sigaud (1976), and Mintz (1985). Caio Prado Júnior observes that, since the early days of the colony, Brazil's economic systems have "brought together a relatively large number of workers under the orders and on the behalf of a single entrepreneur. It is this fact that we should chiefly consider, since it is in this system of organizing labor and property that lies the origin of the extreme concentration of wealth that characterizes the colonial economy" (1963: 140). Note how carefully Prado Júnior refers to command ("orders") rather than control.

23. In this vital tradition, a few initial sources include Gilliam (1974), Twine (1998), Souza Tavares (1998), Bledsoe (2017), Rocha (2012), Harding (2003), Perry (2013), Vargas (2005), Sullivan (2017, 2021), Mitchell-Walthour (2018), Paschel (2016), Caldwell (2007), Williams (2013), Matory (2005), and Smith (2016a, 2016b).

24. Classic documents include Nascimento (1989), Fernandes (1964), Andrews (1991), Hellwig (1992), and Butler (1998). Recent years have seen a flourishing of research on Black solidarity and shared experience across the diaspora, including (in addition to those I have already cited) Conceição Evaristo (2016), Roth-Gordon (2016), Bowen and Brandão da Costa (2010), Goldstein (2013), Kenny (2018), Pinheiro-Machado and Scalco (2014), Collins (2015), Garmany and Richmond (2020), and Burdick (1998).

25. I am grateful to Sean Mitchell for this insight.

26. See Sen's acknowledgment of this problem, which he calls "value-endogeneity" (1988: 20).

Chapter One

1. Linguistic anthropologists have helpfully theorized a *voice* as a performance that links a social persona to a genre of speech. For discussion, see Harkness (2014), Kunreuther (2009,

2014), and Bakhtin (1981). My understanding is deeply influenced by Irvine (1996) and Gal and Woolard (2014). For the notion of "authoritative discourse," see Bakhtin (1981).

2. Interestingly, both Marx and Durkheim suggest that it is the act of communication that produces a sense of the social whole—and, more specifically, a sense of one's place in the whole, that is, the consciousness necessary for forming a class sensibility (Durkheim 2014: 304, 308; Marx and Engels 2005: 52; and Marx and Engels 1978: 178–79). Durkheim evocatively refers to "the pleasure of communicating with one another," which he describes as a force beyond interest that brings people together (2014: xliii–xliv). However, Marx and Durkheim alike tend to present communication as a process that is almost automatic and self-acting, and hence they do not develop their observations into full-fledged theories of semiosis.

3. However, there may be considerable solitude in the labor performed by women who find employment as domestic servants in the cities.

4. This is an interpretation that I learned from landless movement leaders and thinkers. See especially Costa Sena (2007: 17–18). For some such militant intellectuals, a core challenge in building a successful land reform community is breaking with the "plantation mindset" that leads workers to strive to produce little autonomous spaces—one's own field, one's own herd. In the "plantation mindset," according to this interpretation, virtually every attempt at collaboration is understood as an imposition by a boss. Landless leaders express great frustration at the fact that when they initiate collaborative ventures, they themselves are sometimes treated like the boss by other farmers, a treatment that involves both deference and resentment (Mitchell 2017: 50–51). One of the major challenges of landless organizing is thus to invent a different, more democratic mode of cooperation, in land reform farms and in the movement's practice more broadly. On these issues, see Wolford (2010), DeVore (2015,) and Branford and Rocha (2002).

5. I am grateful to John Collins for helping me understand the importance of *chamar*.

6. The same verb, *chamar*, can be used to refer to the act of making a telephone call, but villagers mostly say *ligar* instead.

7. Here, I belabor the analysis of commands, but for a reason. The aim is to suggest that *command* is a better notion than *control* for imagining authority inside economic life. This is so, first of all, for empirical reasons. Control is difficult—maybe impossible—for an observer to witness. How can an anthropologist really know if the boss "controls" a given worker? A command, by contrast, is an observable statement: a phrase spoken, a sign posted on a door, a work policy enacted. Commands are communicative. To focus on command is not to solve all the thorny epistemological questions involved in figuring out where authority resides, but at least we are beginning with recognizable evidence.

A second, deeper reason why I prefer the notion of command to the notion of control is that arguments about control tend to rest on an implicit notion of will: each actor has a clear (and singular) will, and to control others is to impose this will on them and turn them into its agents. The notion of command, however, suggests a fundamentally communicative approach to authority. Here, we begin by focusing on the communicative utterance, not on the actor. We do not start with presuppositions about will, agency, autonomy, or freedom. Instead, we have to define these terms by working though the particular (historical and cultural) encounters we find. Freedom, especially, must be discovered rather than presumed.

The notion of command *does* require that the analyst begin by postulating a relationship and a language in which that relationship can be expressed. For this reason, the command concept fits with a vision that imagines the human world as fundamentally relational and linguistic—social from the start—rather than fundamentally composed of pre-existing discrete actors.

These musings have their ground in the problematic faced by Marxists who strive to theorize class inside modern corporate capitalism. In a large corporation, it is not immediately obvious who owns the means of production. The managers (even the CEOs) are themselves employees, not owners. Who is the dominant class? One response to this question is to allow class analysis to sink into the background and to focus, instead, on the experience of being dominated in a more general sense. Another very influential response was pioneered by Dahrendorf, who used the notion of control as a foothold for retaining the class concept. According to Dahrendorf, classes become visible in the contemporary capitalist firm if one monitors "the relation of factual control and subordination in the enterprises of industrial production" (1959: 21). The dominant class is the class that controls production, not simply the class that owns it.

Dahrendorf's approach is important, but it requires us to presume, from the start, what it means to control another person. The suggestion I offer here is that control can helpfully be supplanted by command, a concept that Dahrendorf also uses; see also Foucault (2012: 166). Command is, moreover, theorized by Weber, opening up a possible bridge between Marx's notion of production and Weber's notion of authority (Weber 1968d: 212). By following the *language* of command—the speech-act of commanding—instead of Weber's less helpful suppositions about commands as expressions of will, analysts may gain a clear view onto economic authority in contemporary capitalism, thus locating Weber's and Dahrendorf's insights inside the frame of a critique of capital.

8. Note the parallel with the "precise system of command" that Foucault detects in disciplinary institutions. Such commands are "injunctions whose efficacy rests on brevity and clarity. The order does not need to be explained or formulated; it must trigger off the required behavior and that is enough [. . .] it is a question not of understanding the injunction but of perceiving the signal and reacting to it immediately" (2012: 166).

9. Mbembe has observed that "commandements" (Mbembe's term) become authoritarian because they cannot be discussed. Nonetheless, Mbembe argues, commandements imply a certain familiarity between the person issuing and the person receiving the command. "I use the term commandement," Mbembe explains, "in the way it was used to denote colonial authority, that is, in so far as it embraces the images and structures of power and coercion, the instruments and agents of their enactment, and a degree of rapport between those who give orders and those who are supposed to obey them, without, of course, discussing them. Hence the notion of commandement is used here of the authoritarian modality par excellence" (1992: 30).

10. I am grateful to Jay Sosa for this insight.

Chapter Two

1. Caio Prado Júnior discusses the historical isolation of the region (1963: 42, 98), and Freyre notes how the ranching system, profoundly influential in the region, could serve as a bulwark against enslavement (1989: 42).

2. A caveat is in order here. My sense is that there is a connection between several trends that took place in the region shortly after midcentury: the rise of coffee as a plantation cash crop, the increase in the price of manioc, the new popularity of manioc as a crop for small producers, and the enclosures at Rio Branco. However, this connection is something of a leap on my part; my interlocutors did not say directly that the enclosures were caused by the new prices for manioc.

3. Fábio Santos was a wonderful speaker and a determined leader, and he continued organizing in the face of death threats. These threats were ultimately fulfilled by gunmen who assassinated him while he was driving; they killed him in front of his wife and daughter. Santos spent

NOTES TO PAGES 77–88

time in Maracujá, and people there knew him well. Most of his organizing, however, took place in the municipality of Iguaí. His death was followed a few years later by the assassination of Márcio Matos, a major landless leader in the region. Matos was the son of the antidictatorship mayor Jadiel Matos. For more details, see the appendix to Morton (2015) and also Morton (2018). Both Santos and Matos had interest in supporting the movement by running for electoral office. This wish—to integrate the claims of landless people peacefully into the political system—may have been deeply threatening to the people who killed them.

4. On *natureza* (nature) as a model for people's selfhoods in rural Bahia, see Johnson 1997: 419.

5. One of the best comments I have ever heard about GDP was spoken by Father Ray Tetrault, a brilliant activist and Catholic priest who honored me by auditing a class of mine on economic growth. Once, I asked the class with me, "What does it mean that France's GDP per capita is eight times larger than Thailand's?" He replied, "It means that the French have eight times more needs."

6. GDP makes it possible to compare a single society across time (Brazil's GDP per capita today is higher than it was twenty years ago), and GDP also makes it possible to compare two societies to each other (Brazil's GDP per capita today is lower than Italy's.) However, these are really not the same sort of comparison, which leads to difficulties that deserve further reflection.

7. This argument owes to Angus Deaton.

8. At least, the tasks described did not add a cent to GDP. Village Sundays are actually filled with accompanying small commerce that does add to GDP.

9. I am grateful to Thomas Morton for this insight.

10. For a discussion of this familial style, see Borges 1992.

11. This is a limitation that Durkheim recognized in the Second Preface to the *Rules of the Sociological Method* (1982; second preface written in 1901). I am grateful to Manuela Carneiro da Cunha for teaching this insight.

12. Bolsa Família has been associated with a wide range of effects, including a decrease in income inequality (Paes de Barros et al. 2006); an increase in the height of five-year-old children (Jaime et al. 2014); an improvement in girls' school attendance (DeBrauw et al. 2015); and a 65 percent drop in child deaths from malnutrition (Rasella et al. 2013), among many other outcomes. The program has been the subject of much excellent ethnographic investigation; for a small sample, see Piperata et al. (2016), Badue and Ribeiro (2018), Ahlert (2013), Ansell (2014), Brandão et al. (2013), Balen and Fotta (2018), Lavra Pinto (2013), Lui and Molina (2013), Pereira and Ribeiro (2013), Pires (2009, 2014, 2013), Pires and Rego (2013), Pires and Silva Jardim (2014), A. Pires (2013), Rego and Pinzani (2013), Rocha (2013), Gomes (2011), and Suárez and Libardoni (2007). For a fascinating comparative assessment of the relationship between labor and cash transfers in another context, see Dubbeld (2021).

13. I am grateful to Dain Borges for this idea.

14. Fontes, Andrade Jacinto, and França (2019) find that Bolsa Família is associated with a 5 percent increase in the likelihood that a migrant from the Northeast will return to the Northeast: the program seems to enable migrants to go home.

15. The foregoing might have the unfortunate consequence of implying a grand ranking system in which some societies appear, on the whole, less cooperative than others. "Cooperation" then reduces to a stigmatizing marker of one's modernity or lack thereof. Such a comparison would be an absurd violation of relativist principles, since the collaborations that ran (for example) a Quechua-speaking ayullu in 1400 CE (Mayer 2002) are in some important way not comparable to Alexandra's relationships in Belo Horizonte. Fortunately, one of the semantic benefits of

the word "growth" is that it refers not so much to states as to changes. We can think of growth as less of a scalar and more of a vector, less like location and more like velocity. What concerns us, as we speak of growth, is the intensification itself: the characteristic changes in relationships that people undertake when they find themselves in the middle of a growth process. Growth is not a kind of cooperation; growth is a wave of enthusiasm about transforming the way you cooperate. What we must describe is not which steady state was more cooperative, but rather how and why people embarked on a recognizable project to *change* the kind of cooperation in their lives.

16. I am grateful to Hannah Appel for this term.

Chapter Three

1. *Selva de pedra*, also the title of two famous Brazilian telenovelas.

2. Weber long ago argued that "work" has a special meaning in capitalist modernity, a meaning that emerged through the mundane new habits that city-dwellers acquired in the city-states of Renaissance Italy (Weber 1968b). There, families began to draw a distinction between their household budgets and their business expenditures. Artisans moved their toil to workshops located outside of their houses. One's home life began to feel different from a separate sphere that could be called "work," and the two spheres were associated with a new refiguring of gender, a refiguring that rendered invisible much of the toil done by women (Waring 1988; Donath 2000; Mies 2014). Labor, in the sense that it appears in growth models, arose through such gestures of separation. Weber's argument here reinforces the words of Pope Leo XIII cited in this chapter's epigraph. Progressives may be accustomed to proclaiming that all capital comes from labor, but the reverse also holds. Capital and labor, as concepts, are born together, through the split that makes them different from each other. At Maracujá and Rio Branco, that split happens on the bus.

3. A long line of scholars have traced the inventions, ideologies, and politics that allowed labor to be depicted with increasing abstraction over the past six centuries. More accurate clocks installed in late medieval bell towers played a role (LeGoff 1980); so did the interaction between colony and metropole (Comaroff and Comaroff 1991, 1997); so did the techniques of mass discipline imposed on enslaved people toiling at sugar plantations, techniques developed in Brazil and the Caribbean and then imported to England's incipient factories (Gorender 2005; Mintz 1985). My own thinking about abstract labor has been shaped, in the deepest way, by the teaching of Moishe Postone (1993). For a recent anthropological retheorization of abstract labor, see Narotzky (2018), Harvey and Krohn-Hansen (2018), and the entire special issue they produced.

4. About homogeneity, see Benjamin (1968) and Chakrabarty (2000).

5. This tension is ably addressed in the field of peasant studies. The tension is already present in the concept of "the peasant": as Robert Redfield pointed out, the "peasant" label applies to small farmers who live in relation to a politically dominant extractive elite, often an urban one (Redfield 1955; see Wolf 1966). Peasant farmers remain always distant from their elite counterparts, never fully separate. The two groups are oriented toward a shared religion, language, communications network, and set of standards for measuring value. The similarity is the basis for both oppression and resistance. (See Edelman 2005).

6. On semiproletarianization, see Wallerstein (2003:26), Burawoy (1976), and Meillassoux (1981, especially part 2, chap. 5), and Parson (1984) on the "peasantariat." Young, able-bodied workers migrate to join an urban workforce, while children and older people support themselves much more affordably in the countryside through a heavy dose of home production. Since these young workers do not have families to support in the city, urban wages remain low, the city is ab-

solved of the costs of social reproduction, and a steady stream of new workers flows in with each new generation. The process relies on hidden female labor, since it is often unpaid women, living in the countryside, who quite literally bring down the price of maintaining a worker through their toil to care for the people who will become urban proletarians (as well as those who have already finished a city career).

7. Note Besky's illuminating description of tea workers in India who return to the countryside after deciding that city work is "not good work." In the countryside, their work schedule allows them to make food for children in the morning and be home when children return from school (2013: 80–81).

8. By Victor e Léo, "Deus e eu no sertão," from the album *Victor e Léo* (2002).

9. See Antônio Cândido's words about rural São Paulo state at mid-century:

The *pareceiro* small farmer must obey a certain work rhythm, inscribed in the different units of time—which are for him the day, the week, and the farm year. For the urban worker, with a fixed workday, the hour and often the minute take on a marked importance. They indicate the immediate output of effort and the temporal elements into which an operation can be decomposed. It is not so for the rural worker, who slogs away from one sun to the next, and whose tasks are completed over longer periods, only concluding, in fact, according to the germination cycle.

For the *colono* worker or the salaried worker, the month is the fundamental unit, regulating the receipt of money. But it is not so for the *aforante* worker, whose accounts close at the end of the farm year, and for whom the thirty days mean nothing. The rhythm of his life is determined by the day, which marks out the alternating moments of effort and rest; by the week, measured by the "revolution of the moon," which suspends toil for twenty-four hours, regulating the occurrence of feast-days and contact with other villages; by the year, which includes inside itself the evolution of the seeds and the plants. (1964: 95)

10. See Thompson's pronouncement: "those who are employed experience a distinction between their employer's time and their 'own' time" (1967: 61).

11. Murilo sounded startlingly like one of Kathleen Millar's interlocutors, an independent recycler (*catador*) toiling on a garbage dump in Rio de Janeiro: "I worked for four years at a photocopier, I worked for six years at a grocer, and after one day of working as a street vendor, I never again wanted that life of having a boss order me around" (2018: 43).

12. Here, I owe a special debt to the literature on relationships of mutuality and autonomy in Brazil's Northeast, especially the intrepid anthropologists who embarked, in the middle of the dictatorship, on the "Pernambuco project" to study systems of production in rural Brazil: Sigaud (2007, 1976), Palmeira (1976), and Leite Lopes (1976), among others. Important subsequent interlocutors include Ansell (2014, 2010), Lanna (1995), De L'Estoile (2014), DeVore (2017, 2018).

13. See Schuster (2015: 53, 134, 210) on the notion of "ajeno" in Paraguay.

14. One can detect, here, the fundamental dilemma identified by Lévi-Strauss—one's dependency on those outside the kinship group, because, thanks to the incest taboo, outsiders are necessary to the reproduction of the inside group (1969). See development and critique in Weiner (1976).

15. To refer to the city, Analis used the word *comércio* (commerce), a usage common among older villagers. The word captured something of the way the city was understood: primarily as a location for buying and selling.

16. For only a few examples, see Ansell (2010, 2014), Leal (2012), Fischer (2008), Mitchell (2017), Goldstein (2013).

17. I am grateful to Tom Morton for this insight.

18. Nussbaum traces this approach from Kant through to a certain infamous radical: "Marx, like his bourgeois forebears, holds that it is profoundly wrong to subordinate the ends of some individuals to those of others. That is at the core of what exploitation is, to treat a person as a mere object for the use of others" (2000: 74).

19. Sweat for liquor: this trope fits in with villagers' frequent comments about lack of blood, breastmilk, and rain, all bespeaking the liquid medical theory ultimately derived from the Greek humoral system and famously so influential in the parched drylands of the Northeast (Sanabria 2009, Mayblin 2013).

Chapter Four

1. Prices in the village, by contrast, derive much of their meaning from a different deictic frame: *I* and *you*, the relationship between the speaker and the hearer, with villagers giving different prices to different people.

2. Village negotiation partners might cajole each other by speculating on the future prospects of the negotiated object. To cite only one example, I once heard a young man regale his skeptical neighbor with enthusiastic predictions about the three-month growth of a particular newborn calf that the young man wanted to sell. The Conquista marketplace was different. It offered today's generic commodities for today's standard prices.

Hence the cool affect of the middlemen, which differs notably from the energy of the vendors found a few blocks away, in the department stores, where salespeople wax eloquent about the uniqueness of each washing machine or blender. The farmer selling a calf—or the used-car dealer peddling a Fiat—may create an enthusiasm that renders their merchandise incommensurably special, an enthusiasm stoked by projecting the object into the vagueness of the future. Middlemen instead adopt the half-bored attitude that gives them the authority to rank objects as commodities on a standard scale of value calibrated to the blunt certainty of the present moment. The middleman carries out the "demystifying" move so characteristically familiar inside capitalist discourses—even inside critiques of capitalism—where any enthusiastic and hopeful rhetoric is pierced by the revelation of a boring and emotionless truth-value that underlies it. We can think of this as the reduction of retail to wholesale. Could such a reduction be the ultimate source of modern cool itself? At any rate, it is enacted in the moment when advertising, hype, and other forms of market energy are revealed to rest on a base valuation system in which the object loses the aura of uniqueness with which it had temporarily been invested, becoming instead utterly indistinguishable from a mountain of other objects in its category, all ranked in relation to other objects. The department store washing machine turns out to come from a warehouse of identical hulks of steel. (One might consider here not only Benjamin [1968], but also the moment in *Bicycle Thieves* [De Sica 1948] when the pawnshop clerk shows Maria the innumerable bedsheets that look like her own.) We discover that we fetishize the commodity because it is a commodity: what we love is not something specific about the commodity itself, but instead its vague and generic capacity to incarnate a quantity of human labor that has been used up in its production and that now becomes a badge of our own power as consumers. This bracing moment of demystification is what happens every day when farmers like Félix watch the reduction of their product to wholesale.

We should note, however, that demystifying analysis has its limits. Such an analysis operates from the position of the middleman: it is the middleman's style of thought that we imitate when we plunge into these jaded totalizations with a cool look on our faces. For whatever important capitalist reality this operation reveals, it does not sum up possible approaches. Not in every form of society does the ultimate truth come from the wholesale warehouse.

3. I am grateful to Thomas Morton for the conversation that led to this insight.

4. This sum, R$50, was double the rate for unskilled day labor at the time in the village. I assume that Félix was following the common village practice of valuing labor with a machine at a much higher rate than regular day labor.

5. See Marx's comment: "The independent peasant or handicraftsman is cut up into two persons [. . .] He exploits himself as wage-labourer" (1969:408).

6. Farmers would make this kind of calculation when I asked them, in interviews, to list their agricultural expenses for the year. In an important sense, I was creating the context for the calculation (although I did not suggest to farmers that they should account their own labor as an expense, and I felt very surprised when they did). Was I influencing the calculation too much with my questions? Worried, I spoke with the always generous Félix. He assured me that farmers did often assign a monetary value to their labor. Why? Félix suggested that he and others at Maracujá had learned the habit from the agricultural extension officials who helped MST farmers apply for loans. This suggestion, while fascinating, did not entirely satisfy me, since I had heard farmers mention their own labor as an expense at Rio Branco, a village with no formal connection to the MST and few links to extension agents.

7. It is perhaps not a coincidence that I heard this aesthetic response—the refusal to calculate—most clearly from older women. Similar words came from the mouths of men, but the rejection of calculation was never as clear as from Dona Lola and Dona Mara.

8. Tarlau has noted that MST ideology aims precisely at this goal. In the MST's (Marxist) analysis, labor relations under capital tend to separate managers from workers, mental from manual labor, those who see the total from those who act on it. "Such separation rejects workers' ability to envision the entire production process [. . .] A major principle of the MST's pedagogical approach is to reject the separation between intellectual and manual labor and, instead, promote the idea of farmer-intellectuals who are both the engineers and laborers of the production process" (Tarlau 2019: 54).

9. Marx uses this example from Burke in *Capital,* chap. 13, "Cooperation" (1976: 440).

10. Weber (2002), Durkheim (2014), Williams (2014), Mintz (1985), Mies (2014), Marx (1976).

Chapter Five

1. Note the connection to classic economic anthropology theory about separate "spheres of value." A conversion is the act of taking an object from one sphere of value and transforming it into something that can circulate in another sphere of value (Bohannan and Bohannan 1968).

2. My debt to Bourdieu (1977, 2011) is obvious here. Readers, if they like, may convert my phrasing into Bourdieu's vocabulary: cultural capital, social capital, fields, and illusio. However, I have reasons for not doing so. Bourdieu, I worry, does not offer enough of a compelling account of what "economic capital" means; its meaning is sometimes taken for granted (Weininger 2005: 87). One possible outcome is that readers may come to see the whole world as fundamentally economistic, with the consequence that return to the countryside can only be understood as a mystification or misrecognition of value, not as a tenuous but genuine step beyond the realm

of value itself. But if Bourdieu's theory sometimes seems pessimistic, his life does not. His commitment to action for social change is admirable—and rare among social scientists who write in cheerier tones of voice—and I hope that my challenges here can do honor to that commitment.

3. If we think of class as a relation to labor, then we are not thinking about class (in the first instance) as a relation to the dominators, to the marketplace, or to the means of production. Instead, we begin by focusing on how people understand their work. This account stands in contrast to the approach adopted by those Marxists who define class as the distinction between people who own the means of production and people who do not (see Marx and Engels 2005: 39n; Turner 1979, 2003). In my view, some difficulties arise when one defines class by reference to the ownership of the means of production. If class is the effect of property relations, then is it not property relations—rather than production itself—that lie at the heart of history? The approach runs the risk of legalism, since it prioritizes the legal question of property. This legalism seems at odds with the Marxist imperative to explain politics as a result of production and not the reverse. Questions only deepen when one observes that the footnote cited above (Marx and Engels 2005: 39n) was written by Engels, in 1888, after Marx's death.

Of course, social class also has its non-Marxist theorists. Weber typically appears as the most decisive of these, and he defines class as one's position in a marketplace, whether that position is determined by one's property or one's capacity to mobilize labor (1968a, 1968c). Weber has become especially famous for his distinction between class, status, and party: he insists that one's market position does *not* correspond in any simple way to one's honor among peers (status) or one's alliance with organized groups that change the social order (party). (In anthropology, see Warner and Lunt [1973]). Perhaps most of all, Weber is engaged by Bourdieu and his interlocutors, who build a bridge to Marx by cataloguing the intricate and always fraught translations between status, party, and class—these three having been rebaptized as cultural capital, social capital, and economic capital.

Although I am fascinated by the Weberian interest in history, in this book I attempt to ground myself more deeply in an alternative Marxist account, which defines social class in terms of the worker's consciousness. On this view, class emerges not from ownership per se, but rather from the relations developed inside the division of labor (Marx and Engels 1978: 160). Anthropologists and their allies, inspired by this approach, have demonstrated how such labor relations presuppose and entail a consciousness, a practical disposition toward the world. Class is thus a matter of consciousness. It is about the relationship between the dominators and the dominated as that relationship is lived out inside a given labor relation. The "consciousness" approach to class has been enormously influential for anthropology, and is powerfully represented by (among an ocean of others) Nash (1993), Thompson (1963), and Davis (2011).

Unlike some consciousness theorists, however, I do not aim to expand the notion of class so broadly that it covers any act of domination. Instead of interrogating domination in general, I ask about how people engage with their work. In other words, I focus specifically on labor (in its abstract mode). Rather than highlighting relations that appear immediately as relations between persons, I emphasize the worker's relationship to time and objects. This relationship is created through a given type of labor. Our imaginations about time and objects do *ultimately* correspond to our relations to other people, I argue, but through the mediation of labor. Rather than moving straight to an assessment of the human link, I attempt to tarry with the mediation, taking it as the problem to be solved. How does our labor connect us with other people—but then blind us to that very connection? (See Kalb 2015: 19.) Inspirational, in this regard, is Lukács's definition, which focuses on class as a reality that emerges from production as a process: "in

Marxism the division of society into classes is determined by position within the process of production" (1999: 46). Even more inspirational is the question that Lukács places immediately following: "But what, then, is the meaning of class consciousness?"

4. Moisés Kopper powerfully suggests that class analysis should consider "the particular imaginative horizons through which distinction and belonging, hierarchy and aspiration, human becoming and materiality, are woven into action," and he urges analysts to "become attentive to how objects and materials pervade middle-class affects" (2019: 82).

5. See Thorkelson's important argument about how class can precede work (2016: 483).

6. "An asset," say Adkins, Cooper, and Konings, "has a particular temporal structure: it requires an upfront investment of (often borrowed) funds and it is meant to generate returns over a particular future timeframe" (2020: 16–17). In what follows, I do not fully embrace the authors' (Weberian?) suggestion that contemporary social classes are defined by asset ownership rather than labor—since I describe workers who find assets to be relevant precisely because those assets can change one's relationship to labor. Nonetheless, the authors' interpretation of asset inequality is fascinating.

7. These paragraphs bear a resemblance to the discussion in Morton (2018b: 118, 121).

8. Similar to independent small farmers, but clustered on the great estates, were the moradores, the live-in workers on a plantation. Moradores had to contend with a split in the objects around them. On the one side stood the plantation master's assets; on the other side stood the morador's personal crops or herds, which the morador grew during off-hours, in spare plots that the plantation master allowed the workers to use. For a morador, improvement might mean devoting less energy to the plantation master's projects and more energy to their personal realm. Moradores thus struggled for space, in a literal sense, against their bosses (Palmeira 1976; Sigaud 1976, 2007; Barickman 1994; Lanna 1995). Consider, here, the example of Margarida Maria Alves, a major peasant leader and martyr, who struggled for rural workers' rights in the state of Paraíba. Her friend Maria de Soledade Leite said that Alves fought for, among other rights, the right to an area of land where a plantation worker could plant their own crops. "The right to a plot, because the bosses planted sugarcane right up to the door of the house. When we would open the door of the house, we would already be in the middle of the sugarcane field. Her struggle was so that the worker could have a little space for the worker's own crops—all in all, to be able to give a dignified life to her or his or their family" (Lourenço 2015).

9. At the time of writing, carteiras had just become digital.

10. See Marx and Engels on the emergence of Europe's medieval towns: "here property consisted chiefly in the labour of each individual person" (1978: 153).

11. This is a classic argument from the sociology of the professions; see Barber (1963: 679) and Greenwood (1957: 47–48). In the pattern of supervision, liberal professionals differed from wage laborers, whose work was measured by supervisors who were *not* their peers. Liberal professionals thus had something in common with peasant farmers, who also judged their own peers' work, devoting endless hours to debate over the best way to free a tangled cow or clear a field. This similarity created a ground for easy alliance between liberal professionals and peasant farmers. Since both groups embraced egalitarianism as a principle for judgment, it was perhaps understandable that Nelson and Mariele mixed liberal professional work with their farming careers. It was understandable, too, that waves of urban teachers, nurses, psychologists, and anthropologists visited the landless villages and felt deeply inspired by the peasant spirit of freedom, a spirit that resonated with the professionals' own sensibilities about independence from bosses. The alliance could only go so far, however. Peasant farmers tended to work alone and

embrace an especially fierce form of autonomy. Liberal professionals, for the most part, depended intensely on the cooperation of others. Indeed, professional jobs consisted largely of efforts to persuade people to act, speak, think, medicate, worship, or vote differently.

12. See a similar example in Morton 2019a: 674.

13. Avon sales, notably, seemed to operate according to a very different logic, as a succession of reiterated private dealings. The villages' Avon vendors set up intimate, often in-home conversations with their customers to determine what products people needed, to deliver the wares, and to collect debts owed. For example, when Nalta sold Avon goods to families that failed to pay her back, she pressured the debtors by sending private letters that her son gave to the offending families at school. The differential gendering of public space in the villages, unsurprisingly, materialized as a relatively low-key but nonetheless unmistakable expression of patriarchal power.

14. See Sites's insightful comment on the contribution of small proprietors to collective autonomy (in a different context): "Small business ownership in this instance represented a precondition for the development of cultural autonomy—not freedom from the dictates of the marketplace but [a] kind of organizational independence" (2020: 154).

15. On this sense of hegemony, see Comaroff and Comaroff (1992: 28–30) and Eagleton (1991: 118).

16. Ferguson offers similar stories about mine workers in the Zambian Copperbelt who must spend a large portion of their lifetime pension savings to pay to move their belongings into villages when they retire (1999: 125, 152).

17. What most stabilized a field was the presence of perennials. Long-term plants like coffee bushes and fruit trees were considered, as Seu Milton explained to me, "goods and fruits [*bens e frutos*]." On the nearby plantations, when a sharecropper planted such crops, they would be guaranteed the right to harvest them permanently; if the plantation's owner wanted to move the sharecropper to another field, the owner would need to pay the sharecropper for the value of the perennials. In Seu Milton's words, "That right there is a field that remains—let's put it this way—that remains for a whole lifetime. [. . .] That field will not end." (See Sigaud 1976; Palmeira 1976; Johnson 1971.)

Chapter Six

1. For Suso's disturbing encounter with racism and police, during a previous move to the city, see pp. 121–22.

2. See Schuster's similar fieldwork observation: "Whenever I inquired if people were saving for anything, they laughed wryly and told me that 'money flies from your pocket' if you let it sit there too long" (2019: 742).

3. My usage of "premio" takes advantage of an ambiguity that arises when translating the Portuguese word *prêmio* (or its Spanish equivalent, *premio*) into English. *Prêmio* means both "reward" and "prize"; it can refer both to remuneration earned over the long term ("a reward for her labors") and to a short-term jackpot ("a lottery prize.") This ambiguity seems well suited to the meaning at hand, since the premio, in the sense it is used in this chapter, is an immediately visible object—a jackpot of sorts—that comes to stand in for or take the place of regular remuneration.

4. For a complementary interpretation of *segurar* in contemporary urban Brazil, see Sullivan (2021).

NOTES TO PAGES 179–206

5. The notion that cattle represent a special kind of wealth, avidly preserved outside of the sphere of capitalist circulation, is a frequent theme in literature from southern Africa (Ferguson 1994; Comaroff and Comaroff 2005).

6. Compare the similar, but not identical, stories in the second English-language preface to Gilberto Freyre, *Masters and the Slaves* (1987). See also Alger (1864: 415).

7. "Inaudible" indicates a part of the recording I could not hear well enough to understand.

8. I am grateful to Bill Sites for this insight.

9. From the song "Casino Nation" (2002), on the album *The Naked Ride Home*.

10. The verbal parallel is a deep one, because female house servants were referred to as *empregadas*, "employed people." When Tamara employed her money, she was doing to that money exactly what her boss did to her.

11. For an important reflection on the idiom of "making a future" in Bahia—here focused on Calon—see Fotta (2019).

12. Canonically, in neoclassical economics, money is understood as having three functions. First, money serves as a *medium of exchange*, allowing person A to trade with person B even if person B does not have any good or service that person A wants. Person B can offer money, which person A can use to make purchases from other people. Money's second function is to serve as a *measure of value*: money acts like a mental measuring-stick that allows the value of any good or service to be compared to the value of any other. The third function of money is to serve as a *store of value*. By using money, you can sell a good or service, then hold on to the resulting value and spend it at a later date. For a textbook discussion, see Samuelson and Nordhaus (2001: 519).

13. The privileging of money's first function is a tendency that has a long history in Europe. John Calvin, the Protestant pioneer, defined money as "a medium of mutual communication among men [. . .] principally employed in buying and selling merchandise" (Calvin [1948: 584]; this is discussed at length in Friedman [2005: 46]). Adam Smith stipulated, "The sole use of money is to circulate consumable goods. By means of it, provisions, materials, and finished work, are bought and sold, and distributed to their proper consumers" (1786: book 2, chap. 3). Smith, of course, is well aware of the possibility of saving, which he mentions at the end of the same paragraph. But, at least in my reading, he considers saving to be a function subordinate to consumption: you save now in order to consume later. This assumption seems far from the idea that saving might have its own reasons—that you might save in order to distance yourself from the market, to enjoy a feeling of safety, to gain power over your own labor process, to create a social group, or to decline contact with others. Similarly, Smith and Calvin's assumption does not seem to allow for the possibility that production itself, rather than consumption, might be one of the goals of economic activity, and that people might save in order to make it possible for themselves to produce in the way they wish to produce (rather than to consume in the way they wish to consume). (Smith is helpfully discussed in Gudeman and Rivera [1990: 178].)

Conclusion

1. There is a voluminous literature on citizenship discourse in Brazil since the dictatorship. Savell (2015) offers a fascinating, complex look at the dialectic between participation and *non*participation. Other helpful sources include Rego (2008), Holston (2009), and Romano et al. (2007). See Sosa (2020) and forthcoming work by him.

References

Adkins, Lisa, Melinda Cooper, and Martijn Konings. 2020. *The Asset Economy: Property Ownership and the New Logic of Inequality*. Cambridge: Polity Press.

Ahlert, Martina. 2013. "A 'Precisão' e o 'Luxo': Usos do Benefício do Programa Bolsa Família Entre as Quebradeiras de Coco de Codó (MA)." *Política & Trabalho* 38: 69–86.

Alger, William Rousenville. 1864. *A Critical History of the Doctrine of a Future Life*. Philadelphia: George W. Childs.

Andrews, George Reid. 1991. *Blacks & Whites in São Paulo, Brazil, 1888–1988*. Madison: University of Wisconsin Press.

Ansell, Aaron. 2010. "Auctioning Patronage in Northeast Brazil: The Political Value of Money in a Ritual Market." *American Anthropologist* 112 (2): 283–94.

Ansell, Aaron. 2014. *Zero Hunger: Political Culture and Antipoverty Policy in Northeast Brazil*. Chapel Hill: University of North Carolina Press.

Appel, Hannah. 2017. "Toward an Ethnography of the National Economy." *Cultural Anthropology* 32 (2): 294–322.

Appel, Hannah. 2019. *The Licit Life of Capitalism: US Oil in Equatorial Guinea*. Durham, NC: Duke University Press.

Aristotle. 1996. *The Politics*. Edited by Stephen Everson. Translated by Jonathan Barnes. Cambridge: Cambridge University Press.

Badue, Ana Flavia, and Florbela Ribeiro. 2018. "Gendered Redistribution and Family Debt: The Ambiguities of a Cash Transfer Program in Brazil." *Economic Anthropology* 5 (2): 261–73.

Baeninger, Rosana. 2012. "Rotatividade Migratória: Um Novo Olhar Para as Migrações Internas no Brasil." *REMHU: Revista Interdisciplinar Da Mobilidade Humana* 39: 77–100.

Bakhtin, M. M. 1981. *The Dialogic Imagination*. Edited by Michael Holquist. Translated by Caryl Emerson and Michael Holquist. Austin: University of Texas Press.

Balen, Maria Elisa, and Martin Fotta. 2018. *Money from the Government in Latin America: Conditional Cash Transfer Programs and Rural Lives*. Abingdon, UK: Routledge.

Baptista, Emerson Augusto, Járvis Campos, and José Irineu Rangel Rigotti. 2017. "Migração de Retorno no Brasil." *Mercator (Fortaleza)* 16: 1–18.

Barber, Bernard. 1963. "Some Problems in the Sociology of the Professions." *Daedalus* 92: 669–88.

Barickman, Bert J. 1994. "'A Bit of Land, Which They Call Roça': Slave Provision Grounds in the Bahian Recôncavo, 1780–1860." *Hispanic American Historical Review* 74 (4): 649–87.

Barth, Fredrik. 2004 [1967]. "Economic Spheres in Darfur." In *Themes in Economic Anthropology*, 149–74. Abingdon, UK: Routledge.

Bear, Laura, Karen Ho, Anna Lowenhaupt Tsing, and Sylvia Yanagisako. 2015. "Gens: A Feminist Manifesto for the Study of Capitalism." *Cultural Anthropology* website.

Benjamin, Walter. 1968a. "Theses on the Philosophy of History." In *Illuminations*, edited by Hannah Arendt, translated by Harry Zohn, 196–209. New York: Schocken.

Benjamin, Walter. 1968b. "The Work of Art in the Age of Mechanical Reproduction." In *Illuminations*, edited by Hannah Arendt, translated by Harry Zohn, 166–95. New York: Schocken.

Bergman, Pär. 2017. *'Modernolatria' e 'Simultaneità': Investigações Sobre Duas Tendências de Vanguarda Literária na Itália e na França às Vésperas da Ia Guerra Mundial*. Translated by Júlio Bernardo Machinski. Joinville, Brazil: Clube de Autores.

Besky, Sarah. 2013. *The Darjeeling Distinction: Labor and Justice on Fair Trade Tea Plantations in India*. Berkeley: University of California Press.

Bledsoe, Adam. 2017. "Marronage as a Past and Present Geography in the Americas." *Southeastern Geographer* 57 (1): 30–50.

Bohannan, Linda, and Paul Bohannan. 1968. *Tiv Economy*. Evanston, IL: Northwestern University Press.

Borges, Dain. 1992. *The Family in Bahia, Brazil, 1870–1945*. Stanford: Stanford University Press.

Bourdieu, Pierre. 1977. *Outline of a Theory of Practice*. Translated by Richard Nice. New York: Cambridge University Press.

Bourdieu, Pierre. 2011 [1983]. "The Forms of Capital." In *Cultural Theory: An Anthology*, edited by Imre Szeman and Timothy Kaposy, translated by Richard Nice, 81–93. Chichester, UK: Wiley-Blackwell.

Bowen, Merle L., and Josilene Brandão da Costa. 2010. "The Struggle for Black Land Rights in Brazil: An Insider's View on Quilombos and the Quilombo Land Movement." *African and Black Diaspora: An International Journal* 3 (2): 147–68.

Branco, Mariana. 2013. "Ministra Destaca Redução da Desigualdade na Última Década." *EBC*, January 29. https://memoria.ebc.com.br/noticias/economia/2013/01/pela-primeira-vez-brasil-esta-dividindo-o-bolo-diz-ministra.

Brandão, André, Rita de Cássia Pereira, and Salete da Dalt. 2013. "Programa Bolsa Família: Percepção no Cotidiano da Escola." *Politica & Trabalho* 38: 215–32.

Branford, Sue, and Jan Rocha. 2002. *Cutting the Wire: The Story of the Landless Movement in Brazil*. London: Latin America Bureau.

Brauw, Alan de, Daniel O. Gilligan, John Hoddinott, and Shalini Roy. 2015. "The Impact of Bolsa Família on Schooling." *World Development* 70 (Suppl. C): 303–16.

Browning, Martin, and Annamaria Lusardi. 1996. "Household Saving: Micro Theories and Micro Facts." *Journal of Economic Literature* 34 (4): 1797–1855.

Burawoy, Michael. 1976. "The Functions and Reproduction of Migrant Labor: Comparative Material from Southern Africa and the United States." *American Journal of Sociology* 81 (5): 1050–87.

Burdick, John. 1998. *Blessed Anastácia: Women, Race, and Popular Christianity in Brazil*. London: Routledge.

Burke, Edmund. 2017 [1795]. "Thoughts and Details on Scarcity, Originally Presented to the Right Hon. William Pitt, in the Month of November, 1795." In *The Works of Edmund Burke*, vol. 5. Altenmünster, Germany: Jazzybee Verlag Jürgen Beck.

REFERENCES

Butler, Kim D. 1998. *Freedoms Given, Freedoms Won: Afro-Brazilians in Post-Abolition, Sao Paulo and Salvador.* New Brunswick, NJ: Rutgers University Press.

Caldeira, Teresa PR. 2000. *City of Walls: Crime, Segregation, and Citizenship in São Paulo.* Berkeley: University of California Press.

Caldwell, Kia. 2007. *Negras in Brazil: Re-Envisioning Black Women, Citizenship, and the Politics of Identity.* New Brunswick, NJ: Rutgers University Press.

Calvin, John. 1948 [1554]. *Commentaries on the First Book of Moses, Called Genesis, Vol. 1.* Translated by John King. Grand Rapids, MI: Wm. B. Eerdmans. (Also see digital edition at Christian Classics Ethereal Library.)

Candido, Antonio. 1964. *Os Parceiros do Rio Bonito: Estudo Sobre o Caipira Paulista e a Transformação dos Seus Meios de Vida.* Rio de Janeiro: Ouro Sobre Azul.

Chakrabarty, Dipesh. 2000. *Provincializing Europe: Postcolonial Thought and Historical Difference.* Princeton: Princeton University Press.

Chu, Julie Y. 2010. *Cosmologies of Credit: Transnational Mobility and the Politics of Destination in China.* Durham, NC: Duke University Press.

Coase, Ronald Harry. 1937. "The Nature of the Firm." *Economica* 4 (16): 386–405.

Collins, John F. 2015. *Revolt of the Saints: Memory and Redemption in the Twilight of Brazilian Racial Democracy.* Durham, NC: Duke University Press.

Comaroff, Jean, and John L. Comaroff. 1991. *Of Revelation and Revolution, Vol. 1: Christianity, Colonialism, and Consciousness in South Africa.* Chicago: University of Chicago Press.

Comaroff, Jean, and John L. Comaroff. 1992. *Ethnography and the Historical Imagination.* Boulder, CO: Westview Press.

Comaroff, Jean, and John L. Comaroff. 1997. *Of Revelation and Revolution, Vol. 2: The Dialectics of Modernity on a South African Frontier.* Chicago: University of Chicago Press.

Comaroff, Jean, and John L. Comaroff. 2005. "Beasts, Banknotes and the Colour of Money in Colonial South Africa." *Archaeological Dialogues* 12 (2): 107–32.

Conceição Evaristo, Maria Aparaceida Salgueiro de Andrade. 2016. "From the Fetus That Sprouts within Me." Translated by Antonio D. Tillis. *Meridians: Feminism, Race, Transnationalism* 14 (1): 84–93.

Costa Sena, Railda. 2007. "A Despolitização do MST Através dos Programas Assistenciais no Município de Vitória Da Conquista—Bahia." Guararema, Brazil: Curso Produção da Teoria—Pensamento Político Brasileiro, Escola Nacional Florestan Fernandes.

Coyle, Diane. 2014. *GDP: A Brief But Affectionate History.* Princeton: Princeton University Press.

Cunha, Manuela Carneiro da. 1985. "Silences of the Law: Customary Law and Positive Law on the Manumission of Slaves in 19th Century Brazil." *History and Anthropology* 1 (2): 427–43.

Dahrendorf, Ralf. 1959. *Class and Class Conflict in Industrial Society.* Stanford: Stanford University Press.

Daly, Herman E. 1996. *Beyond Growth: The Economics of Sustainable Development.* Boston: Beacon Press.

DaMatta, Roberto. 1991. *Carnivals, Rogues, and Heroes: An Interpretation of the Brazilian Dilemma.* Translated by John Drury. Notre Dame, IN: University of Notre Dame Press.

Davis, Angela Y. 1981. *Women, Race, and Class.* New York: Vintage.

Davis, Angela Y. 2011. *Blues Legacies and Black Feminism: Gertrude Ma Rainey, Bessie Smith, and Billie Holiday.* New York: Vintage.

Deaton, Angus. 2004. "Health in an Age of Globalization." Cambridge, MA: National Bureau of Economic Research (NBER).

Deaton, Angus. 2013. *The Great Escape: Health, Wealth, and the Origins of Inequality*. Princeton: Princeton University Press.

De L'Estoile, Benôit. 2014. "'Money Is Good, But a Friend Is Better:' Uncertainty, Orientation to the Future, and 'the Economy.'" *Current Anthropology* 55 (S9): S62–73.

Deloria, Ella Cara. 1998. *Speaking of Indians*. Lincoln: University of Nebraska Press.

De Sica, Vittorio, dir. 1948. *Bicycle Thieves (The Bicycle Thief)*. Film.

DeVore, Jonathan. 2014. "Cultivating Hope: Struggles for Land, Equality, and Recognition in the Cacao Lands of Southern Bahia, Brazil." PhD diss., Department of Anthropology, University of Michigan, Ann Arbor.

DeVore, Jonathan. 2015. "The Landless Invading the Landless: Participation, Coercion, and Agrarian Social Movements in the Cacao Lands of Southern Bahia, Brazil." *Journal of Peasant Studies* 42 (6): 1201–23.

DeVore, Jonathan. 2016. "Reflections on Crisis, Land, and Resilience in Brazil's Politics of Distribution." *FocaalBlog*, October 6. www.focaalblog.com.

DeVore, Jonathan. 2017a. "Odebrecht's Original Sins: Another Case for Reparations: How a History of Land Speculation and Dispossession in Southern Bahia Foreshadowed Odebrecht's Fall from Grace." *NACLA Report on the Americas* 49 (4): 408–15.

DeVore, Jonathan. 2017b. "The Mind of the Copaíba Tree: Notes on Extractivism, Animism, and Ontology from Southern Bahia." *Ethnobiology Letters* 8 (1): 115–24.

DeVore, Jonathan. 2017c. "Trees and Springs as Social Property: A Perspective on Degrowth and Redistributive Democracy from a Brazilian Squatter Community." *Journal of Political Ecology* 24 (1): 644–66.

DeVore, Jonathan. 2018. "Scattered Limbs: Capitalists, Kin, and Primitive Accumulation in Brazil's Cacao Lands, 1950s–1970s." *Journal of Latin American and Caribbean Anthropology* 23 (3): 496–520.

DeVore, Jonathan. 2019. "Devouring the Public Good: Everyday Forms of Financial Extractivism." *NACLA Report on the Americas* 51 (2): 159–66.

DeVore, Jonathan. 2020. "From Sharecropping to Equal Shares: Transforming the Sharing Economy in Northeastern Brazil." *Dialectical Anthropology* 44 (4): 373–95.

Donath, Susan. 2000. "The Other Economy: A Suggestion for a Distinctively Feminist Economics." *Feminist Economics* 6 (1): 115–23.

Drybread, Kristen. 2016. "Documents of Indiscipline and Indifference: The Violence of Bureaucracy in a Brazilian Juvenile Prison." *American Ethnologist* 43 (3): 411–23.

Dubbeld, Bernard. 2021. "Granting the Future? The Temporality of Cash Transfers in the South African Countryside." *Revista de Antropologia* 64 (2): 1–19.

Durkheim, Emile. 1982. *The Rules of Sociological Method*. Edited by Steven Lukes. Translated by W.D. Halls. New York: Free Press.

Durkheim, Emile. 2014. *The Division of Labor in Society*. New York: Free Press.

Eagleton, Terry. 1991. *Ideology*. London: Verso.

Economist. 2020. "Not Just a First-World Problem." January 18.

Edelman, Marc. 2005. "Bringing the Moral Economy Back In . . . to the Study of 21st-Century Transnational Peasant Movements." *American Anthropologist* 107 (3): 331–45.

Enriquez, Falina. 2022a. *The Costs of the Gig Economy: Musical Entrepreneurs and the Cultural Politics of Inequality in Northeastern Brazil*. Urbana: University of Illinois Press.

Enriquez, Falina. 2022b. "Pernambuco and Bahia's Musical 'War': Contemporary Music, Intraregional Rivalry, and Branding in Northeastern Brazil." *Luso-Brazilian Review* 59 (1): 22–60.

REFERENCES

Escobar, Arturo. 1995. *Encountering Development: The Making and Unmaking of the Third World.* Princeton: Princeton University Press.

Ferguson, James. 1994. *The Anti-Politics Machine: "Development," Depoliticization, and Bureaucratic Power in Lesotho.* Minneapolis: University of Minnesota Press.

Ferguson, James. 1999. *Expectations of Modernity: Myths and Meanings of Urban Life on the Zambian Copperbelt.* Berkeley: University of California Press.

Ferguson, James. 2015. *Give a Man a Fish: Reflections on the New Politics of Distribution.* Durham, NC: Duke University Press.

Fernandes, Florestan. 1964. *A Integração Do Negro Na Sociedade de Classes.* São Paulo: Faculdade de Filosofia, Ciências e Letras da USP.

Fernandes, Rubem César. 1985. "Aparecida, Our Queen, Lady, and Mother, Saravá!" *Social Science Information* 24 (4): 799–819.

Fischer, Brodwyn M. 2008. *A Poverty of Rights: Citizenship and Inequality in Twentieth-Century Rio de Janeiro.* Stanford: Stanford University Press.

Fontes, Luiz Felipe Campos, Paulo de Andrade Jacinto, and Marco Tulio França. 2019. "Programas de Transferência de Renda e Migração Interna: Evidências Do Programa Bolsa Família." *Análise Econômica* 37 (72).

Fotta, Martin. 2019. "'Only the Dead Don't Make the Future': Calon Lives between Non-Gypsies and Death." *Journal of the Royal Anthropological Institute* 25 (3): 587–605.

Foucault, Michel. 2012. *Discipline and Punish: The Birth of the Prison.* Translated by Alan Sheridan. New York: Vintage.

Fraga, Walter. 2016. *Crossroads of Freedom: Slaves and Freed People in Bahia, Brazil, 1870–1910.* Translated by Mary Ann Mahony. Durham, NC: Duke University Press.

Freyre, Gilberto. 1987. *The Masters and the Slaves/Casa-Grande and Senzala: A Study in the Development of Brazilian Civilization.* Berkeley: University of California Press.

Friedman, Benjamin M. 2005. *The Moral Consequences of Economic Growth.* New York: Vintage.

Gal, Susan, and Judith T. Irvine. 2000. "Language Ideology and Linguistic Differentiation." In *Regimes of Language: Ideologies, Polities, and Identities,* edited by Paul V. Kroskrity, 35–84. Santa Fe, NM: School of American Research Press.

Gal, Susan, and Kathryn A. Woolard. 2014. "Constructing Languages and Publics: Authority and Representation." In *Languages and Publics: The Making of Authority,* 1–12. Abingdon, UK: Routledge.

Garmany, Jeff, and Matthew A. Richmond. 2020. "Hygienisation, Gentrification, and Urban Displacement in Brazil." *Antipode* 52 (1): 124–44.

Geertz, Clifford. 1963a. *Agricultural Involution: The Process of Ecological Change in Indonesia.* Berkeley: University of California Press.

Geertz, Clifford. 1963b. *Peddlers and Princes: Social Change and Economic Modernization in Two Indonesian Towns.* Chicago: University of Chicago Press.

Gibson-Graham, J. K. 2006. *The End of Capitalism (As We Knew It): A Feminist Critique of Political Economy.* Minneapolis: University of Minnesota Press.

Gilliam, Angela. 1974. "Black and White in Latin America." *Présence Afric aine* 92: 161–73.

Goldstein, Donna M. 2013. *Laughter Out of Place: Race, Class, Violence, and Sexuality in a Rio Shantytown.* Berkeley: University of California Press.

Gomes, Simone. 2011. "Notas Preliminares de Uma Crítica Feminista Aos Programas de Transferência Direta de Renda—O Caso Do Bolsa Família No Brasil." *Textos & Contextos (Porto Alegre)* 10 (1): 69–81.

Gorender, Jacob. 2005 [1978]. "A Forma Plantagem de Organização Da Produção Escravista." In *A Questão Agrária No Brasil: O Debate Na Esquerda—1960-1980*, edited by João Pedro Stedile and Douglas Estevam, 2:147-76. São Paulo: Expressão Popular.

Graeber, David. 2001. *Toward an Anthropological Theory of Value: The False Coin of Our Own Dreams*. New York: Palgrave Macmillan.

Graeber, David. 2011. *Debt: The First 5,000 Years*. New York: Melville House.

Green, James N. 2001. *Beyond Carnival: Male Homosexuality in Twentieth-Century Brazil*. Chicago: University of Chicago Press.

Greenwood, Ernest. 1957. "Attributes of a Profession." *Social Work* 2 (3): 45-55.

Gudeman, Stephen, and Alberto Rivera. 1990. *Conversations in Colombia: The Domestic Economy in Life and Text*. Cambridge: Cambridge University Press.

Guyer, Jane I. 1993. "Wealth in People and Self-Realization in Equatorial Africa." *Man* 28 (2): 243-65.

Haq, Mahbub Ul. 1995. *Reflections on Human Development*. Oxford: Oxford University Press.

Harding, Rachel. 2003. *A Refuge in Thunder: Candomblé and Alternative Spaces of Blackness*. Bloomington: Indiana University Press.

Harkness, Nicholas. 2014. *Songs of Seoul: An Ethnography of Voice and Voicing in Christian South Korea*. Berkeley: University of California Press.

Harms, Erik. 2011. *Saigon's Edge: On the Margins of Ho Chi Minh City*. Minneapolis: University of Minnesota Press.

Harvey, David. 2006 [1982]. *The Limits to Capital*. New York: Verso.

Harvey, Penny, and Christian Krohn-Hansen. 2018. "Introduction. Dislocating Labour: Anthropological Reconfigurations." *Journal of the Royal Anthropological Institute* 24 (S1): 10-28.

Hellwig, David J., ed. 1992. *African-American Reflections on Brazil's Racial Paradise*. Philadelpia: Temple University Press.

Herskovits, Melville J. 1956. "African Economic Development in Cross-Cultural Perspective." *American Economic Review* 46 (2): 452-61.

Hirsch, Eric. 2022. *Acts of Growth: Development and the Politics of Abundance in Peru*. Stanford: Stanford University Press.

Holston, James. 2009. *Insurgent Citizenship: Disjunctions of Democracy and Modernity in Brazil*. Princeton: Princeton University Press.

hooks, bell. 2000. *Where We Stand: Class Matters*. New York: Routledge.

Hunt, E. K. 2002. *History of Economic Thought: A Critical Perspective*. Armonk, NY: M. E. Sharpe.

Instituto de Pesquisa Econômica Aplicada. 2012. *A Década Inclusiva (2001–2011): Desiguladade, Pobreza, e Políticas de Renda*. Comunicados Do Ipea 155. www.ipea.gov.br.

Jaime, P. C., A. C. N. Vaz, E. A. F. Nilson, J. C. G. Fonseca, S. C. Guadagnin, S. A. Silva, and M. F. Sousa. 2014. "Desnutrição Em Crianças de Até Cinco Anos Do Programa Bolsa Família: Análise Transversal e Painel Longitudial de 2008 a 2012." *Cadernos de Estudos—Desenvolvimento Social Em Debate* 17: 49-63.

Johnson, Allen. 1971. *Sharecroppers of the Sertão: Economics and Dependence on a Brazilian Plantation*. Stanford: Stanford University Press.

Johnson, Allen. 1997. "The Psychology of Dependence between Landlord and Sharecropper in Northeastern Brazil." *Political Psychology* 18 (2): 411-38.

Kalb, Don. 2015. "Introduction: Class and the New Anthropological Holism." In *Anthropologies of Class: Power, Practice, and Inequality*, by Don Kalb and James G. Carrier, 1-27. Cambridge: Cambridge University Press.

REFERENCES

Kallis, Giorgos, Christian Kerschner, and Joan Martinez-Alier. 2012. "The Economics of Degrowth." *Ecological Economics* 84: 172–80.

Karim, Lamia. 2011. *Microfinance and Its Discontents: Women in Debt in Bangladesh*. Minneapolis: University of Minnesota Press.

Kenny, Mary Lorena. 2018. *Deeply Rooted in the Present: Heritage, Memory, and Identity in Brazilian Quilombos*. Toronto: University of Toronto Press.

Keynes, John Maynard. 2010. "Economic Possibilities for Our Grandchildren." In *Essays in Persuasion*, 321–32. New York: Palgrave Macmillan.

Keynes, John Maynard. 2016. *General Theory of Employment, Interest and Money*. Atlantic Publishers & Distributors.

Klein, Charles H., Sean T. Mitchell, and Benjamin Junge. 2018. "Naming Brazil's Previously Poor: 'New Middle Class' as an Economic, Political, and Experiential Category." *Economic Anthropology* 5 (1): 83–95.

Klein, Peter Taylor. 2022. *Flooded: Development, Democracy, and Brazil's Belo Monte Dam*. New Brunswick, NJ: Rutgers University Press.

Kopper, Moisés. 2019. "Porous Infrastructures and the Politics of Upward Mobility in Brazil's Public Housing." *Economic Anthropology* 6 (1): 73–85.

Kopper, Moisés. 2020. "Measuring the Middle: Technopolitics and the Making of Brazil's New Middle Class." *History of Political Economy* 52 (3): 561–87.

Kottak, Conrad Phillip. 2017. *Assault on Paradise: The Globalization of a Little Community in Brazil*. Long Grove, IL: Waveland Press.

Kunreuther, Laura. 2009. "Between Love and Property: Voice, Sentiment, and Subjectivity in the Reform of Daughter's Inheritance in Nepal." *American Ethnologist* 36 (3): 545–62.

Kunreuther, Laura. 2014. *Voicing Subjects: Public Intimacy and Mediation in Kathmandu*. Berkeley: University of California Press.

Kuznets, Simon. 1934. "Concept, Scope, and Method" (chap. 1). In *National Income, 1929–32*, 1–10. Doc. 124, 72nd Cong. Washington, DC: US Government Printing Office.

Lanna, Marcos. 1995. *A Dádiva Divina: Troca e Patronagem No Nordeste Brasileiro*. Campinas: Editora da Unicamp. (This work is closely related to the author's 1991 English-language dissertation: "Divine Debts: Exchange Relations in Northeast Brazil," PhD diss., University of Chicago, Department of Anthropology.)

Larkins, Erika Robb. 2015. *The Spectacular Favela: Violence in Modern Brazil*. Berkeley: University of California Press.

Latouche, Serge. 2009. *Farewell to Growth*. Translated by David Macey. Malden, MA: Polity Press.

Lavra Pinto, Michele de. 2013. "O Público e o Privado: O 'baralhamento' No Cotidiano Das Famílias Beneficiárias Do Programa Bolsa Família." *Politica & Trabalho* 38: 157–70.

Leal, Victor Nunes. 2012. *Coronelismo, Enxada e Voto: O Município e o Regime Representativo No Brasil*. São Paulo: Editora Companhia das Letras.

Le Goff, Jacques. 1980 [1963]. "Labor Time in the 'Crisis' of the Fourteenth Century: From Medieval Time to Modern Time." In *Time, Work, and Culture in the Middle Ages*, translated by Arthur Goldhammer, 43–52. Chicago: University of Chicago Press.

Leite Lopes, José Sérgio. 1976. *O Vapor do Diabo: O Trabalho dos Operários do Açúcar*. Rio de Janeiro: Paz e Terra.

Leo XIII. 1891. "Rerum Novarum." https://www.vatican.va/content/leo-xiii/en/encyclicals/documents/hf_l-xiii_enc_15051891_rerum-novarum.html.

Lévi-Strauss, Claude. 1969. *The Elementary Structures of Kinship*. Translated by James Harle Bell, John Richard von Sturmer, and Rodney Needham. Boston: Beacon Press.

Lewis, W. Arthur. 1955. *The Theory of Economic Growth*. Homewood, IL: R. D. Irwin.

Li, Tania. 2014. *Land's End: Capitalist Relations on an Indigenous Frontier*. Durham, NC: Duke University Press.

Livingston, Julie. 2019. *Self-Devouring Growth: A Planetary Parable as Told from Southern Africa*. Durham, NC: Duke University Press.

Loera, Nashieli Rangel. 2010. "'Encampment Time': An Anthropological Analysis of the Land Occupations in Brazil." *Journal of Peasant Studies* 37 (2): 285–318.

Lourenço, Luana. 2015. "Conheça a História de Margarida Alves, Que Inspira a Marcha Das Margaridas." *Revista Fórum*, August 13. https://www.geledes.org.br/conheca-a-historia-de-margarida-alves-que-inspira-a-marcha-das-margaridas/.

Lucas, Robert E. 2002. *Lectures on Economic Growth*. Cambridge, MA: Harvard University Press.

Lucas, Robert E. 2004. "The Industrial Revolution: Past and Future." 2003 Annual Report. Minneapolis: Federal Reserve Bank of Minneapolis.

Lui, Gabriel Henrique, and Silvia Maria Guerra Molina. 2013. "Benefícios Sociais e Transição de Modos de Vida Rurais: Uma Análise Do Bolsa Família e Da Aposentadoria Rural Entre Pequenos Produtores Na Amazônia." *Politica & Trabalho* 38: 137–55.

Lukács, György. 1999 [1923]. *History and Class Consciousness: Studies in Marxist Dialectics*. Cambridge, MA: MIT Press.

Marx, Karl. 1969 [1863]. *Theories of Surplus Value*. Edited by S. Ryazanskaya. Translated by Renate Simpson. London: Lawrence & Wishart.

Marx, Karl. 1976 [1867]. *Capital: A Critique of Political Economy, Vol. 1*. Translated by Ben Fowkes. New York: Vintage.

Marx, Karl. 1994. "Economic and Philosophic Manuscripts of 1844." In *Social Stratification*, edited by David Grusky, 65–69. Boulder, CO: Westview Press.

Marx, Karl, and Friedrich Engels. 1978. "The German Ideology, Part I." In *The Marx-Engels Reader*, edited by Robert Tucker, 146–202. 2nd ed. New York: W. W. Norton.

Marx, Karl, and Friedrich Engels. 2005 [1848]. *The Communist Manifesto*. Edited by Phil Gasper. Chicago: Haymarket Books.

Matory, J. Lorand. 2005. *Black Atlantic Religion: Tradition, Transnationalism, and Matriarchy in the Afro-Brazilian Candomblé*. Princeton: Princeton University Press.

Mattos, Hebe. 1995. *Das Cores Do Silêncio: Os Significados Da Liberdade No Sudeste Escravista—Brasil, Século XIX*. Campinas, Brazil: Editora Unicamp.

Mauss, Marcel. 1967 [1925]. *The Gift: Forms and Functions of Exchange in Archaic Societies*. Translated by Ian Cunnison. New York: W. W. Norton.

Mayblin, Maya. 2013. "The Way Blood Flows: The Sacrificial Value of Intravenous Drip Use in Northeast Brazil." *Journal of the Royal Anthropological Institute*, special issue: *Blood Will Out: Essays on Liquid Transfers and Flows*: S43–S56.

Mayer, Enrique. 2002. *The Articulated Peasant: Household Economies in the Andes*. Boulder, CO: Westview Press.

Mbembe, Achille. 1992. "Provisional Notes on the Postcolony." *Africa* 62 (1): 3–37.

McKittrick, Katherine. 2013. "Plantation Futures." *Small Axe* 17 (3): 1–15.

Meek, David. 2020. *The Political Ecology of Education: Brazil's Landless Workers' Movement and the Politics of Knowledge*. Morgantown: West Virginia University Press.

REFERENCES

Meillassoux, Claude. 1981. *Maidens, Meal, and Money: Capitalism and the Domestic Community*. Cambridge: Cambridge University Press.

Menezes, Catarina Agudo, Bianca Machado Muniz, and Maria Angélica da Silva. 2013. "Os Engenhos de Açúcar e a Construção do Patrimônio Cultural Alagoano." In *VI Colóquio Engenhos de Açúcar*, 10–20. Maceió, Brazil.

Mies, Maria. 2014. *Patriarchy and Accumulation on a World Scale: Women in the International Division of Labour*. London: Zed Books.

Millar, Kathleen M. 2015. "The Tempo of Wageless Work: E. P. Thompson's Time-Sense at the Edges of Rio de Janeiro." *Focaal* 73: 28–40.

Millar, Kathleen M. 2018. *Reclaiming the Discarded: Life and Labor on Rio's Garbage Dump*. Durham, NC: Duke University Press.

Mintz, Sidney Wilfred. 1973. "A Note on the Definition of Peasantries." *Journal of Peasant Studies* 1 (1): 91–106.

Mintz, Sidney Wilfred. 1985. *Sweetness and Power: The Place of Sugar in Modern History*. New York: Viking.

Mitchell, Sean T. 2017. *Constellations of Inequality: Space, Race, and Utopia in Brazil*. Chicago: University of Chicago Press.

Mitchell, Timothy. 1998. "Fixing the Economy." *Cultural Studies* 12 (1): 82–101.

Mitchell, Timothy. 2002. *Rule of Experts: Egypt, Techno-Politics, Modernity*. Berkeley: University of California Press.

Mitchell-Walthour, Gladys. 2018. *The Politics of Blackness: Racial Identity and Political Behavior in Contemporary Brazil*. Cambridge: Cambridge University Press.

Mokyr, Joel. 2017. *A Culture of Growth: The Origins of the Modern Economy*. Princeton: Princeton University Press.

Morissawa, Mitsue. 2001. *A História da Luta pela Terra e o MST*. São Paulo: Expressão Popular.

Morton, Gregory Duff. 2013. "Acesso à Permanência: Diferenças Econômicas e Práticas de Gênero em Domicílios que Recebem Bolsa Família No Sertão Baiano." *Política e Trabalho* 1 (38): 43–67.

Morton, Gregory Duff. 2014. "Protest before the Protests: The Unheard Politics of a Welfare Panic in Brazil." *Anthropological Quarterly* 87 (3): 925–33.

Morton, Gregory Duff. 2015a. "Leaving Labor: Reverse Migration, Welfare Cash, and the Specter of the Commodity in Northeastern Brazil." Chicago: Department of Anthropology and School of Social Service Administration, University of Chicago.

Morton, Gregory Duff. 2015b. "Managing Transience: Bolsa Família and Its Subjects in an MST Landless Settlement." *Journal of Peasant Studies* 42 (6): 1283–1305.

Morton, Gregory Duff. 2018a. "Blood on the Land in Brazil." *New York Review of Books Daily*, March 5. www.nybooks.com.

Morton, Gregory Duff. 2018b. "Types of Permanence: Conditional Cash, Economic Difference, and Gender Practice in Northeastern Brazil." In *Cash Transfers in Context: An Anthropological Perspective*, edited by Jean-Pierre Olivier de Sardan and Emmanuelle Piccoli, 113–40. New York: Berghahn Books.

Morton, Gregory Duff. 2019a. "How Work Counts: Time, Self-Employment, and Wagelessness in Rural Brazil." *Anthropological Quarterly* 92 (3): 663–96.

Morton, Gregory Duff. 2019b. "The Power of Lump Sums: Using Maternity Payment Schedules to Reduce the Gender Asset Gap in Households Reached by Brazil's Bolsa Família Conditional Cash Transfer." *World Development* 113: 352–67.

Morton, Gregory Duff. 2019c. "Saying No: Bolsa Família, Self-Employment, and the Rejection of Jobs in Northeastern Brazil." In *Money from the Government in Latin America*, by Maria Elisa Balen and Martin Fotta, 178–92. Abingdon, UK: Routledge.

Munn, Nancy D. 1992. *The Fame of Gawa: A Symbolic Study of Value Transformation in a Massim (Papua New Guinea) Society*. Durham, NC: Duke University Press.

Narotzky, Susan. 2018. "Rethinking the Concept of Labour." *Journal of the Royal Anthropological Institute* 24 (S1): 29–43.

Nascimento, Abdias Do. 1989. *Brazil, Mixture or Massacre? Essays in the Genocide of a Black People*. Houston, TX: Majority Press.

Nash, June C. 1993 [1979]. *We Eat the Mines and the Mines Eat Us: Dependency and Exploitation in Bolivian Tin Mines*. New York: Columbia University Press.

Navarro, E. A. 2005. *Método Moderno de Tupi Antigo: A Língua do Brasil dos Primeiros Séculos*. São Paulo: Global.

Nørgård, Jørgen S. 2013. "Happy Degrowth through More Amateur Economy." *Journal of Cleaner Production* 38: 61–70.

North, Douglas. 1991. "Institutions." *Journal of Economic Perspectives* 5 (1): 97–112.

Nussbaum, Martha. 2000. *Women and Human Development: The Capabilities Approach*. Cambridge: Cambridge University Press.

O'Dougherty, Maureen. 2002. *Consumption Intensified: The Politics of Middle-Class Daily Life in Brazil*. Durham, NC: Duke University Press.

Oliveira Soares, Venozina de, and Celso Donizete Locatel. 2011. "A Territorialização Da Reforma Agrária Em Barra Do Choça: Os Assentamentos Mocambo, Canguçu e Pátria Livre." *Revista Geográfica de América Central*, special issue: 1–16.

Ondetti, Gabriel A. 2008. *Land, Protest, and Politics: The Landless Movement and the Struggle for Agrarian Reform in Brazil*. University Park: Pennsylvania State University Press.

Oulton, Nicholas. 2012. "Hooray for GDP!" *CentrePiece* (magazine of the Centre for Economic Performance, London School of Economics).

Paes de Barros, Ricardo, Miguel Nathan Foguel, and Gabriel Ulyssea. 2006. "Desigualdade de Renda No Brasil: Uma Análise Da Queda Recente." Vol. 1. Brasília: IPEA. http://repositorio.ipea.gov.br/handle/11058/3249.

Pahnke, Anthony. 2018. *Brazil's Long Revolution: Radical Achievements of the Landless Workers Movement*. Tucson: University of Arizona Press.

Palmeira, Moacir. 1976. "Casa e Trabalho: Nota Sobre as Relações Sociais na 'Plantation' Tradicional." *Actes du XLIIème Congrès International des Américanistes* 1:205–315. (Reprinted in *Camponeses Brasileiros: Leituras e Interpretações Classicas*, edited by Clifford Andrew Welch, Edgard Afonso Malagodi, Josefa S. B. Cavalcanti, and Maria De Nazareth Baudel Wanderley [São Paulo: UNESP, 2009].)

Parson, Jack. 1984. "The Peasantariat and Politics: Migration, Wage Labor, and Agriculture in Botswana." *Africa Today* 31 (4): 5–25.

Paschel, Tianna S. 2016. "How Are They Dying? Politicizing Black Death in Latin America." *World Policy Journal* 33 (1): 38–45.

Paulson, Susan, and Jonathan DeVore. 2006. "'Feeding the Nation' and 'Protecting the Watershed': Forces and Ideas Influencing Production Strategies in a Brazilian Agricultural Community." *Culture & Agriculture* 28 (1): 32–44.

Pereira, Milena Cassal, and Fernanda Bittencourt Ribeiro. 2013. "No Areal Das Mulheres: Um Benefício Em Família." *Política & Trabalho* 38: 87–104.

Perry, Keisha-Khan Y. 2013. *Black Women against the Land Grab: The Fight for Racial Justice in Brazil*. Minneapolis: University of Minnesota Press.

Pimenta, Denise Moraes. 2012. "Ensaio Sobre a Promessa: Circulação de Devotos, Palavras, Graças e Objetos." Diss., Universidade de São Paulo.

Pinheiro-Machado, Rosana, and Lucia Mury Scalco. 2014. "Rolezinhos: Marcas, Consumo e Segregação no Brasil." *Revista Estudos Culturais* 1: 1–21.

Piot, Charles. 1999. *Remotely Global: Village Modernity in West Africa*. Chicago: University of Chicago Press.

Piperata, Barbara Ann, Kendra McSweeney, and Rui Sergio Murrieta. 2016. "Conditional Cash Transfers, Food Security, and Health: Biocultural Insights for Poverty-Alleviation Policy from the Brazilian Amazon." *Current Anthropology* 6: 806–26.

Pires, André. 2013. "Relações de Troca e Reciprocidade Entre Os Participantes Do Programa Bolsa Família Em Campinas (SP)." *Política & Trabalho* 38: 171–95.

Pires, Flávia. 2009. "A Casa Sertaneja e o Programa Bolsa-Família: Questões Para Pesquisa." *Política & Trabalho* 27: 1–15.

Pires, Flávia. 2013. "Comida de Criança e o Programa Bolsa Família: Moralidade Materna e Consumo Alimentar No Semiárido." *Política & Trabalho* 38: 123–35.

Pires, Flávia F. 2014. "Child as Family Sponsor: An Unforeseen Effect of Programa Bolsa Familia in Northeastern Brazil." *Childhood* 21 (1): 134–47.

Pires, Flávia Ferreira, and George Ardilles da Silva Jardim. 2014. "Geração Bolsa Família: Escolarização, Trabalho Infantil e Consumo Na Casa Sertaneja (Catingueira/PB)." *Revista Brasileira de Ciências Sociais* 29 (85): 99–112.

Pires, Flávia Ferreira, and Walquiria Domingues Leão Rego. 2013. "10 Anos de Programa Bolsa Família: Apresentação Do Dossiê." *Politica & Trabalho* 38: 13–19.

Pollin, Robert. 2018. "De-Growth vs. a Green New Deal." *New Left Review* 112: 5–25.

Postone, Moishe. 1993. *Time, Labor, and Social Domination: A Reinterpretation of Marx's Critical Theory*. Cambridge: Cambridge University Press.

Prado Júnior, Caio. 1963 [1942]. *Formação Do Brasil Contemporâneo—Colônia*. São Paulo: Editôra Brasiliense.

Rasella, Davide, Rosana Aquino, Carlos A. T. Santos, Rômulo Paes-Sousa, and Mauricio L. Barreto. 2013. "Effect of a Conditional Cash Transfer Programme on Childhood Mortality: A Nationwide Analysis of Brazilian Municipalities." *Lancet* 382 (9886): 57–64.

Rebhun, Linda-Anne. 1999. *The Heart Is Unknown Country: Love in the Changing Economy of Northeast Brazil*. Stanford: Stanford University Press.

Redfield, Robert. 1947. "The Folk Society." *American Journal of Sociology* 52 (4): 293–308.

Redfield, Robert. 1955. "The Social Organization of Tradition." *Far Eastern Quarterly* 15 (1): 13–21.

Rego, Walquiria Leão. 2008. "Aspectos Teóricos Das Políticas de Cidadania: Uma Aproximação Ao Bolsa Família." *Lua Nova: Revista de Cultura e Política* 73: 147–85.

Rego, Walquiria G. Domingues Leão, and Alessandro Pinzani. 2013. *Vozes Do Bolsa Família: Autonomia, Dinheiro e Cidadania*. São Paulo: Editora UNESP.

Rocha, Luciane de Oliveira. 2012. "Black Mothers' Experiences of Violence in Rio de Janeiro." *Cultural Dynamics* 24 (1): 59–73.

Rocha, Sandoval Alves. 2013. "O Programa Bolsa Família: Subjetividade e Integração Social Em Maracanaú-CE." *Politica & Trabalho* 38: 197–213.

Rogers, Douglas. 2005. "Moonshine, Money, and the Politics of Liquidity in Rural Russia." *American Ethnologist* 32 (1): 63–81.
Romano, Jorge Osvaldo, Maristela de Paula Andrade, and Marta Antunes. 2007. *Olhar Crítico Sobre Participação e Cidadania: A Construção de Uma Governança Democrática e Participativa a Partir Do Local.* Vol. 1. São Paulo: Expressão Popular.
Roth-Gordon, Jennifer. 2016. *Race and the Brazilian Body: Blackness, Whiteness, and Everyday Language in Rio de Janeiro.* Berkeley: University of California Press.
Sahlins, Marshall. 1972. "On the Sociology of Primitive Exchange." In *Stone Age Economics*, 185–276. Chicago: Aldine-Atherton.
Sahlins, Marshall. 1994. "Cosmologies of Capitalism: The Trans-Pacific Sector of 'The World System.'" In *Culture/Power/History: A Reader in Contemporary Social Theory*, edited by Nicholas B. Dirks, Geoff Eley, and Sherry B. Ortner, 412–58. Princeton: Princeton University Press.
Sahlins, Marshall. 2013. "On the Culture of Material Value and Cosmography of Riches." *HAU* 3 (2): 161–95.
Salisbury, Richard Frank. 1962. *From Stone to Steel: Economic Consequences of a Technological Change in New Guinea.* Melbourne: Melbourne University Press on behalf of the Australian National University.
Samuelson, Paul, and William Nordhaus. 2001. *Economics.* 17th ed. New York: McGraw Hill.
Sanabria, Emilia. 2009. "Alleviative Bleeding: Bloodletting, Menstruation and the Politics of Ignorance in a Brazilian Blood Donation Centre." *Body & Society* 15 (2): 123–44.
Sargent, Adam. 2020. "Working against Labor: Struggles for Self in the Indian Construction Industry." *Anthropology of Work Review* 41 (2): 76–85.
Sargent, Adam. 2021. "Ideologies of Labor and the Consequences of Toil in India's Construction Industry." *Signs and Society* 9 (3): 300–323.
Savell, Stephanie. 2015. "'I'm Not a Leader': Cynicism and Good Citizenship in a Brazilian Favela." *PoLAR: Political and Legal Anthropology Review* 38 (2): 300–317.
Schumacher, E. F. (Ernst Friedrich). 1973. *Small Is Beautiful: A Study of Economics As If People Mattered.* London: Blond & Briggs.
Schuster, Caroline. 2015. *Social Collateral: Women and Microfinance in Paraguay's Smuggling Economy.* Berkeley: University of California Press.
Schuster, Caroline. 2019. "The Indebted Wage: Putting Financial Products to Work in Paraguay's Tri-Border Area." *Anthropological Quarterly* 92 (3): 729–56.
Sen, Amartya. 1988. "The Concept of Development." In *Handbook of Development Economics*, by H. Chenery and T. N. Srinivasan, 1:9–26. New York: Elsevier.
Sen, Amartya. 1992. *Inequality Reexamined.* New York: Russell Sage.
Sen, Amartya. 1999. *Development as Freedom.* New York: Alfred A. Knopf.
Sigaud, Lygia. 1976. "A Percepção do Salário entre Trabalhadores Rurais no Nordeste do Brasil." *Actes du XLIIème Congrès International des Américanistes* 1:317–30. (Reprinted in *Capital e Trabalho no Campo*, edited by Paul Singer and Jaime Pinsky, 42–68 [São Paulo: HUCITEC, 1977].)
Sigaud, Lygia. 2007. "'Se Eu Soubesse': Os Dons, as Dívidas e Suas Equivalências." *Ruris: Revista Do Centro de Estudos Rurais* 1 (2): 123–53.
Silverstein, Michael. 1993. "Metapragmatic Discourse and Metapragmatic Function." In *Reflexive Language: Reported Speech and Metapragmatics*, edited by John A. Lucy, 33–58. Cambridge: Cambridge University Press.

REFERENCES

Singer, Paul Israel, and Fernando Henrique Cardoso. 1972. *A Cidade e o Campo*. Vol. 7. São Paulo: Centro Brasileiro de Análise e Planejamento.

Sites, William. 2020. *Sun Ra's Chicago*. Chicago: University of Chicago Press.

Smith, Adam. 1786. *An Inquiry into the Nature and Causes of the Wealth of Nations*. London: Printed for A. Strahan, and T. Cadell.

Smith, Christen A. 2016a. *Afro-Paradise: Blackness, Violence, and Performance in Brazil*. Champaign: University of Illinois Press.

Smith, Christen A. 2016b. "Facing the Dragon: Black Mothering, Sequelae, and Gendered Necropolitics in the Americas." *Transforming Anthropology* 24 (1): 31–48.

Solow, Robert M. 1956. "A Contribution to the Theory of Economic Growth." *Quarterly Journal of Economics* 70 (1): 65–94.

Sosa, Joseph Jay. 2019. "Subversive, Mother, Killjoy: Sexism against Dilma Rousseff and the Social Imaginary of Brazil's Rightward Turn." *Signs: Journal of Women in Culture and Society* 44 (3): 717–41.

Sosa, Joseph Jay. 2020. "Choreographing Exclusion: Protest, Race, and Place in São Paulo." *Latin American and Caribbean Ethnic Studies* 15 (3): 325–35.

Sousa Tavares, Julio Cesar de. 1998. "Gingando and Cooling Out: The Embodied Philosophies of the African Diaspora." PhD diss., University of Texas, Austin.

Stack, Carol. 1996. *Call to Home: African Americans Reclaim the Rural South*. New York: Basic Books.

Stein, Stanley. 1985 [1958]. *Vassouras: A Brazilian Coffee County, 1850–1900: The Roles of Planter and Slave in a Plantation Society*. Princeton: Princeton University Press.

Stiglitz, Joseph E., Amartya Sen, Jean-Paul Fitoussi, and Commission on the Measurement of Economic Performance and Social Progress (France), eds. 2010. *Mismeasuring Our Lives: Why GDP Doesn't Add Up*. New York: New Press.

Suárez, Mireya, and Marlene Libardoni. 2007. "The Impact of the Bolsa Família Program: Changes and Continuities in the Social Status of Women." In *Evaluation of MDS Policies and Programs. Results 2*, edited by Jeni Vaitsman and Rômulo Paes-Sousa, 117–60. Brasília/DF: Ministério do Desenvolvimento Social e Combate à Fome. https://www.eldis.org/document/A63600.

Sullivan, LaShandra. 2017. "Black Invisibility on a Brazilian 'Frontier': Land and Identity in Mato Grosso Do Sul, Brazil." *African and Black Diaspora: An International Journal* 10 (2): 131–42.

Sullivan, LaShandra. 2021. "Holding the Wave: Black LGBTI+ Feminist Resilience amidst the Reactionary Turn in Rio de Janeiro." In *Precarious Democracy: Ethnographies of Hope, Despair, and Resistance in Brazil after the Pink Tide*, edited by Benjamin Junge, Alvaro Jarrin, Lucia Cantero, and Sean T. Mitchell. New Brunswick, NJ: Rutgers University Press.

Tarlau, Rebecca. 2019. *Occupying Schools, Occupying Land: How the Landless Workers Movement Transformed Brazilian Education*. Oxford: Oxford University Press.

Taussig, Michael T. 1980. *The Devil and Commodity Fetishism in South America*. Chapel Hill: University of North Carolina Press.

Thompson, Edward P. 1963. *The Making of the English Working Class*. New York: Vintage.

Thompson, Edward P. 1967. "Time, Work-Discipline, and Industrial Capitalism." *Past and Present* 38: 56–97.

Thorkelson, Eli. 2016. "Precarity Outside: The Political Unconscious of French Academic Labor." *American Ethnologist* 43 (3): 475–87.

"Trabalhadores Rurais são assassinados por jagunços em Vitória da Conquista - BA." *Solidariedade*:

Órgão Informativo da Solidariedade Popular (Sorocaba). November 1994. www.cpvsp.org.br /upload/periodicos/pdf/PSOLISP111994006.pdf.

Trouillot, Michel-Rolph. 1992. "The Caribbean Region: An Open Frontier in Anthropological Theory." *Annual Review of Anthropology* 21: 19–42.

Tsing, Anna Lowenhaupt. 1993. *In the Realm of the Diamond Queen: Marginality in an Out-of-the-Way Place*. Princeton: Princeton University Press.

Tsing, Anna Lowenhaupt. 2005. *Friction: An Ethnography of Global Connection*. Princeton: Princeton University Press.

Turner, Terence. 1979. "Anthropology and the Politics of Indigenous Peoples' Struggles." *Cambridge Anthropology* 5 (1): 1–43.

Turner, Terence. 2003. "The Beautiful and the Common: Inequalities of Value and Revolving Hierarchy among the Kayapó." *Tipití: Journal of the Society for the Anthropology of Lowland South America* 1 (1): 11–26.

Twine, France Winddance. 1998. *Racism in a Racial Democracy: The Maintenance of White Supremacy in Brazil*. New Brunswick, NJ: Rutgers University Press.

Vargas, João H. Costa. 2005. "Genocide in the African Diaspora: United States, Brazil, and the Need for a Holistic Research and Political Method." *Cultural Dynamics* 17 (3): 267–90.

Vargas, João Costa, and Jaime Amparo Alves. 2010. "Geographies of Death: An Intersectional Analysis of Police Lethality and the Racialized Regimes of Citizenship in São Paulo." *Ethnic and Racial Studies* 33 (4): 611–36.

Vettese, Troy. 2018. "To Freeze the Thames." *New Left Review* 111: 63–86.

Wallerstein, Immanuel. 2003 [1983]. *Historical Capitalism with Capitalist Civilization*. London: Verso.

Waring, Marilyn. 1988. *If Women Counted: A New Feminist Economics*. San Francisco: Harper & Row.

Warner, William Lloyd, and Paul S. Lunt. 1973 [1941]. *The Social Life of a Modern Community*. Westport, CT: Greenwood Press.

Weber, Max. 1968a [1922]. "Class, Status, Party." In *Economy and Society*, edited by Guenther Roth and Claus Wittich, 2:926–40. Berkeley: University of California Press.

Weber, Max. 1968b [1922]. "Household, Enterprise, and Oikos." In *Economy and Society*, edited by Guenther Roth and Claus Wittich, 1:370–84. Berkeley: University of California Press.

Weber, Max. 1968c [1922]. "Status Groups and Classes." In *Economy and Society*, edited by Guenther Roth and Claus Wittich, 1:302–10. Berkeley: University of California Press.

Weber, Max. 1968d [1922]. "The Types of Legitimate Domination." In *Economy and Society*, edited by Guenther Roth and Claus Wittich, 1:212–52. Berkeley: University of California Press.

Weber, Max. 2002. *The Protestant Ethic and the "Spirit" of Capitalism and Other Writings*. Translated by Peter Baeher and Gordon C. Wells. New York: Penguin.

Weiner, Annette B. 1976. *Women of Value, Men of Renown: New Perspectives in Trobriand Exchange*. Austin: University of Texas Press.

Weiner, Annette B. 1992. *Inalienable Possessions: The Paradox of Keeping-While-Giving*. Berkeley: University of California Press.

Weininger, Elliot B. 2005. "Foundations of Pierre Bourdieu's Class Analysis." In *Approaches to Class Analysis*, edited by Erik Olin Wright, 82–118. Cambridge: Cambridge University Press.

Williams, Eric. 2014. *Capitalism and Slavery*. Chapel Hill: University of North Carolina Press.

Williams, Erica Lorraine. 2013. *Sex Tourism in Bahia: Ambiguous Entanglements*. Champaign: University of Illinois Press.

Wolf, Eric R. 1955. "Types of Latin American Peasantry: A Preliminary Discussion." *American Anthropologist* 57 (3): 452–71.

Wolf, Eric R. 1966. *Peasants*. Englewood Cliffs, NJ: Prentice-Hall.

Wolford, Wendy. 2010. *This Land Is Ours Now: Social Mobilization and the Meanings of Land in Brazil*. Durham, NC: Duke University Press.

Yan Qinghua. 2014. "The Theory of Division of Labour in Chinese History." In *The History of Ancient Chinese Economic Thought*, 181–93. London: Routledge.

Zelizer, Viviana A. Rotman. 1994. *The Social Meaning of Money*. New York: Basic Books.

Index

abstract labor. *See* labor
accounting practices, 124–33, 161, 164–68, 231n7
accumulation, 11, 30, 136, 143, 200, 207–8
advice (as a speech act), 29, 37, 50–52, 207
African enslavement. See enslavement
Afro-Brazilian identity. *See* Black identity
agrarian reform. *See* land reform
agriculture on large farms. *See* plantations
agriculture on small farms, 13–14, 75, 127, 141–43, 164–66, 229n9, 234n17; agriculture and small-farm marketing, 29; fences and enclosures, 72, 83; small-farm labor, 40, 69 124–27, 145; wage labor on small farms, 40, 43, 55–56, 59–60, 107–8, 124, 128–29, 140. *See also* bistunta; price negotiations
alienation. See Marx, Karl
Alves, Margarida Maria, 233n8
assassination: of Márcio Matos, 74, 226–27n3; of Fábio Santos, 74, 226–27n3
assets, 144, 178, 233n6; asset chain, 10, 30, 141–60, 163–64, 169–70; asset chain and premio, 174–76, 182; household durable goods as assets, 167–68, 174–75; houses as assets, 30, 145–46, 156, 182–87; livestock as assets, 30, 145–46, 174–75, 178. *See also* cattle; houses; premio
atravessadores. *See* middlemen
authoritative discourse, 37, 50–62, 123–24, 194, 225n1, 225–26n7. *See also* advice; calling on; commands
autonomy, 6, 10, 11, 14, 24–25, 29, 42, 55, 63, 69–70, 107, 112–15, 118, 134, 145–46, 190–91, 224n18, 233n11, 234n14; autonomy or citizenship, 206–207. *See also* distance; freedom

Bahia, 6; discrimination against Bahian identity, 22, 191

bars and small stores, in villages, 3, 11, 12, 13, 42, 51, 61, 71, 152–58, 166
Belo Horizonte, 1–2, 26–28, 35, 51, 147, 191
bistunta (marketing practice), 29, 118, 129–33, 136
Black identity, 21–22
Bolsa Família, 23, 45, 85–86, 207, 224n19; measured effects of Bolsa Família, 227n12, 227n14
Bomfim, Manoel, 74
boss, 29, 38, 42, 54–55, 56–60, 60–63, 97, 106–110, 114–15, 123, 169, 183–85, 191, 194, 196, 225n4, 225n7; boss and measurement of skill, 148; boss and self-employment, 135–36, 233n11
Brazilian history. *See* history, of Brazil
bus, 90; long-distance bus rides, 1, 29, 48, 93–101; rural bus service, 73, 76, 119, 211

calling on (as a speech act), 29, 37, 50, 52–54, 61, 136, 207
capabilities approach. *See* growth
cattle, 11, 30, 69, 71, 129, 141, 164–65, 169, 174, 235n5; cattle and enclosure, 72
chamar. *See* calling on
chores. *See* domestic laborers
churches, 12, 13, 42, 69–70, 71, 73, 122, 150–51, 173, 183, 213
cities and urbanity, 23–24, 99, 111–12, 121–22, 206–7
citizenship, as political concept, 23
clandestine merchandise: counterfeit phones, 49; Pokémon (unregistered) vehicles, 162–63; unregistered cattle, 11
class. *See* social class
clientelism and coronelismo, 108–9. *See also* boss
coffee: as a beverage to consume, 19, 40, 99, 127, 203–4; as a crop, 71–72, 124, 190, 205, 226n2; plantation labor, 13, 20, 40, 55, 87–88, 102, 188, 205

commands, 10, 11, 19, 28–29, 37, 54–60, 61–63, 122–24, 132, 133–34, 193–94, 207, 224n22; command vs. control (theoretical argument), 225n7
commodity (as concept), 182–83, 203n2; decommodification, 45–46, 163
conselhos. *See* advice
construction work, 36, 54, 60, 139–40, 148, 153, 165, 184, 191
cooperation, 8–11, 29, 37, 38–39, 42–43, 46, 68, 69, 72, 87–91, 129, 133–36, 208, 225n4, 227–28n15, 233n11; definition of cooperation, 88. *See also* growth
cows. *See* cattle
credit: 186; from moneylenders, 154–55; from traveling mascate traders, 73, 166–68; from village bars/stores, 153, 157–58, 166

day labor. *See* agriculture on small farms; plantations
decommodification. *See* commodity
degrowth, 8. *See also* growth
deictics, 57–58, 122–23, 132, 193, 230n1
democracy, 25, 46, 64, 84, 86, 205–7, 225n4. *See also* autonomy
development, 221n6. *See also* growth
DeVore, Jonathan, 64, 206, 224n18, 224n21
Dilma Rousseff. *See* Rousseff, Dilma
dispossession, 6, 111–13, 222n8
distance, as a concept and strategy, 20, 29, 49, 63–64, 95–97, 103, 117–18, 127, 128, 132–34, 146. *See also* autonomy
domestic laborers: paid, 3–5, 21, 26, 38, 101, 107, 174, 183–84; unpaid, 1, 9, 17, 40–41
durability. *See* permanence and durability
Durkheim, Emile, 9, 67, 89, 134, 225n2, 227n11

earmarking, 165–66
ecological and environmental analyses, 79, 222n11
economic growth. *See* growth
empreita (labor contracted by the job), 108, 128–29, 136
enslavement, 19, 21–22, 42, 67, 224n22, 226n1, 228n3
enthusiasm and intensity, 8–10, 11, 29, 45, 68, 133–34, 208, 230–31n2
exchange, 76, 108–109, 120, 120–21, 131–32, 154, 174, 185, 190–91, 194–95, 199–200, 229n14. *See also* bistunta; hospitality; marketplace; price negotiations
exploitation, 109–13, 144, 159–60, 169

factory labor, 10, 48, 63, 88, 101, 103, 110, 147
family. *See* household; kinship
feminist analyses, 79, 222n11, 231n7. *See also* domestic laborers; gender relations

food: diet and consumption, 40–41, 54
freedom, 6, 10, 19, 21, 64, 101, 104, 109, 136, 152, 224n18, 225n7, 233n11. *See also* autonomy; DeVore, Jonathan

gender relations, 17–18, 177, 234n13; gender and the management of credit, 167–68; gendered division of labor, 40–41. *See also* domestic laborers; feminist analyses; household
Gross Domestic Product, 78–81; debates about GDP, 222n11; GDP and the problem of incomparability, 227n6
growth: anthropological theories of growth, 222n12; arguments against growth, 8, 136, 222n11; arguments in favor of growth, 7, 222n10; boom and bust cycle, 11, 20, 63, 91, 201; Brazilian growth in 2000s, 2–3, 9, 22–26; Brazilian recession of the mid-2010s, 3, 11, 185, 187; definitions of growth, 8–10, 29, 37, 38–39, 76–91, 221n6, 222n11, 227–28n15; degrowth, 8; growth and capabilities approach, 86, 148–49; growth and cooperation, 8–10, 42–43, 38–39, 42, 46, 60, 62, 68, 72, 77, 87–91, 133–34; growth and democracy, 46, 64, 86, 205–7; growth and permanence, 10, 187; growth and social class, 143, 169–70; growth models, 23, 25–26, 43; human capital and growth, 81–83, 148–49; institutions and growth, 83–84; racism and growth, 22

history, of Brazil: from sixteenth to nineteenth centuries, 19–20, 90–91, 224n22; from twentieth to twenty-first centuries, 22–26, 205–7. *See also* inflation
history, of local villages, 29, 39, 67–77, 188–89, 226n1
homogeneity. *See* labor: abstract
household, 69–70, 164–65, 166–68; composition, 13, 17, 69–70; gender relations, 17, 167–68; household durable goods as assets, 166–68, 174–75. *See also* domestic laborers; gender relations; kinship
hospitality, 13, 14, 16, 17, 27, 42, 53, 99–100, 195, 203–5, 208–9
houses, 30, 69–70, 139, 145, 156, 160, 174, 182–87, 195, 204
human capital. *See* growth
hunger, 27–28, 84–85, 157

inalienability. *See* permanence and durability
income inequality: decrease in Brazil in 2000s, 2, 9, 22–26, 143; inside villages, 13, 14–15
Indigenous Brazilians, 19, 67
inflation: hyperinflation of the 1980s, 30, 176, 179
institutional theories of growth. *See* growth
intensity. *See* enthusiasm and intensity

INDEX

kinship, 1–2, 5, 7, 22, 26–28, 30, 31–32, 35–36, 59–60, 61–62, 68, 69–70, 158, 164–65, 176–77, 178, 195, 227n10. *See also* domestic laborers; household

labor: abstract, 10, 29, 59, 95–99, 109–15, 123–27, 133–136, 199, 228n2, 230n2; abstract labor, conclusions about, 96–98, 135–36; abstract labor and premios/saving, 176, 195, 199; average, 133–34; gendered division of labor, 40–41, 228n2; ideology of labor (theoretical concept from Adam Sargent), 168; labor and objects, 141; labor and the definition of social class, 143–44, 168–70, 232n3; leaving labor, 10, 30, 43, 106, 117, 182, 184; manual and intellectual labor, 231n8; rotating labor exchange (voluntary), 40. *See also* agriculture on small farms; plantations
landless people, 14, 222n11. *See also* MST
land reform, vii, 12, 64; expropriation, 12, 25, 74–75, 224n17. *See also* MST
language. *See* advice; authoritative discourse; calling on; commands; deictics; price negotiations; social class
LGBTQ+ people, 18
Lula da Silva. *See* Silva, Luiz Inácio Lula da

malnutrition. *See* hunger
marketplace, 119–24, 166, 230–31n2
Marx, Karl, 9, 59, 78–79, 81, 96, 134, 199, 225n2, 225–26n7, 230n18, 231n8, 232n3, 233n10; Marx and alienation, 181–83, 195. *See also* dispossession; permanence and durability
mascates (itinerant merchants), 70, 73, 166–68
Matos, Márcio, 74, 226n3
McKittrick, Kathleen, 20
meia partnernships. *See* partnerships
middlemen, agricultural, 120–121, 122–24, 127–33, 230–31n2
migration: from city to countryside (reverse and return migration), 2, 16, 19, 20, 23, 24–26, 54, 60, 75, 93–94, 106, 139–43, 153, 160–61, 185, 207, 227n14; from countryside to city, 2, 15, 22–26, 42, 94–95, 104, 111–12, 206–207; from villages to plantations, 71, 87–88, 91, 107; migration and democracy, 25, 227n14; push and pull factors, 5
mimetic convergence, decline, 222n6
minimum wage. *See* wages
Mintz, Sidney, 20, 134, 207, 228n3; and the "permanently unbalanced oscillation," 20, 207
money, 30, 80, 104, 120, 128, 140–43, 145, 155–56, 158, 161–70, 176–181, 185; money's function as a store of value, 199, 235n12, 235n13. *See also* accounting practices; exchange; marketplace; middlemen; price negotiations; remittances; saving

moradores. *See* plantations
MST (Movimento dos Trabalhadores Rurais Sem Terra, Brazil's landless movement), 14, 15–16, 25, 121, 206, 213–14, 224n17, 226–27n3, 231n8; Costa Sena's analysis of plantation mindset, 225n4; land occupations, 16, 55, 73–76, 95; land settlements, 12, 39, 46; militantes, 150, 211; professional development, 150. *See also* land reform
musicians, rural, 36, 70, 94–95, 187–95
mutirão (voluntary rotating labor exhange), 40, 43, 69, 73

na meia partnerships. *See* partnerships
nannies. *See* domestic laborers

objectives, personal (goals), 7, 27–28, 31, 142, 224n26
other people (as a conceptual category), 43, 107–9
ownership. *See* assets

Partido dos Trabalhadores (PT). *See* Workers Party
partnerships, *na meia* and *sociedade*, 129, 133–34, 136
paying the times (*pagar os tempos*). *See* plantations
peasants, 20, 117–36, 141–43, 144–46, 150, 222n11, 224n18, 228n5, 98, 228–29n6; peasants and assets, 145–46, 163–68; similarities to and differences from liberal professionals, 233n11
permanence and durability, 144–46, 158, 163–68, 175–76, 178, 182–95, 234n17. *See also* segurar
phone call. *See* telephone
plantations, 2, 13, 19–20, 25, 40, 42–43, 55, 68–76, 81, 87–88, 102–4, 110, 179, 196, 224n22, 225n4; moradores (resident laborers), 42, 68–69, 71, 74, 107, 184, 233n8, 234n17; paying the times (*pagar os tempos*, a job-ending benefit for moradores), 184–85
plastic economy (theoretical concept from Kathleen Millar), 30, 142, 168, 207
premio (theoretical concept for understanding assets), 10, 30, 174–76, 181–95, 234n3
price negotiations, language of, 120–21, 122–24, 131–32, 167, 191–94
primitive accumulation. *See* dispossession
property. *See* assets

Queer identity. *See* LGBTQ+ people

racialization, 17, 20–22, 121–22
racism, 20–22, 121–22
recession. *See* growth
religion. *See* churches
remittances, 27–28, 161–62
return migration. *See* migration
reverse migration. *See* migration

roads (in countryside), 29
Rousseff, Dilma, 23

Santos, Fábio, 74, 226n3
São Paulo, 6, 21, 22, 36, 44, 47–48, 54, 56, 60–62, 73, 93–95, 104, 106, 111–12, 115, 119, 160–61, 162, 183–84, 187–95
saudades (emotion), 35–37, 48–49
saving, 30, 161, 174–81, 195–200; theories of saving, 198–99. *See also* premio
segurar (holding on), 145, 178, 234n4. *See also* permanence and durability
servants. *See* domestic laborers
Silva, Luiz Inácio Lula da, 22–23, 85
slavery. *See* enslavement
small farms. *See* agriculture on small farms
small stores. *See* bars and small stores
Smith, Adam, 9, 62–63, 88, 177, 235n13
social class, 9, 30, 143–60, 168–70; class and communication/language, 225n2, 225–26n7; class and time, 103; definitions of class, 10, 30, 141, 143–44, 158–60, 232n3
social welfare programs, 23, 25, 45, 64, 75–76, 85, 140–41, 150, 156, 157, 186, 207, 224n19; paying the times (*pagar os tempos*, a job-ending benefit for moradores), 184–85. *See also* Bolsa Família
sociedade partnerships. *See* partnerships
speech acts. *See* advice; calling on; commands
supervisor. *See* boss

telephone, 28–29, 35–37, 61–62; cellphone, 39, 44–46, 47, 49, 50; pay phone (orelhão), 38–39, 41–45, 46–47, 51, 207
time: and asset chains, 141, 144–160; class, 143–60, 169, 231n3; time and hospitality, 13, 204–5, 208–9; time-labor discipline, 3–5, 96, 100–104, 114–15, 124–27, 228n3, 229n7. *See also* plantations: (paying the times)
total (how to see the whole), 127–33, 231n8
traveling merchants. *See* mascates

urbanity. *See* cities and urbanity

value, in anthropological theory, 11, 123, 136, 142, 166, 186, 230n2, 231n1, 231n2
violence, 7, 51, 74

wage-labor. *See* agriculture on small farms; plantations
wages, 35, 40, 61, 112 124–27, 140; minimum wage, 23, 110
welfare state. *See* social welfare programs
whiteness, 17, 21, 22
Wolf, Eric, 20, 228n5
Workers Party, 22–26, 45, 64, 84–85, 150, 205–6, 226–27n3
world, as concept, 19, 122, 224n21

Zilda, Maria, 74